W9-BSE-441

AMERICAN MOTHER

BOOKS BY GREGG OLSEN

Starvation Heights

DETECTIVE MEGAN CARPENTER SERIES
Snow Creek
Water's Edge
Silent Ridge
Stillwater Island

PORT GAMBLE CHRONICLES
Beneath Her Skin
Dying to Be Her

Lying Next to Me
The Last Thing She Ever Did
The Sound of Rain (Nicole Foster Thriller Book 1)
The Weight of Silence (Nicole Foster Thriller Book 2)

AMERICAN MOTHER

**THE TRUE STORY OF A TROUBLED FAMILY,
MOTHERHOOD, AND THE CYANIDE
MURDERS THAT SHOOK THE WORLD**

GREGG OLSEN

GRAND CENTRAL
PUBLISHING

NEW YORK   BOSTON

For Hayley Snow Klein and Sarah Webb

Copyright © 1993, 2002, 2022 by Gregg Olsen
Cover design by Lisa Horton. Cover images from Shutterstock.
Cover copyright © 2022 by Hachette Book Group, Inc.

Hachette Book Group supports the right to free expression and the value of copyright. The purpose of copyright is to encourage writers and artists to produce the creative works that enrich our culture.

The scanning, uploading, and distribution of this book without permission is a theft of the author's intellectual property. If you would like permission to use material from the book (other than for review purposes), please contact permissions@hbgusa.com. Thank you for your support of the author's rights.

Grand Central Publishing
Hachette Book Group
1290 Avenue of the Americas, New York, NY 10104
grandcentralpublishing.com
twitter.com/grandcentralpub

Previously published by Warner Books in 1993 and St. Martin's Press in 2003 as *Bitter Almonds*. Published in 2022 by Bookouture, an imprint of StoryFire Ltd.

First Edition: November 2022

Grand Central Publishing is a division of Hachette Book Group, Inc. The Grand Central Publishing name and logo is a trademark of Hachette Book Group, Inc.

The publisher is not responsible for websites (or their content) that are not owned by the publisher.

The Hachette Speakers Bureau provides a wide range of authors for speaking events. To find out more, go to www.hachettespeakersbureau.com or call (866) 376-6591.

Library of Congress Control Number: 2022941934

ISBNs: 9781538724859 (trade pbk.)

Printed in the United States of America

LSC-C

Printing 4, 2023

From the Author

All characters depicted in *American Mother* are real people. There are no composites. Some have passed away, a few are still living. This book was crafted through hundreds of hours of interviews that survive both in print and on film and thousands of pages of court records (federal and local). Circumstances described are true.

Prologue

Though only half an hour drive away, the South King County cities of Auburn and Kent are worlds away from high-rises loaded with tech workers that make up Washington State's largest metropolis, Seattle. Surrounded by the Olympics, the Cascades, and both the waters of Puget Sound and sailboat-specked Lake Washington, Seattle is as beautiful and as cosmopolitan as the Northwest gets: galleries, symphony, opera, and the home addresses of tech titans like Bezos and Gates.

All of that is glitz and glamour.

The milky, glacial-fed White River roars down from snow-clad Mt. Rainier to meet the meandering Green River near Auburn and Kent. This is the Pacific Northwest of Boeing factories and warehouse jobs. It's pool tables and darts. It's a world of overpriced tract homes and the region's last stand for trailer parks and mobile homes on acreage.

Pleasures might be smaller here, but dreams can be big.

And sometimes dreams morph into nightmares.

At 5:02 p.m. on June 5, 1986, a volunteer fire department Plectron radio receiver announced an emergency. A man was in the throes of a seizure at his residence, a mobile home off Lake Moneysmith Road in the hills above Auburn. His name was Bruce Edward Nickell. His wife, Stella, had made the call for help.

Volunteers Lori and Bob Jewett drove with practiced urgency, lights flashing. Adrenaline pumping. Though they were familiar with the area, finding the address proved difficult. No street markers pointed the way, and mailboxes were huddled in a cluster, away from addresses written on reflective tape with Sharpies.

Woodsy with thick stands of firs and alders, privacy had been part of the dream for those who lived there.

After turning onto a narrow road, Bob stopped the aid car in front of a mobile home.

"It didn't seem like the right place," Lori later remembered. "Usually there is somebody at the end of the driveway waving their arms . . . just can't wait for you to get down the dirt road."

At that particular address, no one was there to greet them.

After what seemed like a minute or so, the screen door slowly creaked open, and a woman who identified herself as Stella Nickell waved them over. She was mid-forties, with long dark hair, and a thick smear of apple red lipstick on her lips. She dressed in dark jeans and a button-down western shirt. Silver drop earrings swung from her ears as she moved.

She led them to her husband who was still damp from a shower and clad in a terry bathrobe. On his back in front of a living-room couch, Bruce's eyes were fixed, but he was struggling to breathe. His mouth gaped like a caught salmon.

"After his shower, he went over to the sliding glass door to the deck to watch the hawks," Stella said. "He turned to me and said, 'Stella, I'm feeling light-headed' . . . then he fell."

"Is he on any medication?" Bob asked.

Stella shook her head.

"Just aspirin," she answered.

She went on to explain Bruce had taken a couple of Excedrin capsules and, as had been his custom of late, had retreated to the deck to relax and watch the hawks circle the sky above their property. Throughout her explanation with its multiple references to Excedrin, Bruce continued to gasp. It was not only audible, it was wrenching enough to be felt.

It was not a symptom the volunteers had ever seen before. Neither was Bruce's strange two-tone coloration. He was cherry red from the neck up, white below. It was such a contrast, it looked as though a line had been drawn separating red and white. It was baffling. If this were carbon monoxide poisoning the victim would be red from head to toe. Bruce had a pulse, but he wasn't breathing. Just gasping.

When paramedics arrived moments later, they bagged the lanky man with thinning dark hair and the calloused hands of a mechanic with an oxygen mask and called for a helicopter.

Within minutes, he was loaded onto a helicopter and was bound for Harborview Medical Center in Seattle.

Everything happened so fast. Lightning fast. The arrival of the volunteer fire department, the paramedics, and the speedy ride to a landing zone on a nearby pasture for a helicopter—all of it was a blur.

All but one thing.

Stella's behavior when the Jewetts first arrived. There had been no urgency. No calling for help. Stella hadn't rushed out to greet them. In fact, she had done the opposite. She took her sweet time. It was strange. *Watched through the screen door. Drank coffee?* She stood behind the door, motionless.

It was almost as if she was stalling.

Later, some would wonder if Stella Nickell had been waiting for her husband to die.

Chapter One

At fifteen, Hayley Snow still called her mother "Mommy." By that age, all of Hayley's peers had switched to the less endearing, but more grown-up, "Mom." Sue was proud her daughter still called her that. It affirmed what they both knew. They were as close as a mother and daughter could be.

Little notes. Secrets. Inside jokes.

That close.

Sue kissed Hayley and called "I love you" as she went to her bathroom off the master bedroom to get ready for work.

In her own bathroom Hayley stepped into the shower, the start of the routine of another school day. She heard her mother turn on the faucet through the walls.

It was about 6:30, June 11, 1986.

"I heard something drop while I was in the shower," Hayley recalled later. "At first, I panicked, the second I heard it. Then I thought, "That's really stupid, she's not going to just fall on her face. So I ignored it, got out of the shower, and continued getting dressed."

Hayley was applying her eye makeup when she realized the water in the master bathroom sink was still running. She knew her mother's pattern from hearing her every morning through the bathroom walls.

Weird. Something is wrong.

She went to find out what was going on.

That's when she found her.

Sue, wearing a zippered purple robe with a white stripe down the front, lay on her back. The water was nearing the top of the sink, so Hayley shut off the spigot and dropped to her knees.

What's happening?

"Mommy?"

Her mother's hazel eyes were fixed, frozen at the corner of the room. Her head rested on the sliding track of the shower door; her hand was across her breast. Her red lacquered nails curled backward sharply and unnaturally.

Hayley tried to figure out what had gone wrong.

"Mommy, wake up!"

The teen struggled to remember what she had learned in health class and checked to see whether her mother was breathing while she hurried to the kitchen phone and dialed 911.

It was 6:43 a.m.

"What's the matter?" the dispatcher asked.

"I think my mother fell while I was in the shower ... and she's breathing and everything, but something's wrong with her."

The dispatcher gathered more detail on Sue's condition. "How is her coloring?"

"Um, hold on a sec, okay?"

Hayley returned and said her mother was red.

The dispatcher instructed her to shake her hand. "Tell her to talk with you. See if she will. Come back and tell me."

"Okay. Hold on ..."

Back and forth to the phone, to her mother on the bathroom floor.

"Mommy, Mommy, please talk to me. Mommy ..." Her voice got louder as she tried harder and harder to wake her.

"Mommy, won't you please talk to me? Mommy. Mommy, please talk to me."

"She won't talk to me ..." she cried into the phone.

The dispatcher reassured her.

"We've got the aid car on the way, okay? I want you to keep on the phone with me. What is she doing now? Is she still breathing normally?"

"It's not really normal." Hayley started to lose it. "It's just breathing."

The fire department arrived at 6:47 a.m.

In tears, Hayley directed the men to the bathroom, where they found Sue in the throes of agonal respiration—a gasping, snorting respiration, eyes still fixed, and dilated. The firemen attempted to ventilate Sue by using a bag mask, a device with a facepiece fitting over the nose and mouth and a plastic reservoir the EMT squeezes to facilitate breathing.

Sue was deteriorating.

It was near the end of the shift when paramedic Debbie Ayrs and Medic 6 officer Randy Bellon answered the call of a "woman down" in Auburn. They arrived just after the firefighters. Hayley took them to her mother. The firefighters lifted Sue, arms dangling, from the bathroom to the bedroom, where there was more room to work on her.

Debbie remembered it all years later: "We started doing our resuscitation, but it wasn't going right. We would give her something to help her cardiac rhythm and it wouldn't help. She was neurologically intact, she was acting like a head injury, but she wasn't exhibiting any of the things that go along with that."

"Has this ever happened before?" she asked Hayley.

"No."

"Does she have any history of depression? Suicide attempts?"
"No."
"Was your mother on any drugs?"
"No."
She was asked again about possible drug use.
"No! My mother's not a druggie!"
The waste basket in the bathroom was examined for drug paraphernalia.
There wasn't any.
An unresponsive Sue was placed onto a stretcher for the ride to the landing zone on a tiny stretch of runway passing for Auburn's small municipal airport. No one thought she was going to survive.
Hayley set off to Harborview with Karen Inoue, a family friend.

Seattle's Harborview Medical Center is the Northwest's finest trauma center, and the county hospital where the indigent come for care. Gang fights. Knifings. Murder. It is a place where the saddest of stories often end. Desperate measures were used to save Sue's life when she was airlifted there that morning.

Hayley and Karen arrived at 7:30. They sat in a waiting area, wondering where her stepfather, trucker Paul Webking, was working and if someone had contacted him. Hayley's own father, Connie Snow, was on the job at Boeing in Auburn—not the easiest place to track down someone.

A doctor came in and said that something was the matter with her mother's brain. *Swollen*, she thought she heard the man say. A few minutes later, the doctor returned and said Sue was still in a coma.

"We're trying everything we can," he said. "We're going to run some more tests. Is your father coming?"

"I think so," Hayley said.

There is no way to measure time in a hospital waiting room, but what seemed like a short time later, the doctor returned with a dire update

"I'm sorry. Your mother is brain-dead."

Paul Webking was loading his truck at Safeway's Distribution Center in Bellevue, just east of Seattle, when a salesman from the Metro Freight office told him that his wife had been rushed to Harborview.

"Sue has been working so hard," Paul said. He wondered aloud if she had suffered some kind of anxiety attack, caused by the stress of her job as a vice president of the North Auburn branch of Puget Sound Bank.

She had even taken some medication to calm her nerves, though what the pills had been eluded him just then.

Paul and his boss left for the hospital. Their conversation was so unconstrained, they were distracted enough to lose their way to the hospital. Paul wasn't worried, and he certainly didn't exhibit much concern. After all, whatever medical problem his wife was suffering was being handled.

Paul entered the hospital through the emergency-room entrance. Hayley would later say that his demeanor seemed casual. She thought she saw him carrying a book, as if he was going to have time to get a little reading in.

"Hey, what's going on?" he asked.

"Mommy's brain-dead," she said.

The color immediately drained from Paul's face, and he hugged her.

Just after 11:00 a.m. the doctors asked if they could remove Susan Kathryn Snow from life support. They said it was the family's decision, but there was absolutely no hope for recovery. Only forty, Sue was gone.

The family agreed.

Hayley went into the hospital room. The woman lying there no longer looked like her mother. In her hospital gown, Sue looked like an inflatable mannequin. Her fingernail polish had been removed. Her toes were swollen and sticking out from under the sheet. Sue's eyes were tiny slits and there was tape and tubing all over her arms. Her chest rose and fell with the machine. It made Hayley ill. She took one more look and left.

Chapter Two

Sue and Connie Snow had made their home in a mobile-home park in Sumner, a small Pierce County town within an easy commute of the Auburn Boeing plant. Though she had spent her whole life in the desert of the Southwest, Sue adjusted to the Northwest in short order. The green and the rain agreed with her.

It was June 1969 when Sue took a job at the Pacific East Valley branch of Puget Sound National Bank. She later told people the reason she took the teller's job was that she figured "anybody could do it" and that meant she could. She was young and smart. Too smart, some who worked with her at the time believed, to be stuck at the teller's window.

Over the next few years, she moved up to credit and later, repossessions. She wasn't thrilled with the repo job, which occasionally involved stealing cars back for the bank, but she knew she had to do it in order to move up. By then, she had earned her GED, but her lack of additional credentials embarrassed her. Yet she was determined: she would make up for her lack of credentials with hard work and her personality, which many, especially men, found irresistible.

Sue was young and vibrant, and since she got pregnant at sixteen with Exa, she had missed all the fun of running around. When her second daughter was born, Sue named her after Hayley Mills, the actress known for her role as a set of identical twins in the Disney classic *The Parent Trap*. Motherhood the second time around was a special joy. Hayley was an easy, loving baby and toddler. That sweetness balanced Sue's relationship with her tumultuous child, Exa. Connie, who loved Exa every bit as much as if she were his own, recalled instances when Exa and Sue nearly had knock-down drag-outs over the littlest things. It was true Sue was strict with Exa, but it was only because she wanted to make sure Exa didn't make the same mistakes she herself had. More than anything, she wanted her daughters to go to college.

"It bothered her that she didn't go on to school, she felt she had missed out. She had the brains and the smarts to do things," Connie said.

In the typically independent fashion that the family would come to expect of her, Exa stopped calling herself Clayton and went by the Snow surname. Like her mother, she liked the last name Snow.

And though they were separated by hundreds of miles, Sue and her identical twin sister, Sarah, remained as close as ever. They talked on the phone daily. When Sue made noises that her marriage wasn't working out, Sarah was the first to hear of it—even before Connie Snow. When there were other men, Sarah got the blow by blow. Sarah thought Connie Snow was wonderful, a good husband and father, but still she understood her sister's infidelities.

"Years later she told me that she was never faithful to Connie. I think she sort of outgrew Connie. She was real smart. She was real pretty. You know, men liked her. She was outgoing. Connie was a homebody. He came home and slept on the couch," Sarah said later.

As the Snow marriage began to fall apart, Sue and her girls left Seattle for New Mexico to care for her daddy, who'd had a stroke and was in a Roswell rehab center. She enrolled Exa in elementary school and took a job at a Roswell bank. The money was terrible, but it was good to be back in New Mexico.

About a year after she left him, Connie sent Sue money to return to Washington, half hoping she'd come back to him. It was not to be. After she returned, Sue asked Connie to fish some change out of her purse. Inside, he found a love letter his wife had written to a co-worker at the bank.

"That was the beginning of our crumble," Connie later said. Connie knew Sue was a bit of a flirt, but he never expected anything to come of it. She was just being charming…and it seemed to be working. Sue had received more promotions than anyone else at the bank.

Devastated, Connie nevertheless continued to put himself in situations that would drive home the point. He would sneak out of the plant during lunch to spy on his wife and her boyfriend. He even drove to the Motel 6, where Sue was living, to see if his car was parked alongside hers. It was.

Stress and a near-ulcer eventually put him in the hospital. He knew he couldn't go on; he loved Sue and doubted he'd ever love any woman as he loved her. Their marriage, however, was over.

She asked him to stay, but Connie had more pride and brains than that.

"I just felt like if I couldn't trust her if she was fifteen minutes late getting home…And that's not a marriage; when you're having to question somebody about where they are all the time," he said.

They didn't file for divorce for eight more years.

Sue and her girls moved into some apartments in Puyallup, where Exa made what she later claimed was the biggest mistake of her life: She introduced her mother to Paul John Webking.

Love him or hate him, nobody was ambivalent about Paul Webking. The Bremerton, Washington–born, though South Bay, Los Angeles–raised, long-haul trucker was stretched out down by the pool at the Meridian Firs apartment complex when Exa introduced him to her mother in the spring of 1978.

Exa, and Paul's son, Damon, were students at Kalles Junior High when she offhandedly told him she thought his father was good-looking and should meet her mother. Though Sue, now a bank manager's secretary, seemed to favor dating doctors and lawyers at the time, she was intrigued enough to agree to meet the man down at the pool.

He wasn't a tall man, but he still seemed big. His hair was long, scraggly, and blond. His eyes were the bluest she'd ever seen.

Paul had done everything from digging ditches and handling customer-service complaints for a gas company to tending bar, before he went to truck-driving school in Fresno in 1974. By the time he had eventually found his way back up to Washington in 1976 to take a job as a long-haul driver for Hayes Truck Lines, he had divorce decrees from three ex-wives. It was shortly after his move to the Puget Sound area that he met Sue.

On the surface, Paul and Sue wouldn't seem even close to a suitable couple, but friends would later say it was easy to see how their personalities complemented each other. Paul was demanding. He was the kind of man who would tell a salesclerk in no uncertain terms that she had better learn the meaning of the word "service."

"I want to speak to your manager!" he'd boom, and then watch the befuddled clerk scurry for the boss.

Sue was taken aback by his outbursts. Paul thought the world was sinking into a dangerous abyss of apathy. He found the human race to be lazy and selfish. Paul shook Sue up—challenged her. Paul found her to be an eager student, to test, to try, to influence.

Sarah, still in conservative Artesia, was in daily contact with her twin, and began to see changes in Sue as the result of Paul's influence.

"We thought alike. She would show me things, to make me have an opinion. Sue was exposed to more of that; this was a dead-end town. She just put a lot of things in my head that would not have got in there. A lot of it was Paul. Sue became Paul."

With Paul, Sue could also let her hair down, and set aside the cheerful smile she felt forced to maintain all day.

"Being cheerful requires a lot of energy, and she would get very tired of being cheerful. When I met her," Paul remembered, "one of the things that probably attracted her to me and me to her was that she was not able to go beyond being cheerful. She always had to be cheerful, and she was suffering from being cheerful. She never learned to, you know, to say no. She was able to relax with me."

The next year, Sue and her daughters moved to a town house at 2019 N Street N.E., Auburn, and though she and Paul had broken up, they'd started to date again. By then, things had fizzled somewhat with a doctor Sue had been seeing. As with the man from the bank, the fellow wouldn't leave his wife.

To those outside, the relationship seemed somewhat strange. Sue sometimes traveled with Paul on weekend trips. Paul was the cook, the house cleaner, the domestic. He and Hayley formed an immediate bond.

In 1981, they made it official and Paul finally moved in. Exa, who did not like sharing her mother with Paul, left for the University of New Mexico.

Chapter Three

Sue Snow's body was under a thin white hospital sheet when Dr. Corinne Fligner, the assistant medical examiner for King County, went to work, aided by pathologist's assistant Janet Miller. There was a great mystery surrounding the woman from Auburn. She was only forty. She was not a drug abuser. She just got up one morning and dropped dead.

After a scalpel made its way through Sue's skin, Janet Miller looked up, her brow knitted in thought.

"I smell cyanide," she said to Dr. Fligner, who was busy recording findings. "You know, it might sound crazy, but did this woman take Tylenol?" she added, referring to the infamous Chicago poisonings.

Miller recalled later, "There was no doubt in my mind that I had smelled cyanide. Once you've smelled it, you can recognize it. I just didn't know the significance of it at the time, because she didn't have any of the classic symptoms of cyanide poisoning. She was as pale as a white shirt. The other cyanide case that I had seen, he was cherry red, just like he was supposed to be."

The M.E. offered no comment on her assistant's suggestion of cyanide, being unable to smell it herself. Janet Miller, as a technician, didn't press the point. Dr. Fligner made a note, however, to check for cyanide in the toxicology screen.

Later, another technician focused on Sue's morning routine. He was especially concerned with her curling iron and whether she had potentially been electrocuted.

Hayley remembered the running water, the curling iron, and her mother's fall, which she had told no one about. She hadn't seen any burns on her mother's hands when she uncurled her fingers.

She wondered, wouldn't there be burns? Paul adamantly declared the electrocution theory nonsense.

"Sue was not electrocuted. We have a ground fault in the bathroom. Nobody reset it, and it still works. If there had been a short, it would have shut down the ground fault. There was no way it was electrical."

Dr. Fligner offered another theory. She was polite and compassionate. But to Paul Webking, her tone felt patronizing and evasive. She said her office had not found any discernible cause of death. She suggested Sue's death might be related to a "heart rhythm" problem that interrupted the flow of blood to her brain.

Sarah interjected that her sister had been complaining of stress-related headaches. She wondered if those symptoms might be related to something like a stroke.

Dr. Fligner didn't know.

"Could she have died of capsule poisoning?" Paul asked.

"I don't see how," the doctor said.

"We found a freshly opened bottle of Excedrin capsules in the cupboard, and Sue obviously took two before she died. Perhaps that's a possible reason," he explained.

Dr. Fligner dismissed it as being "far-fetched."

In a daze, Hayley went to school the next day. She didn't know what else to do. At least there she would be rid of all those clingy people back at the house. She loved them, but everyone seemed so intense. She later heard a cruel rumor that she must not care about her mother because she went to school the day after she died.

She was fifteen. It was hard for her to accept what happened. Or how it could have happened.

Later, she and her sister and her aunt would fixate on the theory that Paul had advanced.

Where did it come from?

Chapter Four

At thirty-five, Auburn police detective Mike Dunbar was a quiet man of few words, the kind who commanded attention as listeners strained to hear what he had to say. It was Monday morning, June 16, when he learned Sue Snow, the pretty bank manager from North Auburn, had been murdered.

Even more disturbingly: she was the victim of cyanide poisoning.

He phoned Dr. Fligner, who told him they had been unable to determine a cause of death during the autopsy, but that a technician thought she had smelled cyanide. Toxicology tests confirmed a fatal level of cyanide in the blood. Dr. Fligner went on to explain that cyanide was so fast-acting that it was consistent with the time frame outlined by Sue's youngest daughter. It was possible, she added, that Sue had been poisoned with a tainted Excedrin capsule.

"Snow's husband, Paul, told me his wife took two Extra Strength Excedrin capsules the morning of her death. I'm not sure if he saw her take them or if he just assumed she did. He said she routinely took them for chronic headaches."

Hayley had last seen her mother at 6:20 a.m. About ten minutes later—long enough for a gelatin capsule to dissolve—the woman collapsed.

Mike Dunbar knew he would have to move quickly.

At the Snow/Webking house, Sue's survivors were in the midst of preparing to leave for her burial at Mountain View Cemetery on the west side of the valley. Though Sarah Webb wanted to help with the decision of what her twin would wear, her brother-in-law had already made up his mind. He selected a black-and-white-checked suit. The rings she had worn at the memorial service on Saturday were removed.

Sarah thought her sister looked lovely, though she felt Sue had been dressed according to Paul's taste, rather than Sue's own. Sue had told her before her death that Paul preferred her to dress in tailored suits.

Most of the dozen or so people were in the kitchen area drinking coffee when Paul took a call from Mike Dunbar telling him that, in fact, his wife had been poisoned, that an investigation was now underway, and that he needed to interview family members.

Paul hung up, visibly upset, but made no mention of the poison. He did tell everyone, however, that something had come up and after the service they would all need to return to the house.

Detectives Dunbar and John Calkins had expected a somber group returning from Mountain View. Instead it seemed like a celebration.

"Everyone was there for the funeral … it was like a party atmosphere … 'Hey, I'm going for pizza, what does everybody want?' Everyone was firing out their orders. It struck me as kind of strange," he later said.

In the center of it all was Paul Webking.

At 12:04 p.m., Paul signed a consent to search the residence. Donning rubber gloves, the Auburn detectives went through the house and loaded all prescription and non-prescription bottles into evidence bags. Partial packages and bottles of Dexatrim, various vitamins and antacids, Excedrin PM tablets, and some tranquilizers were collected.

"All we had was a bottle with no cap, no packaging. I went through every bit of garbage in the house. They had a trash compactor. They had a garbage can in the garage. I went through it all piece by piece," Dunbar later recalled.

Of the headache remedies, which also included a bottle of Albertson's store-brand aspirin, all were tablets. The detective noted that only the Extra Strength Excedrin bottle Sarah Webb had moved to a higher shelf the day her sister died contained capsules.

Sarah nudged Exa Snow when she heard Paul tell Dunbar: "Sue always bought capsules."

"That was bullshit," Sarah said later. "He told some big lie. I knew it wasn't true."

Detectives also searched the garage, pulling anything— such as an insecticide—that might contain cyanide. Paul went with them, pointing things out.

Paul told the investigators that he and Sue had met eight years before and had lived together for the past five years. They'd married on Thanksgiving Day of 1985.

Hayley was the only other person who lived with Sue and Paul. Exa and Damon were occasional visitors at the house. Mike Dunbar asked Paul for an explanation of his whereabouts around the time of his wife's death.

"I left for California on Sunday, June 8, at about one o'clock in the afternoon. I took two Excedrins before I left. I noticed we were getting low, and I mentioned it to Sue. She said they were on her list."

His delivery was unemotional, matter-of-fact. Though it had been five days since his wife died, Detective Dunbar thought it was strange.

Paul said he returned to Auburn Tuesday evening, June 10.

"On the morning of June 11, before I left for work, I took two Excedrin capsules from a nearly new bottle in the kitchen cupboard. The lid was already gone."

Paul explained that Sue always tossed the packaging—including the cap—so she didn't have to mess with the clutter. He also said he and Sue took two Excedrin nearly every morning for the caffeine.

"I don't know if she took any on Tuesday, because she was still in bed when I left. She took vitamins every morning too. But I didn't see her take them that morning."

Paul said he knew nothing more until his boss from Metro Freight told him he was needed at Harborview. Mike Dunbar asked about their marriage.

"Sue and I had been getting along very well," he answered. "We had not argued since September 1985, when I told her about an affair I had with Mary, an old girlfriend…on a trip to California."

Later, the two men would offer differing accounts of what was really said during the interview in the basement on N Street.

"When we got home," Paul later said, "Calkins and Dunbar took me downstairs into the den and started questioning me about the house and what I had said on the phone. Dunbar kept accusing me of saying 'cyanide.' 'How did you know it was cyanide that had killed her?' I said I didn't remember saying it and look, if I would have said cyanide in front of twelve people, everybody would have turned their heads around. I don't remember anybody reacting."

Detective Dunbar left wondering about Paul Webking's statement. The medical examiner had said the man's original story was that his wife suffered from "chronic headaches" and took Excedrin "every morning." Now he was saying he and his wife both took it for the caffeine.

By the end of the afternoon, most family members had given statements either at the house or down at the police station. There had been some jockeying about what was personal and what wasn't.

Sue had been the one to hold the family together, to calm the storms. She had been dead only five days, but loyalties were disintegrating and fear was spreading.

Hayley felt it immediately.

"Right after they told Paul it was murder, he pulled me aside," she said later. "He said, 'Get ready. They are going to think it was either you or me. They are going to consider us the prime suspects. You were here. So was I.'"

Chapter Five

Midway through the year before her murder, Sue learned her husband had had a fling with Mary, a high-school girlfriend from California. It shattered her. Paul insisted it meant nothing And more than anything, Sue wanted to believe him.

The couple started seeing a counselor to sort things out and, after a while, it appeared to work. On Thanksgiving Day 1985, Sue and Paul surprised everyone by going to Reno in the truck and coming back husband and wife.

Sue called Sarah with the news. There was no doubt by the sound of her voice that she was elated. No matter what he had done, she knew her sister loved Paul.

While going through her sister's clothes after the funeral, Sarah Webb found evidence that Sue's jealousy hadn't completely faded.

She found an old notebook scribbled with an angry hand: "Fuck Paul! I hate Mary! I hate Paul."

Sarah left the notebook where she found it, and never told anyone it existed. The discovery, however, started her thinking about the last months of her twin sister's life and what was really going on there.

"When she called, sometimes she was mad. Sometimes she was devastated. She thought she was losing him. She did love Paul. 'I can't have him, so I really want him.' I know you are that way in high school, but you are supposed to outgrow it."

Sarah just listened. She never encouraged her sister to leave her husband. She knew Sue didn't want to leave him. During one of their marathon phone conversations, Sue told her Paul had claimed he had slept with Mary only once.

"Sometimes I don't believe the son of a bitch," she said, between tears.

"Sue thought that it was only once, and that was real important to her. It wouldn't have made a difference to me —one or a thousand times. It was important to her. It really was," Sarah recalled.

As always, Sarah supported her twin. Sometimes that meant keeping her mouth shut. She saw her brother-in-law as a master manipulator and controller. She wondered how Sue had fallen for a man like him in the first place.

When her answer came, it was from a television program.

"About the time Sue and Paul were having that trouble with Mary, there was a show on *Donahue* that we all watched: 'Women Who Fall for Shitty Men.' One point they made was that the way we are raised, we don't feel like we are worthy of accepting our success, so we fall for some man who will bring us down a notch or two."

Sue had not kept Paul's affair secret from her daughters, either.

One time Sue and Hayley considered gathering all of Paul's belongings and piling them out on the front lawn. He'd get the message when he returned home. In the end, neither could quite bring herself to do it.

Heated arguments, which had never been the norm between Sue and Paul, became more common.

"I remember her being very, very upset and they would fight a lot," Hayley recalled. "I remember hearing them yelling at each other, which is something they never, never did. The only time I was really scared, they had a big fight, and Paul threw the phone."

Sue refused to let Paul's little girlfriend shanghai her man, and she wasn't the type to let things run their course. Hayley witnessed her mother's determination to keep Paul.

"I think my mother and Mary had it out on the phone. My mother—she has a mouth on her when she's mad—I think she called Mary every name in the book. I saw her do the whole thing. At least one phone call, I was there listening in the room."

Paul's affair changed Sue. For months, it was all she could talk about. She complained of stress and had bouts of irritability that some didn't think were like her at all. She suggested her bad moods were the result of the demands of her job.

She told people she wanted to hate Paul but couldn't.

*

It was a little after 8:00 p.m. on June 16, when the FDA completed analysis of the Excedrin capsules recovered from Sue's kitchen. Depending on the number taken by the victim, either nine or eleven of the capsules had been tainted with potassium cyanide. The sixty-count bottle had fifty-six remaining.

Sue had been murdered, of course, but the horror of the discovery was that there could be other bottles of tainted capsules in area stores, or worse, in the medicine chests of local residents. The city of Auburn had no blueprint, no information manual on how to handle a product-tampering murder. With the exception of Chicago, where seven had died of tainted Tylenol, it was doubtful any other place would either. The seizure of bottles was the next life-saving step.

Mike Dunbar returned to N Street to confirm the tainted-capsule news to Sue's family. Paul was not surprised in the least.

"That's what we expected," he said.

The detective was put off by the response.

Could it be that Paul had put it there, which was why he already knew what the results of the tests would be?

Other aspects of Paul's statement continued to bother Dunbar. Paul said he took two capsules out of the same bottle that held the tainted ones. Nobody had seen him do that. Police had only his word.

"He takes the first two, she takes the second two off the top, and she drops dead. Do you believe it or not? It's suspicious," he said later, back at the station.

Further, Paul had told the Auburn detective he had mentioned the possibility of tampered Excedrin to a doctor at Harborview, and that the doctor had suggested the prospect to Dr. Fligner after his wife's autopsy.

And there was the question of whether Sue had taken the Excedrin for headaches or as some kind of a caffeine upper. Paul had suggested both reasons. Which was the truth?

As the hours and days passed, Mike Dunbar became more and more convinced Paul was his wife's killer.

That evening, while Auburn police began to plan the seizure operation—recovering and taking the Excedrin out of circulation—they did not know the FBI had jurisdiction over consumer-product tampering, the result of a federal law passed after the Chicago Tylenol murders.

In fact, the FBI had already been notified of the case by the FDA.

*

The Auburn City Council was meeting in their chambers in the building adjacent to the police headquarters. As was his custom, J.D. "Jake" Evans, Auburn Police Chief, sat in on the meeting. He, Mayor Bob Roegner, and City Attorney Jack Bereiter had all been advised of the possible tampering case.

Just after 8:00 p.m., a messenger alerted the chief that the capsules had, without any doubt, been laced with cyanide.

"I didn't feel comfortable, based on the telephone call we took in the morning, that we had a cyanide case and a possible tampering case in doing a seizure operation, but I sure as hell planned for it," Chief Evans later recalled.

The mayor, the city attorney, and chief of police retreated to the mayor's office, just behind Council Chambers. When they returned moments later, Mayor Roegner declared a state of emergency and ended the council meeting.

To recall or seize all bottles of Excedrin capsules was a tough decision to make. After all, Chief Evans and Detective Dunbar knew it could ultimately cost manufacturer Bristol-Myers millions of dollars. And it was possible that Sue Snow's murder was an isolated incident.

"But we can't take the risk," Mike Dunbar insisted. "If there's another bottle out there, it might wipe out a whole family." In the end, it was the only decision to make.

Though stores were all closed and nothing more could be seized, work continued on the tampering case. Around midnight, an FDA investigator boarded a plane with the tainted capsules at SeaTac bound for the FDA labs in Cincinnati. There, with any luck, chemists would be able to determine the source of the poison.

Calendars had already rolled over to the next day when Mike Dunbar tried to sneak through the lobby past the press swelling around the justice center. He was grabbed by a patrol sergeant who knew that Dunbar's least favorite duty was speaking to reporters.

"Here's the guy you want to talk to," the sergeant said. A microphone was jammed into his face. "How do you investigate something like this?"

Detective Dunbar gave his standard response: "You knock on a lot of doors and ask a lot of questions..."

The next day, *Good Morning America* aired his comment, but the detective didn't catch the show. He had more pressing things to do.

The Seattle office of the Food and Drug Administration went public with the announcement that Sue Snow's death had been caused by cyanide-laced Extra Strength Excedrin. Investigators from several jurisdictions continued their sweep of South King County retail stores, pulling Extra Strength Excedrin bottles, with particular attention being paid to lot #5H102.

Excedrin manufacturer Bristol-Myers initiated a nationwide recall, though the FDA stressed that the Auburn tampering was the only known incident.

"Only one bottle involved," a spokesperson naively emphasized.

Later that morning, Exa Snow was brought in for question-ing. She was a striking young woman: beautiful and clearly smart—she said she was finishing up a degree in tax law in New Mexico.

Exa told the detective how she and a boyfriend had stayed at a motel the night before her mother died. She came home that night to get some things, and then left. Everything was fine. She dispelled any notion of a disturbance at the house that night. "Paul barbecued … everyone was just having a good time. We used the hot tub. There was no drinking."

She said that after shopping, her mother routinely would set out an empty grocery bag and fill it with the wrappers and containers not needed from the things she had just purchased.

"The garbage man comes on Tuesdays," she said.

Great, the detective thought, *the day she died, the packaging was sent to some landfill.*

"There's another thing I want to tell you," she said, just before leaving. "Mom never used capsules. She always used tablets. I have never seen her use capsules in my entire life."

In the early afternoon that same day, an employee from the bank called to say she had seen a box of Excedrin in the garbage at work. The timing was lucky. By now, the packaging had become critical. First, it might lead to where Sue Snow had purchased the capsules—if indeed she had purchased them. (Detective Dunbar and others considered the possibility that the tamperer was a disgruntled pharmaceutical employee who had sought revenge against the manufacturer.) Second, investigators needed to either verify or disprove Paul Webking's statement that Sue always took capsules

An interview with the bank employee said that Sue was a bright, attractive, and extremely popular woman. Although the women employees and customers had nothing but glowing things to say about her, her real success was with men.

"A lot of our customers liked to deal exclusively with Sue. They liked the way they were treated," she said.

The co-worker was unsure about where she had seen the Excedrin. She thought it might have been in the employee break room's garbage, but of course, it was long gone.

The detective was told about a man Sue had enraged when she turned him in for embezzlement some six months earlier. Sure, he had motive, the detective thought. But how in the world would he get tainted capsules into her kitchen cabinet?

There was something else, but it happened so long ago that the woman said she was reluctant to bring it up. Several years ago someone had left a nasty note for Sue.

"It read, 'To the whore of Puget Sound Bank.'"

For the next several hours, detective Dunbar met with some of Sue's admirers, all prominent members of the Auburn community. All were adamant that they had dated Sue before she was married to Paul.

Detective Dunbar ended the afternoon of that day on an odd note. That morning, he had asked Exa to return to the station for more questioning and was on the phone when she later arrived—with an attorney.

He wondered what was going on that she thought she needed an attorney. Even more peculiar, she refused to wait for him to get off the phone.

"I was only on the phone a minute or so," he recalled later.

Back on N Street, neighbors jumped into the fray. One man recounted a secondhand story of screaming and crying heard at the Snow/Webking house at 3:00 a.m. the morning Sue Snow collapsed.

Detective Dunbar followed up on that one. The neighbor who had originally told the story cleared it up: it was a cat that was yowling early that morning that woke her. Like the old game of "telephone," the story had become so twisted that the cat had turned into Sue screaming for her life.

Everywhere he went, he learned a little bit more about Sue and Paul's relationship. Paul was not a popular guy. Another neighbor told him Sue had said, "Paul wouldn't let her talk to anyone. Paul was jealous."

By the end of the day, the FBI had sent a busload of agents to Auburn, enough men and women flashing badges around town that it was obvious to Mike Dunbar that working together would serve everyone's purposes. He knew that with the FBI would come manpower and federal money. If the product tamperer was identified, Auburn would have its murderer.

However, in American history, no product-tampering murder had ever been met with an arrest.

The city police detective learned that the FDA's testing of the Excedrin bottles collected from Auburn store shelves showed no others laced with cyanide. In addition, Dunbar was told that of nine contaminated capsules, six had been passed on to the FBI for latent prints examination.

That meant prints were needed from anyone who might have access to the tainted capsules. That meant Hayley, Exa, Sarah, Sue, and, Paul.

The FBI suggested the prints were needed for "elimination" purposes. Or maybe as Hayley and her aunt wondered, to catch the killer who lived there under the same roof.

Chapter Six

Assigned to the patrol unit based out of the Southeast Precinct off of the Maple Valley Highway, King County police officer Edward Sexton was on his break when he was radioed that a hysterical woman had called in to report that her husband had recently died and she had discovered a bottle of Excedrin capsules that matched the lot number of the one that had killed Sue Snow.

The dispatcher said that the woman was so upset, she was nearly unintelligible.

At 5:30, Sexton left in search of an address off Lake Moneysmith Road, just outside of the Auburn city limits. Though he hadn't been involved in the capsule-seizure operation, he was well aware of the Snow case.

Forty-five minutes later, when he finally found the place, he parked by a work shed next to a Honda Goldwing. A woman came out of a wooded area just behind the mobile home to meet him.

Years later, Officer Sexton fumbled trying to describe Stella Nickell.

"Real nice-looking. Had nice slacks on. I believe she was dressed mostly in black, a black top on, kind of a sports jacket on."

If she had been in a panic when she called, that extreme emotion had passed. She was calm as she introduced herself.

Sexton suggested they go inside where he could listen and take notes on what she had to say.

"I'm sorry I sounded so hysterical on the telephone," she said, taking him to the trailer's back door. "I was watching the news report on Mrs. Snow…"

Over the din of the television, Stella drank a Coke and recounted how she had heard about Sue Snow's death and the lot numbers of the tainted Excedrin capsules. Her husband had taken Excedrin capsules with the same lot number two weeks prior—and he had died at Harborview.

"Did they do an autopsy to determine the cause of death?" Sexton asked.

Stella nodded. "They did, but it isn't finished. They gave me a preliminary report, but not a final one," she answered, adding that the preliminary report stated Bruce Nickell had died of emphysema.

She doubted their findings. "He was healthy… he had a check-up… there wasn't any emphysema."

Ed Sexton requested the names of Bruce Nickell's doctors at Harborview and said he'd contact them.

"Will you call me and let me know what you find out?"

"As soon as I do, I'll let you know."

Stella went to the kitchen cabinet near the sink and returned with a nearly empty bottle of Excedrin. Only eight capsules remained. "Bruce had been complaining of bad headaches lately. He was taking three or four capsules a day for pain for a little over a week."

Stella proffered an additional bottle, still in its original box, with a price sticker of $3.39.

"You might as well take these, too," she said. "I don't want any of these around the house."

The cap was loose on the second bottle, but it was practically full to the top.

The black-haired woman sipped her pop and said she had purchased the bottles two weeks apart. The first somewhere in Auburn, the second at Johnny's on the Kent East Hill.

Sexton returned to the precinct and told his supervisor what he had picked up from the kitchen of the Nickells' single-wide mobile home. The bottles were to be entered into evidence.

He phoned Harborview, but none of the doctors who had worked with Bruce Nickell were available.

Sexton called Harborview again the next morning.

"We closed that case two days after Nickell died," a doctor said. "Mrs. Nickell knows the results." He wondered why Stella had said she received only a preliminary report.

"Did you test for cyanide poisoning?" Sexton asked.

"No. Why would we? There was no reason to suspect foul play."

"Are you going to?"

"He's dead and buried."

Frustrated, Sexton made another call, this one to the King County medical examiner's office. Dr. Fligner got on the line and told the officer that she understood a tube of blood from Bruce Nickell's eyes was available at the eye bank.

"I wouldn't say she was interested, but she seemed open to the subject of testing to see if there was foul play," Ed Sexton later recalled.

The next day, Sexton was brought to talk with an FDA supervisory investigator named Kim Rice. He wanted to know about the Excedrin bottles Sexton had collected from Stella.

Hours later, preliminary FDA lab tests showed that both bottles contained cyanide-laced capsules. It was likely that Stella's husband was actually the first of the two known victims.

And the woman had two bottles of the stuff!

Mike Byrne assigned SA Ike Nakamoto to join the FDA's Kim Rice, who planned to head out to interview Stella Nickell. Nakamoto and Rice discussed the interview the afternoon before at FDA offices and, in what was a breach of investigative protocols, called Stella to let them know they were coming the next morning. She was the widow of a tampering victim. SA Nakamoto and investigator Rice agreed sympathy and a gentle touch were warranted.

Neighbor Sandy Scott was jolted by a news report that a second cyanide death was being investigated by federal and county authorities. Across the road from the five-acre spread where she lived with her husband Harold, a King County police officer (nicknamed "Scottie"), and their son Brandon, was the Nickell place. She recalled Bruce Nickell and the emphysema ruling that didn't make sense to her or to his widow. Rather than mulling over possibilities, Sandy cut to the chase and called Stella.

"I just heard on the news …"

Before she could finish, Stella answered the question she must have known was coming.

"It's Bruce," she said.

Sandy offered condolences again and wondered out loud how something like that could happen in the first place. Did Stella need anything? No, she said she'd be all right. But later that day, a rambling Stella phoned her neighbor saying she had changed her mind.

"The FBI and FDA are going to come out tomorrow morning, and the medical examiner is going to announce Bruce's name to the media this afternoon. They told me reporters will probably show up, and I don't want to see anyone. Will you come down and stay with me?"

Sandy said she would. She made arrangements for her son to spend the afternoon with a friend, who was renting the Scotts' camping trailer.

A reporter purporting to be with a big-time news agency had wormed his way into Stella's mother Cora Lee's trailer under the pretext of using the telephone. He was already asking questions when Stella sent Sandy over to ask him to leave.

"I'm worried about Mother's heart," she said.

Stella needn't have worried. Cora Lee, whom Sandy thought of as a hard-boiled Ma Kettle, was giving the reporter a piece of her mind. A big piece. The reporter seemed glad to leave.

The fence and Joe, Bruce's Labrador, fended off more of the media as they lined the dirt road in front of the Nickells' property. Three Seattle TV stations and one from Tacoma overloaded the lane.

"You can't trust me with the press if Ted Koppel shows up," Sandy joked.

Stella laughed. "If Koppel shows up, you can talk to him."

While asking the local media to leave, Sandy repeated one of Stella's lines. "Please go away. Mrs. Nickell doesn't want to see anyone. No pictures. She feels like her husband has died all over again."

When it looked as if she'd be spending the night, because Stella didn't want her to leave, Sandy asked her husband to bring her pajamas.

Until that evening, the two had been hardly more than neighborly acquaintances. Yet Stella had asked Sandy to help her in her hour of need, and Sandy, always eager to get involved in something interesting, did so gladly.

In the end, Sandy got more than she bargained for.

Stella passed the evening guzzling iced-tea-sized glasses full of Tanqueray gin and 7-Up. If it had been she who was drinking, Sandy knew without a doubt she'd be under the table. The booze didn't seem to affect Stella in the least.

The two women talked and watched the news, flipping the channels for more information on the cyanide murders.

Stella said she had put two and two together when a news report broadcast Paul Webking's description of his dying wife's symptoms.

"They matched Bruce's," she said.

Stella was concerned the media would show pictures of Bruce or herself on TV. She told her mother to stay in her trailer and not to answer the door again. Stella was afraid TV people would find out she had been videotaped at a mobile-home-park rent strike centering on cable TV charges a couple of years before.

"I know they got pictures of me," she kept repeating. "I'm just waiting for them to dig that footage out and show it."

When one station showed an old photograph of Bruce, Stella questioned where the producers had got it.

"I didn't give them permission to use that picture."

The answering machine was left on automatic as the media called, one after another. Stella told Sandy not to bother answering it.

The only person she picked up the receiver for was a friend named Jim McCarthy.

Sandy was surprised by who *didn't* call. Stella's daughter Cindy had certainly been out to the property plenty of times. Sandy thought it was odd that Stella had asked her, and not her own daughter, to be there.

While pouring another gin, Stella discussed Bruce's winning battle against alcoholism.

"She got almost defensive. 'We kept the booze here because he wanted to be strong enough to have it in the house and still not drink it,'" Sandy recalled Stella telling her.

Stella opened up about her first marriage, which had had problems from the start: she had been pregnant with Cindy, whom she said had been conceived through rape. It was her mother-in-law who told the little girl that her daddy wasn't really her father.

"She's been nothing but problems since then," Stella said.

Sandy felt sorry for her neighbor. How could all this happen to one person?

Just before taking a sleeping spot on the couch around 3:00 a.m. Sandy made a trip to the bathroom. She noticed that the roll for the toilet paper was empty.

"You're out of TP!"

"Oh, it's under the sink," Stella called from the kitchen.

Sandy opened the cabinet under the sink and saw a bottle of Extra Strength Excedrin capsules. Right in front. Surprised, she picked it up and examined it. It was full of red capsules. As she put it back, she wondered if it was the deadly lot number. A twinge of panic set in.

The FBI is coming tomorrow, and ... Oh God. I touched it!

She set the red-and-white plastic bottle down and decided not to mention it.

Chapter Seven

Media attention unleashes the 220s—police code for average citizens with tips on a crime. Often, calls involve someone calling about a suspect they know or have seen. Auburn police detective Mike Dunbar had never seen anything like the national media attention that the product tampering case produced. While the FBI agents were gearing up to see Stella Nickell, Detective Dunbar went to work, sifting through a deluge of call slips.

People called to accuse. Many left a specific name. Others said they had seen someone acting strangely at the grocery store.

At the Snow/Webking house, it was a repeat of more questioning, but this time it was the FBI asking Paul, Sarah, Hayley, and Exa the questions. The special agents took each person into a separate room. Hayley and Paul added little, if anything, to what they had told Mike Dunbar.

A special agent named Randy Scott sought insight from Sarah Webb into Paul and Sue's marriage. "Were they getting along?"

"It seemed so," Sarah answered somewhat cautiously. He also wanted to know about Paul's personality.

"Was he violent?"

She shook her head. "He just screamed and hollered a lot."

Throughout the interview Sarah spoke softly. She was afraid her voice would carry into the room where Paul was being questioned. She didn't want him to hear anything she had to say. When SA Randy Scott concluded the interview, he warned Sarah not to disclose what they had discussed with anyone. "Especially not to Paul," he said.

That same day, Auburn police detectives conducted more interviews with employees of the Auburn North branch of Puget Sound National Bank.

A loan specialist told detectives that within two days of Sue Snow's murder, Paul Webking had asked for the "entire contents of Sue's desk." Other employees complied with the request.

A woman who had worked with Sue for several years emphasized that Sue carried a large bottle of Excedrin tablets in her purse at all times.

"Never capsules."

The two employees agreed that, at least professionally, Sue had been on top of the world. She had just closed a deal on a five-million-dollar account with a local trucking firm.

Just before lunchtime, Mike Dunbar met with a woman who worked with Sue at the bank. The woman was deeply troubled by what had happened to Sue, whom she considered a good friend.

She said Sue was a flirtatious woman with a bit of a hot temper. She rattled off a list of men she had known. All were customers of the bank.

"Sue only went to lunch with customers—never dinner. She did have a lot of lunch dates, but that was business. Sue always was a flirt, but not serious. Sometimes people took it seriously, but it wasn't meant to be," she said.

She also talked about Paul: "Paul was a jealous man who thought that money was important ... It bothered Paul that Sue made more money than Paul, that she was more successful."

As far as the Excedrin was concerned, the woman insisted that Sue always kept a bottle of tablets in her purse and she took them for menstrual cramps or headaches associated with stress.

She knew nothing of a caffeine habit.

Dunbar got the impression this woman knew Sue very well. It was clear she knew about the problems that Sue and Paul had—at least, Sue Snow's version. She seemed to suggest that it was a possibility that Paul had reason to kill his wife.

Detective Dunbar went to Paul's employer, Metro Freight, in Kent. He had a search warrant allowing him to examine his 1985 Kenworth.

A trip log seemed to back up the man's account of his whereabouts the days before his wife was murdered. His truck was fueled in Kent on June 6 and three days later in Redding, California.

Dunbar found some pills—vitamins, and maybe an amphetamine or two—but nothing to move the investigation any further.

Nonetheless, he returned to N Street to talk to Paul anyway.

"You want to explain this?" Dunbar held the plastic bag.

"What are you talking about? Hey, I'm a truck driver. I've taken bennies…" Paul, his blue eyes bugging out, identified the pills. "The red one is a One A Day and the others are vitamin C."

Nobody could accuse trucker Paul Webking of being stupid. If Paul had an inkling that FBI agents and Auburn police had suspected he had been the tamperer, by the time Mike Dunbar left after discussing the baggie in the truck, he was totally convinced.

Once Dunbar had left the premises, Paul turned to his sister-in-law. "I have some Excedrin in there and they didn't find it," he told Sarah.

Paul's brother, a professor from Canada, was there, and Paul spent most of his time with him. When Paul announced he was going to his truck to look for the capsules, Sarah hoped he would take her along. But it was his brother who went. When the men returned a short time later, Sarah met them at the door.

"Did you find it?"

"Yeah," Paul answered. "They weren't hidden, Sarah. They were in a pocket in the truck. Dunbar should have seen them."

Sarah Webb didn't really care where the capsules had been.

"I want to see them, Paul, I want to see what they look like," Sarah said. She had never taken a good look at the capsules she had moved in the kitchen. She wanted to know what they smelled like. Capsules had killed her sister, and she wanted to know why Sue had taken them in the first place. Shouldn't she have noticed something?

Years later, Sarah could never really be sure if she saw them—Paul flashed something by her face so quickly.

"I really don't care to involve myself in it anymore. If you guys think they [the recovered capsules] are important, take them and give them to the police," Paul said to Sarah and his brother. They couldn't agree either, so Paul, looking every bit a guilty man, trashed them.

"He went straight into the bathroom and locked the door and flushed the toilet immediately. He did not have a bottle in his hand. What I really think he did is throw the bottle in the Green River and looked at the capsules and then flushed them down the toilet. But he didn't tell me that."

Paul later would insist he had disposed of the red capsules by grinding them in the garbage disposal.

"At this point, I didn't want ..." he said later, his voice trailing. "I had had enough and I knew where everybody was going. So I had this bottle of Excedrin in the truck and they missed it in the search. Or they did see it and didn't care, I don't know."

Sarah still wrestled with one more question: what had really made Paul throw away the bottle of Extra Strength Excedrin?

*

The house on N Street had been split in two. Since the FBI investigators and the Auburn detectives had centered many of their questions on Paul and Sue's relationship, it was clear where the investigation was headed.

Whenever Paul left the house, Sarah and Hayley and Exa—while she was still in Washington before returning to college—spent hours trying to decide whether to tell the FBI about Paul's trip to the truck for the Excedrin. If he did the crime they sure as hell wanted him to pay for it, but if he was innocent and was only trying to take unnecessary heat off himself, they didn't want to add to his troubles.

Finally, Sarah and Hayley gathered the courage to call the FBI. Afraid to use the telephone with Paul around, they waited until he left the house. Sarah asked for Randy Scott, but he wasn't in the office. He called back two hours later.

"By that time we really lost our nerve ... We chickened out."

Sarah, more than Sue's daughters, contended Paul had killed her twin. She wanted to believe it. Guilty of the tampering or not, Paul had been the one who told her sister to use capsules. Sue did not use them. Sarah kept going back to the tablets in Sue's purse in contrast with how Paul had capsules in his truck.

They all knew Paul claimed to have taken two capsules the morning Sue died. Sarah considered that another big lie. "He might have chucked them," she told her nieces, "or maybe he knew which ones to take?"

Hayley didn't know what to think. In many ways she loved Paul. Though her father Connie was only a few miles away, and had been a good father, Paul was the one she had lived with. She could see so much of Paul in herself: his sense of humor, his way of battling for what was right.

Hayley could see Sarah's unique loss, but she had lost her mother too; the idea of Paul killing her was inconceivable. Yet Aunt Sarah kept pushing it whenever they were alone.

Sarah considered Paul's affair as part of the motive, but she didn't think that was as viable as another, more obvious factor—money. To her way of thinking, Sue and Paul spent like there was no tomorrow. Sue earned under $40,000 a year, her husband less, yet they never went without. Paul had even gone out on a financial limb and purchased a new Kenworth.

"They were spending money like they were rich... took their credit cards to the max. Sue had been buying all those new clothes at his request," Sarah said later.

"He did it for the money, because everything was Sue's."

Even though her sister's suspected killer slept in the bedroom next to hers, Sarah stayed in the house. She never thought he'd kill her too. He didn't have anything to gain, and Paul was not one to waste the effort on something that wouldn't benefit him.

Only once, however, did doubt creep in.

One night Paul offered Sarah a tranquilizer to help her sleep. A half hour later, she stood woozy and dizzy in the kitchen. "You guys... I swear to God, I think I'm dying..."

"How much did you take?"

"Just one," she answered.

"Sarah," Paul said, narrowing his eyes, "you're supposed to cut it in half…"

Why hadn't he told her that?

Chapter Eight

Stella Nickell was ready for the FDA and FBI by 7:30 a.m. on June 19. Though she could have scarcely slept more than a few hours and had drunk more than her share of gin, she seemed refreshed, eager to get on with it. She dressed in her best jeans and a western-style shirt. Her long black hair was clipped back with a girlish barrette. She looked good. Stella and neighbor Sandy drank coffee, smoked cigarettes, and filled the hours with small talk.

One person got through on the phone. It was Anna Jo "A.J." Rider, a friend and co-worker from SeaTac Airport, where she and Stella screened passengers for Olympic Security. A.J. had called from her mother's in Yakima after hearing a news report that Bruce was a possible cyanide victim.

"Stella, did Bruce die of cyanide poisoning?"

"Well, that's what they're saying."

"How do they know that?"

"I had an autopsy of Bruce," Stella said. "They didn't throw out a specimen, and when they retested they found cyanide."

SA Ike Nakamoto and the FDA's Kim Rice arrived at the Nickell place about 9:45 a.m. Though Sandy felt she would be a nervous wreck in similar circumstances, Stella was calm and had her wits about her. She answered background questions with a directness that Sandy had come to know from the previous evening.

Stella was one self-assured person.

They sat at the dinette table, and with the speed and frequency that had come from years as a "stew" for United Airlines, Sandy poured coffee.

Stella told the investigators that on June 5 her husband had gone to work as usual and returned at 4:10 that afternoon. She was making dinner when he took a shower and came out to watch TV.

He took four Excedrin capsules and went into the den. Later, she said she saw him walk to the deck, go outside, and return to the space in front of the couch. He collapsed, and she called 911.

"During that time she said his breathing nearly stopped," SA Nakamoto later said. "After giving the information to the 911 operator she went back, found he was still breathing, although in a funny, strange manner, I guess a deep type of breathing, waited for the aid unit to come, which they did, and basically the aid unit took over from there and worked on Bruce for about an hour. He was then transported to the Red Barn Ranch, where he was airlifted to Harborview."

"Bruce had been suffering from recurring headaches for a couple of months," Stella explained, adding later that Excedrin was the only pain reliever Bruce took. He usually took four. She kept all of her medicines in the kitchen cabinet above the sink.

While discussing the two cyanide-laced Excedrin bottles she had given to King County officer Ed Sexton, Stella remarked that she, too, had taken some of the capsules from the very bottle that poisoned her husband.

"I came home from Bruce's funeral with a horrible backache, and I took two capsules. My God, can you believe it? I could have taken some with cyanide in them too," she said.

Stella admitted she had a difficult time accepting that her husband had died of emphysema—the pathologist's initial ruling. She even called the medical examiner's office twice—June 7 and 13. There had been some kind of a mix-up, she told Nakamoto. She never got the final results.

A third phone call was made, she said, after she heard the news of Sue Snow's death.

Though the investigators were concerned with the source of the poisoned capsules, the FDA's Rice, in particular, wanted to pinpoint where the bottles had been purchased.

"Where do you do your shopping?" he asked.

She answered: Auburn's Albertson's North, Pay 'N Save South, and the Johnny's Market in Kent.

"Any idea when you bought the bottles?"

Stella said it was likely she purchased them on one of her days off from her job at the airport.

In all likelihood, she said, the opened tainted bottle had been purchased two weeks prior to her husband's death, either at Albertson's North or the Johnny's Market. But Stella conceded she couldn't be certain.

The unopened bottle, however, had been purchased at Johnny's in Kent, a couple of days before Bruce died.

They also talked about Bruce. The Nickells had first lived together in 1974 and married in 1976. At the time of his death, her husband was a heavy-equipment operator for the State Department of Transportation. He had recently passed a state physical examination in order to become a permanent employee.

SA Nakamoto, who had been a police officer and an investigator for the state, asked about insurance.

As far as she knew, Bruce was covered by a single policy from the state. She went to the desk under the fish tanks and produced a statement from the State Employees Insurance Board. She gave it to Nakamoto and he took notes.

She was uncertain about its value.

Later, SA Nakamoto recalled Stella saying her husband had applied for an additional $100,000, but since he had not taken a mandated physical or missed an appointment, or there had been a problem due to delayed delivery by the post office, he was turned down. Bruce had been depressed about that.

The policy indicated that state employees had $5,000 basic life, $5,000 accidental death and dismemberment. Optional coverages were available, including optional life for $25,000, and there was an additional $100,000 accidental death and dismemberment, for a total possible coverage of $135,000.

Stella said she did not know the full amount. Ike Nakamoto asked if there were any other policies on Bruce's life.

Stella told him that she and Bruce had both applied for an additional $20,000 from Bank Cardholders of America. Stella produced a wallet card from her saddlebag-style purse. It had her name as the insured. She said she had called a toll-free number for the insurance company but learned that through a clerical error her policy was the only one issued—not one for Bruce. Her attorney, Bill Donais, had the certificates at his office in Auburn.

"Ike, I've got something you need to see," an agent called from the hallway near the bathroom. It was the sixty-count bottle of Excedrin capsules that Sandy Scott had seen the night before.

Kim Rice recognized the lot number immediately—5H102, expiration date August 1988—as the same as that on the bottle recovered from Sue Snow's kitchen.

Kim Rice asked Stella what she knew about the bottle.

She just looked completely blank.

"I've never seen it before," she said.

Sandy blurted out that her fingerprints were on it.

The FDA investigator would later say Stella Nickell's surprised reaction seemed completely genuine. He put the bottle in an evidence bag.

Next Kim Rice asked if Stella had any grocery receipts from May or June that might help determine where the bottles had actually been purchased. Stella wasn't sure, but she said she and Bruce saved receipts for income tax purposes. She went to her desk in the living room and pulled out various drawers and a shoe box, trying to locate receipts. An Albertson's receipt included an item for $3.39, the same price as the one stickered onto the forty-count bottle Ed Sexton had taken from Stella.

Although minutes before Stella had said she purchased the bottle at Johnny's in Kent, the FDA man didn't ask about the conflict.

Just as the FBI seemed to be finishing up, Stella's daughter Cindy Hamilton and a trucker boyfriend pulled onto the property. Since the door was locked, Sandy Scott got up from the kitchen table to let them inside. Sandy had met Cindy only a couple times before, but she recognized her immediately: the young woman's photograph was displayed prominently in the den.

"How could they suspect my mother of killing Bruce? I don't understand," she said, angrily pushing past her mother's neighbor.

"Nobody's accusing your mother of anything," Sandy replied, not knowing what to make of the comment. Why would Cindy have thought anyone was accusing her mother of murder?

Stella went to her daughter, and for the only time during the morning, became teary-eyed. A few words were exchanged, and the widow took her place back at the kitchen table.

Sandy noticed Stella's muscles tighten as the agents swept through her trailer, her mother's trailer, and Bruce's work shed looking for evidence. The woman was under an incredible amount of stress, and Sandy Scott felt sorry for her.

Sandy cornered Cindy in the kitchen.

"Your mother hasn't eaten anything since yesterday afternoon. She's looking tense and not too well. Why don't you try to get her to eat something?"

Cindy shrugged. "She's a big girl. If she wants something to eat, she can get it herself."

Sandy Scott's jaw dropped. She couldn't understand Cindy's apparent lack of concern for her mother. "The animosity in the retort was so out of character for what the circumstances were," she later said.

The agents involved in the search did so meticulous a job, it even impressed Sandy Scott, whose husband was a cop. An agent brought out the laundry detergent and sifted through it for some hidden evidence.

Another agent said someone might have gained access to the Nickells' house and planted poison there.

When some powder in a sandwich bag taken from one of Bruce's toolkits was shown to Stella, she wasn't able to identify it.

"It might have some use in welding," she offered, getting up from her chair to examine it.

Later, out of earshot of the FBI, she turned to Sandy and said, "I hope it isn't drugs. Cindy's boyfriend borrowed the toolkit recently."

SA Cliff Spingler seated Cindy in the Nickells' spare bedroom, where she talked about family history, including Bruce's battle with the bottle.

"Bruce was a weekend alcoholic, and several years ago my mom gave him an ultimatum—either her or the bottle. She took him into treatment, and he hasn't had a drink since."

Cindy explained that her stepfather suffered a bout of headaches after he was laid off from his job at McDonald Industries in Kent some time ago. He used Excedrin exclusively.

"He figured if two was the recommended dosage, then four was better."

Cindy said there were no problems with the Nickell marriage, and if there had been any financial worries, those had been behind them for better than a year. Her mother loved her stepfather. There were no extramarital affairs.

The agents' train of cars left around the time family friend Jim McCarthy and attorney Bill Donais arrived at the property to help Stella.

Slightly winded from the walk up the hill, Donais stood on the roadside and spoke to the media. "It's been a real shock to her. If it hadn't been for the unfortunate aspect of Mrs. Snow dying, Mrs. Nickell would be dead."

A reporter asked why.

"Apparently, they found cyanide in the last four or five capsules in bottom of the bottle, and both Mr. and Mrs. Nickell used it. If she hadn't been warned, she might have very well taken it herself."

By the end of the day, the FBI had also paid a visit to Bruce's place of employment in Seattle. His toolbox was searched for evidence, the idea being that a disgruntled co-worker could have spiked Nickell's Excedrin with poison.

By then, the FBI also had a code name for the case: Seamurs, for Seattle murders. It was a nickname that paid homage to the Chicago Tylenol case: Capmurs, for capsule murders.

Chapter Nine

The morning nine days after Sue Snow died was filled with minor developments and useless leads.

The bulk of the day was spent going through canvas bags full of the stored garbage from Sue's bank office. No evidence of any Excedrin was found during the three hours Detective Dunbar and FBI agents pawed through the material in a department conference room.

By the end of the week, the FDA lab in Cincinnati had determined that the cyanide contaminating the Snow and Nickell bottles had come from the same source. In a way, that was good news. At least a copycat wasn't at work. Not yet, anyway.

The *Seattle Times* published a story headlined:

ALERT WIDOW AVOIDED FATE OF HUSBAND

The same paper ran an article announcing a $300,000 reward for information offered by the Proprietary Association, a consortium of the drug companies that had been bruised and beaten by this kind of a maniac more than a dozen times. But the rewards offered had been no help in solving the other tamperings, and drug companies continued the withdrawal of capsule medicines.

The Webking/Snow house got its share of calls from strangers. Some were oddballs calling only to say that they had seen the articles; others called with a purpose.

Paul took a phone call from a Colorado man who said he wanted to join in a lawsuit with Sue's estate. He said he had proof that x-rays could convert acetaminophen, one of the ingredients in Excedrin, into cyanide. He had even written a paper on it.

Paul's brother listened in on the extension.

"It occurs when they x-ray bottles for consistency in packaging," the man said. "There is a possibility that the radiation emitted from Chernobyl caused the conversion…"

A call from the household's second phone line was made to the police regarding the man with information on the tamperings. An Auburn police officer responded at 10:25 p.m. The officer stood in the hallway, while Paul tried to keep the caller on the line in an attempt to get as much information as possible.

The officer's radio irritated Paul.

"Turn the fuckin' radio off," he whispered, his hand over the receiver.

The officer shrugged. "Just give me the phone, and let him talk to a real person."

"Why don't you get the fuck out of here!" Paul bristled.

The officer left, telling the family to "have Mr. Personality call me when he settles down."

Later Paul reported the call to the FBI, but he felt they dismissed his information. He told family members that if the authorities were looking for Sue's killer, they were looking for him on "their time—not on the killer's time."

The Auburn officer who responded to the harassing call was one of the first to have a run-in with "Paul the Hothead." As the days passed, others would experience it for themselves.

Mike Dunbar later put it this way: "Paul has the type of personality that doesn't endear him to you. Some people might be guilty, but you want to believe they are innocent. You look for the good, the positive, because of personality. Paul didn't have the kind of personality that made you want to help the guy out. Given all the circumstantial evidence, there wasn't a lot of motivation to want to try and clear the guy."

One afternoon, local news cameras recorded the awkward moment Hayley, Sarah, and Paul accepted a plaque from a loyal bank customer. It had been inscribed with a tribute and a photograph of Sue.

The fifteen-year-old girl with cropped blonde hair and a set of light-catching braces looked and sounded very much her age. "Thanks a lot. I mean, it's really nice and neat that you've done this for us and you remember her ... everyone will remember her in this way."

A store off Auburn Way North was one of two Pay 'N Save drugstores located in Auburn. It was next door to the Albertson's grocery store where investigators believed Sue might have purchased her tainted bottle of Extra Strength Excedrin.

Mike Dunbar too paid a visit to the Albertson's store where Snow shopped and confirmed that both tablets and capsules had been available when she did her shopping. It was possible that she might have picked up the wrong bottle.

But next door to Albertson's, around noon on Tuesday, June 24, 1986, store manager of Pay 'N Save, Jim Nordness, his staff, and two FBI agents continued their examination of inventory to ensure the removal of the banned capsules from the shelves.

A fifty-count bottle of Maximum Strength Anacin-3 quickly became the subject of great interest. It had been found earlier in the day sitting on a can of peanuts, two rows from where it should have been in the pharmacy's over-the-counter medications display. Not only was it in the wrong section, but further examination showed it was in the wrong store. It had been price-stickered on the end flap with a red "As Advertised" label over an orange price tag not used by Pay 'N Save.

And there was more. After going through store inventory schematics, Nordness discovered that the Pay 'N Save store didn't even carry the fifty-count size in the first place.

The FBI took the bottle off to the lab. By the end of the day the flames of panic were fanned again as the word got out: the tamperer had struck again—this time it wasn't Excedrin, but Anacin-3.

Chapter Ten

FBI Special Agent Roger Martz, a chemist in the chemistry toxicology unit of the Washington, D.C., forensic laboratory, was given five tainted bottles from South King County. The latent-print examiners had come up with only one unknown latent on all the bottles, and none on the tainted capsules themselves. It was a good bet the tamperer had worn gloves. It was Martz's task to find out where the poison had been manufactured and where the tampered capsules had been sold.

The information concerning each bottle was recorded in meticulous detail.

Bottle No.1, from Sue Snow's kitchen, had no outside wrappings, no box, not even a cap. Of the sixty Excedrin capsules purported to be inside, fifty-six remained; nine contained cyanide. Of the nine, four contained green specks.

Bottle No.2, a sixty-count Excedrin, was from Johnny's in Kent. Though in a box, it's safety seal around the neck of the bottle had been cut. Of fifty-six capsules found in the bottle, four contained cyanide mixed with little green specks.

Bottle No.3 was the forty-count Excedrin from the Nickell home. The lip of the bottle had been pared, making it loose. It contained seven capsules, two with cyanide, and one of those had the foreign green material.

Bottle No.4 had a box, though no safety seal around the bottle neck. It was the second one turned in by Stella, and like its companion, was a forty-count. Only thirty-five remained. Four capsules contained cyanide, all of which were mottled with green specks.

The last bottle was the Anacin-3, found at Pay 'N Save. The bottle was in a box, but the box, SA Martz determined through chemical analysis, had been re-glued. Martz also noted that the box had two price stickers, one red, the other orange. The aluminum safety seal on the top of the bottle had been partially removed, as had the polyethylene heat seal. Of the fifty capsules supposed to be inside, only forty-five remained. Four capsules were tainted. All four had the green material.

The sixty-count Excedrin bottle retrieved from under Stella's bathroom sink was completely clean, and was not considered evidence.

While the source of the potassium cyanide had yet to be determined, one thing was clear. With the capsules averaging 700 milligrams of cyanide, they were lethal.

It was SA Martz's job to determine what the green particles in seventeen of the twenty-three tainted capsules were.

*

Fifteen members of the Auburn police gathered in Conference Room #3 at headquarters at 9:00 a.m., Wednesday, June 26, for what had become their answer to the FBI's daily briefings.

A preliminary psychological profile created from the bureau's work on the Chicago tampering case suggested the tamperer was a person who lived locally, might visit the stores to check on the sales of the tampered bottles, and finally, in an act of ghoulishness, might even visit victims' graves.

Detective Dunbar told the group about a disgruntled Pay 'N Save employee who was being investigated by the FBI. He also reported that federal chemists were trying to "fingerprint," or determine the source of, the cyanide.

"It's contaminated with some green crystals of some kind," he said.

The investigators had learned how easy it was to purchase a poison as lethal as cyanide. Chemical supplies stores sold it, while high school chemistry classes, photographers, and jewelers used it.

The FBI knew the tampering had been done after the bottles left the manufacturing plant, and that the case appeared to be local.

Officers went over the victims' files. Very little time was spent on the Nickell case. It was true that Stella Nickell was being investigated, but she didn't seem as viable a suspect as Paul Webking.

Sue was a tablet user.

Paul said he took two capsules before he left.

How could Paul know Sue had taken two capsules when he wasn't even there?

And what about Paul's conversation with Dr. Fligner?

The circumstances piled up ...

The new widower has a double-indemnity life insurance policy on his wife.

The fact that the Anacin-3 had two price stickers—one from Pay 'N Save, the other from Associated Grocers.

A truck driver would have easy access.

An officer wondered if it had been a coincidence that Sue had died on garbage-pickup day, leaving no evidence in the home except for the Excedrin bottle.

The Auburn officers even batted around the idea of a family conspiracy. The quack caller had been from Colorado; Sarah lived in Colorado...

SA Randy Scott phoned Paul Webking for a list of the people who attended Sue's funeral. The FBI planned to review it for possible leads. Though he didn't say it, the implication was clear: Sue's killer might have been at the service.

When the agent showed up later, however, he didn't mention the list.

"You know," he told Paul as he took a seat in the living room, "we can stop bothering you. I know you're innocent. We all know you're innocent. We could really put it to bed if you took a polygraph."

Paul's face grew red and the veins in his neck strained at the surface of his skin. Sarah had seen the look before, as had Hayley. Usually he directed it at some kind of incompetence that frustrated him to the point of an eruption.

"I've never refused to talk to you people yet. You're beginning to piss me off. So if you continue to come back like this, I am not going to talk with you anymore, I'll talk to somebody else."

Randy Scott tried to defuse the anger.

"I know you're not guilty, but if you take a lie detector test, it will free us up to pursue others. I just want you to know that in another case there is a person who refused to take a lie detector test and we still suspect him as the person who did it."

"Why did you have to come out here under the subterfuge of wanting to look at the funeral list? I've been racking my brain thinking about the people who were at the funeral. Here I am trying to help you, and you're trying to bullshit me."

With or without a polygraph, some at the FBI office weren't convinced of Paul Webking's guilt. One of the doubtful was Special Agent Ron Nichols.

A mechanical engineer in his forties, Nichols was a "tech" and computer expert who enjoyed the challenge of the paper chase. He could organize information in a system that worked, not only for himself, but for others.

As the end of June approached, SA Mike Byrne assigned Nichols the task of taking all case interview reports, teletypes, and memoranda, and organizing them in a way to ensure every detail had been covered, nothing missed. Byrne knew Nichols was the right one for the job—they had worked on dozens of other cases.

For the Snow-Nickell murders it was time to regroup.

Paul might be a dead point due to lack of evidence; at least SA Nichols thought so. There was talk and worry on the seventh floor of the Federal Building that the FBI was going to be left with yet another unsolved product tampering. None of the scores of agents on the case could live with that.

Chapter Eleven

After SA Randy Scott had angered Paul Webking with his maneuvering to get the polygraph, Jack Cusack stepped in to fix things up. SA Cusack made Sue's widower his business. He talked with everyone from the medical examiner's office, doctors at Harborview, agents who had interviewed other family members. There were plenty of people, like Sarah Webb, who were sure that Paul was the killer.

Though Paul Webking looked promising, Cusack had long since learned it was a mistake to allow one statement to sway an investigation. He knew that traps can lead to the wrong conclusion. Only one statement is worth hanging everything on: "I did it."

Paul insisted he didn't do it.

SA Cusack drove down to 1404 N Street N.E. in Auburn wondering if Paul was going to be openly hostile. After all, he had made it clear for days that he was tired of the FBI "fucking with" him and saying that they should get on with the case and find his wife's killer.

Paul employed an unusual directness in everything he said. Indeed, he was blunt. His eyes didn't dart. And his answers were always given with a somewhat reserved hesitation. Some might have found it to be the way of a man who carefully thinks out what he is going to say; others found his style of delivery suggestive of a man giving calculated responses.

The FBI agent did his best to smooth out any ruffled feathers Randy Scott might have left behind. Cusack told Paul he would be handling him from now on; he would be the one to administer the polygraph.

"We'd like you to come downtown for a polygraph, so we can eliminate you as a suspect."

"I'll think about it," he said.

SA Cusack thanked him and left, feeling fairly certain Paul Webking would come around.

A short time later, Paul called and said he'd do the polygraph.

He was in fine form when he showed up at FBI headquarters. Though he came there voluntarily, he was still mad at Randy Scott.

"Randy Scott is a weasel, and I really don't want to deal with him," he said.

"You won't have to," Cusack promised.

As they talked, Cusack told Paul about the polygraph, and how by taking the test, he'd be "able to put all of this behind you."

They talked for an hour or so.

Throughout a pre-test interview, Cusack always simply observed. Did the subject try to steer him away from critical areas? Was he omitting facts from his statement? Was he being evasive?

Paul was not trying any evasive tactics. Components attached to his fingertips, tubes around his chest, and a blood pressure cuff on his arm, SA Cusack went on with the polygraph.

Paul sat stiffly in the chair.

"Did you cause the death of your wife on June 11, 1986?"

Paul didn't blink. "No," he said.

"Did you put any cyanide in any Extra Strength Excedrin capsules?"

Again, another no.

Several questions later, and after some analysis—not much was needed—SA Cusack could see what the results indicated.

"Paul," he said, "it is my conclusion after this examination that you're not involved in the cyanide product tampering in any way."

Paul looked satisfied and relieved.

"I only have one thing to say about this case," he said, finally.

"What's that?"

"You guys will never solve this case."

Fleetingly, SA Cusack wondered what he could have missed during the polygraph.

"Why?"

"I'm just telling you …" His voice trailed off. "You guys just won't catch the guy who killed Sue."

When her brother-in-law returned to Auburn and announced he had "passed" the polygraph, Sarah embraced him as though she was glad for him, sorry for what he had been through. Inside, however, she still had doubts.

"I thought he was so manipulative that he could lie during a polygraph," she later said. When Auburn detective Mike Dunbar heard Jack Cusack's news, he couldn't believe it.

"There's got to be something wrong," he told colleagues at the department. While he had no qualms about Cusack's ability as a polygrapher, he was convinced Paul Webking had been his wife's killer.

Meanwhile, the chemical analysis to establish exactly the source of the poison proved to be a major disappointment for the Seamurs team. Following the cyanide from its source to its distributor ultimately could lead to the tamperer. Though only three manufacturing sources of potassium cyanide were available to the American consumer—Du Pont, DeGasa, and ITI—sodium from the irksome green specks made it impossible to "fingerprint" the manufacturer. The green specks made it impossible to trace the manufacturer, as they contained sodium, which was the trace element in the potassium cyanide that SA Roger Martz needed to determine the source of manufacture. The presence of sodium in the green specks interfered with this process and made identification of the source impossible.

The FBI was out of luck. Chemists could not even determine if all the capsules had been tainted by the same batch of cyanide.

More than ever it looked as if Paul Webking's assertion at the end of his polygraph was on point. The death of his wife would be another in the string of unsolved tampering murders. No one at the Seattle office would say it outright, but many thought so.

Roger Martz's chemical analysis found that the specks were made up of monuron, simazine, and atrazine. All three were algicides (chemicals used to kill algae).

After a battery of tests, Martz determined that the green specks were an aquarium product called Algae Destroyer. No other such product used by tropical fish fanciers held the exact same chemical makeup.

The message was passed on to the Seattle field office.

"You know," a special agent offered when he heard the news, "out at the interview at Mrs. Nickell's, I noticed she had a couple of fish tanks."

SA Cusack's polygraph of Paul Webking had essentially cleared Sue's husband and sent investigators digging deeper into the other likely suspect: Stella Maudine Nickell.

SA Nichols was the first to be convinced that the Auburn woman's story needed further scrutiny. He flat out said she was guilty. But the agents who went out to Nickell's place for the interview said she seemed believable. She had nothing to hide.

"Why would a woman who killed her husband come forward if she was home free?" one asked. "She had the goddamn death certificate stating natural causes before Snow's death."

Among the materials piled on Ron Nichols's desk, he found a newspaper clipping that started him thinking. It stated that Stella had purchased the two tainted bottles at different stores and at different times.

He grabbed a pen and wrote *What? How can that be?* In the margin. It was true, it didn't make sense. But the information was also reflected in Ike Nakamoto's report.

"If Stella is to be believed, she purchased the only two forty-count boxes of poisoned capsules. No one could be that unlucky," Nichols said.

The only possibility to explain it away was if SA Nakamoto had gotten it wrong or, worse, unwittingly prompted Stella Nickell with store names. That, too, was taken into account.

SA Cusack met with King County officer Ed Sexton at the precinct in Maple Valley to learn if the officer had detected any hesitation when Stella Nickell told him where she had purchased the capsules. Sexton remarked that Stella had been confident.

There were other things about Stella that worried the investigators.

As the agents understood it, Stella would inherit about $135,000 from her husband's death if deemed accidental, and only $5,000 if he died of natural causes.

Investigators thought it odd that if Bruce Nickell had been taking handfuls of capsules for severe ongoing headaches, his wife would purchase the smallest, forty-count size.

Stella said she purchased the forty-count size because it did not have the plastic wrapping that her husband found bothersome.

Sue's bottle was a sixty, as was the one under the Nickell's bathroom sink first found by Sandy Scott. Was that one simply a spare no longer needed?

SAs Cusack and Nichols also discussed the possibility that Stella Nickell kept the poisoned bottle and wanted an unopened box to show police officers.

"Maybe she was afraid that when the police came out to see and she showed them the nearly empty bottle, they'd say, 'You put those pills in that bottle!'

"If she had another bottle, she could say, 'No, I didn't. In fact, I have another bottle here in the house.'"

"She kept the second to cover any suspicion on the first?"

"It could be."

FBI agents speculated that Stella called 911 for two reasons when she heard of Sue's death. One, she knew there were three more boxes and others could die, and two, she possibly would get more money if her husband died an accidental death.

Could it have been that after Stella Nickell identified all three stores in which she placed poisoned capsules, she returned to Pay 'N Save and moved the Anacin-3 to the peanut aisle so someone would find it?

If it had been there from the beginning, Jack Cusack figured it would have been discovered sooner. It had the wrong price tags. It was in the wrong place.

Maybe Stella, if she was the killer, had felt guilty and moved the bottle because she didn't want someone else to die? No one was looking for Anacin, only Excedrin.

The FBI report from the Nickell search indicated that the agents had found a bottle of Maximum Strength Anacin capsules in the kitchen but didn't seize them.

In another conflict with the widow's story, A.J. Rider (Stella's friend and co-worker from the airport) told the FBI, "No one but Bruce took any Excedrin caps." Stella Nickell had claimed to have taken at least five from the bottle that killed her husband.

Further questions plagued the detectives. Had Stella Nickell ever used Algae Destroyer? Did she have access to cyanide? Could store inventory records prove she bought two bottles of forty-count Excedrin on two different days at Johnny's?

Chapter Twelve

On June 5, 1986, Stella Maudine Nickell was on overdrive without any fuel. She and her mother sat in a waiting area at Harborview Medical Center. Both seemed anxious, ready to kill for a smoke. Cora Lee Rice, her thick braids streaked with gray, sat stonily with her daughter, the very picture of the tough bird her family always said she was.

While her husband, Bruce, lay unconscious, Stella excused herself to make a phone call and sneak a cigarette. Cowboy boots clacked on the scuffed linoleum floor as she walked away.

At 8:45 p.m., Bruce Edward Nickell was pronounced dead, and without hesitation, his wife released his body to hospital pathology for an autopsy.

The two women returned to Stella's pickup for the drive home to Auburn. The next morning there would be places to go, people to see. First on her list was to phone her husband's boss, Dick Johnson, at the Department of Transportation office in Seattle. "Bruce won't be in today. He died." The man offered condolences and asked as many questions as he could to show concern and to satisfy curiosity. When he hung up, he was still struck by Stella's brusqueness.

Next, Sella had to visit Bruce's adoptive parents, Walter and Ruth, over in Wenatchee.

She drove to the elderly couple's apartment, only a few miles away. Bruce's parents were in their nineties and were shocked by the news of their only child's sudden death.

After listening, Walter Nickell immediately went into a back bedroom to study photographs of his only son... Conflicted memories came back alongside his tears.

After fourteen years of trying to conceive, Walter, an apple farmer from Winthrop, Washington, and Ruth, his second-grade-schoolteacher wife, adopted a boy from a Seattle maternity home. They named the week-old baby Bruce Edward, and brought him home in June 1934.

Many years later, Walter remembered his wife's joy. "She was real happy with him. He was a beautiful baby. Actually, I think he was the prettiest baby I ever did see."

Since the new baby was allergic to cow's milk, Walter happily took up the chore of milking a goat every day. He and his wife never wanted anything so much as that little baby. They did everything they could for the child.

Bruce grew up on a twenty-acre Red and Golden Delicious apple orchard in arguably one of the prettiest spots in a state known for its unsurpassed rugged, natural beauty.

Though he had the kind of childhood Norman Rockwell portrayed on canvas, Bruce started drinking at fifteen.

"I never accused him of it, but he knew how I felt about drinkin'. It was something I didn't do. I never have. Don't say I'm a teetotaler, but drinkin' is something I didn't do," Walter said.

Alcohol seemed to be the cause of nearly every misstep their son made in life. Before he met Stella, he had married Ruby, Linda, Mary, and Phyllis. None had worked out. He had two sons by his previous wives, but became completely estranged from both boys. He did a stint in the Marines, but was discharged without honor after going AWOL.

Even so, Walter and Ruth never talked to Bruce about his drinking. They didn't figure it would do any good.

Chapter Thirteen

Like a noose-knotted necklace, the ties that bind choke. This was the way from the very beginning with the Stephenson clan.

Before she was known as Cora Lee Rice, the Stephenson matriarch was called Alva Georgia or "Jo" Duncan. Jo and her husband, George Stephenson, had had a son and three daughters prior to Stella Maudine's birth in Colton, Oregon, in the summer of 1943. She was a beautiful baby with dark hair that curled in ringlets. Stella looked like her father, a tall, olive-skinned lumberman with dark curls that would make any person envious. He had the big, dirty hands of a main sawyer who made his living off timbers felled in the forests of the Pacific Northwest.

Texas-born Jo Duncan was no typical beauty, but she was a striking woman with a strong jawline. She told her children she had some Cherokee and Apache blood, and the braids she wore in her hair backed up her contention—at least her children thought so.

George Stephenson knew little other than how to work the sawmill and drink until he dropped. Jo would not always tolerate his ways, regularly dragging him out of their local tavern.

Eldest daughter Georgia Mae would never forget the routine that often left her in charge.

"… My dad would come home from work and he'd want to go, and my mom would want to chase after him. I took care of the kids and done the chores," she later said.

The Stephenson home was neither the best nor the worst of the places Stella would call home. They did not have hot and cold running water—fifty-five-gallon oak barrels and a stove did the job. Even so, Jo Stephenson made sure there was always food on the table. Anyone who knew Jo, knew she cared about her children. They were hers. Not hers and her husband's. Hers alone.

Yet by the time Stella was born, the household had fallen into a vicious pattern of abuse and neglect, and possibly molestation. Georgia Mae later claimed her father sexually abused her from age six to nine. She never told anyone about it and no other children ever made similar claims, at least not publicly.

The marriage between their parents ended with a fight that would remain memorable to the children.

"Dad got drunk, been out playing poker with the guys, and he came home and had a big fight with Mother. He grabbed a shotgun and Mother told us kids to run, and we ran to the neighbors. Mother took off out of the house and Dad shot a couple of shots at us with the shotgun. That was the final blow," Berta, the sister closest to Stella's age, later remembered.

Stella would have no memories of her father, only what Jo Stephenson thought was important enough to pass on.

When it was time to leave Oregon, Jo and her children caught a servicemen's boxcar for Leadville, Colorado. World War II was just ending.

Jo told her children she took them to Colorado to keep them away from their father. He'd threatened to take the kids and run. Jo didn't doubt it, though if she had thought about it, she'd have realized there was no way any of those kids would stay with their father.

So she scattered her brood among her sisters—Hazel, Lucille, and Dorothy—and her parents, and returned to Oregon to divorce George.

For Stella's sister Berta, Colorado was a nightmare. The young girl couldn't convince Aunt Dorothy that she appreciated her home cooking. When her aunt became angry, she booted Berta outside to eat on the porch with the dogs.

When she felt it was safe to do so, Jo and her children returned to Oregon and moved into a tent house just below a sawmill. Jo began working as a mill worker, the only woman among them. She told her kids she could do the job as well as a man.

By 1949, Jo Stephenson thought her life had taken a turn for the better. She answered an ad for an assistant to a logging truck driver placed by a Molino, Oregon, man named Colver "Dewey" Kelly. She was hired, and a short time later married her boss. But he was not the answer to her prayers. Jo Kelly ended up locked in a repeat of her previous marriage—abuse and drunken rages.

Jo and Dewey—when he was sober enough—worked the pea harvest, cutting and driving trucks in Eastern Washington from Walla Walla to Wapato. Jo wore men's clothing and kept her hair hidden in a dirty old bandanna. Tucked over her truck's sun visor, she kept a Coke bottle handy to wallop any man who made an inappropriate advance toward the only woman running a pea truck.

But Jo was always searching for other opportunities. Following promises of work, the family moved to the Anacortes and La Conner area on Puget Sound, north of Seattle.

On New Year's Day, 1952, Little Joe Kelly was born. By then, the family of eight lived in a two-room house below a rendering plant near La Conner, Washington. The children slept in the bedroom, and Dewey and Jo slept in a double bed adjacent to the kitchen stove.

In the battles between Jo and Dewey Kelly, Jo had the upper hand, though her children probably saw it as an even match. She didn't drink to excess, and she could swing a fist when called for. Dewey had a mean streak, and whenever it struck him, he'd show it by beating his wife.

Stella recalled one fight in particular. "The side of the refrigerator was bloodied where he hit her in the mouth. He broke her front teeth; she had on dentures, and they went through her lower lip. And she leaned up against the refrigerator and just laid her head on her arm for a minute and the blood just drained down the side of the refrigerator. And when she come away from the refrigerator, she laid into him."

Dewey Kelly didn't stick around Anacortes. He told Jo he was going off to make some real money in Alaska. Later, Stella and her sisters heard Kelly impregnated a girl out there and was unable to return. But none of that mattered. By the time Jo divorced him, the family was scarcely getting by on welfare and living in a little place on 16th and B streets in Anacortes.

By 1955, it was clear Jo Kelly was going nowhere fast in Anacortes. She finally decided the small town held few opportunities for a single mother. The winter months, when field work was not available, were especially hard. When her son James enlisted in the service, she knew it wasn't going to get easier.

She packed up her three girls and moved into the North Star Motel on Seattle's Aurora Avenue N. The room had a kitchenette, making it seem more like an apartment than its name implied. Jo found a job waiting tables; she told the girls the tips weren't half-bad. It wasn't easy, but somehow they got by.

Stella Maudine Stephenson grew up fast.

By the time she hit her teens, she knew how to use her body and looks to her advantage. Imbued with self-confidence from a young age, she never went through a gawky phase. She always felt more mature than her peers and, in particular, boys her age.

"They were childish. And there was absolutely no way that I could even think of going out with one of them."

Missouri-born farm boy Ricky Slawson liked what he saw when he first laid eyes on Stella. Though he was seventeen and she was only thirteen, he didn't pay that any mind.

The two started hanging out around the Northgate area. Jo even approved of Ricky enough to lend him her 1950 Chevrolet so he could take her daughter around town.

Jo moved herself and her daughters out of the North Star Motel and into a house in Seattle. She dated a couple of men after Dewey, but none were marriage material. And though they sometimes lived with her, she never depended on them. She never asked for anything for herself or her daughters.

Jo's daughters all had different qualities. Georgia Mae, with her flaming red-rinsed hair, was the pretty one; Berta at six feet was the sensitive and gentle giant; and Mary, with a love of caring for the kids and cooking, the little mother. Stella was the one with a wild streak.

One time when Berta wouldn't get off the telephone when Stella decided it was her turn, Stella grabbed her sister's arm and bit hard enough to draw blood.

And though she was running around with boys, Stella dreamed of being a veterinarian or a nurse.

Her dreams would not come to pass. At fifteen, Stella Stephenson found herself pregnant.

How it happened, and just exactly who was the father, would be the subject of much family discussion over the years. Stella claimed she had been gang-raped.

She said it happened while she was visiting a boyfriend named Russell. His mother left the two alone to do some grocery shopping, and Russell got on the phone.

"He told me he had a friend that he'd like me to meet. Then, when his friend came over, they proceeded to carry me upstairs. Russell tied my hands behind my back with his belt while the other kid held my feet and raped me."

One sister believed the story, because a similar attack had happened to her.

Stella was four months along when she determined she was pregnant, and like many young girls, tried to hide the pregnancy as long as she could. Finally she told her mother. Jo's solution was for her daughter to marry the baby's father.

"I won't marry him if he's the last man on earth," Stella told her. She refused to let the bastard who had attacked her and was complicit in raping her be a part of her family. Stella never saw Russell or her rapist again.

Nevertheless, Stella wanted her baby to have a name, so she enlisted Ricky Slawson in a charade. Luckily, Ricky never saw it that way. Whether naive or a liar, he told people the baby was his.

In the summer of 1959, Stella and Ricky showed up at Georgia Mae's Holly Park housing-project apartment in Seattle looking for a place to stay. Single after a failed marriage, Stella's older sister was working several jobs. She knew nothing about the rape and thought Slawson was the baby's father.

Stella said their mother had thrown her out, but Georgia figured Stella had probably just run away as she had so often before. Every time Jo turned around, Stella was gone.

Living with her sister wasn't the best solution for either party. On one occasion, Georgia whipped Stella after accusing her of stealing a silver dollar and a wedding ring.

"She stole my one-carat engagement ring, and my 1934— year I was born—silver dollar. She didn't deny it. So I took a belt to Stella. I turned her over on my bed and spanked her worse than my own kids. I was afraid I had injured the baby, but I was so mad at her. I was so upset."

Stella didn't stay for another round. She and Ricky left the next day and moved in with Berta and her husband, south of town, until the baby was born.

Stella gave her last name as "Slawson" when she had her baby girl on October 23, 1959. Ricky wanted to name her Cynthia, and Stella chose the middle name Lea.

By the time Cynthia was born, Alva Georgia "Jo" Duncan Stephenson Kelly had married for the third time, to a retired Navy man named Bill Street. The new couple took off south and moved into a small house in Stanton, Orange County, California.

Stella's mother now felt she was in the position to do something for her daughter. She wanted to adopt Cindy and raise her as her own.

*

"Stella, you aren't ready for this," Jo told her daughter. "I want you to have the life of a teenager."

Stella wasn't convinced but Jo didn't wait for an answer. She went to work on gathering the information needed for adoption. Yet when she sent for her own birth certificate, the name that came with it was Cora Lee Duncan—not Alva Georgia.

From that day forward, she adopted her original name, a name she never knew.

"I'm Cora Lee," she'd correct people.

It was as if Alva Georgia or Jo had never existed.

When it came to the wedding, Berta told would-be brother-in-law Ricky that courthouse employees wouldn't ask for ID and he should tell them he was twenty-one. "That way you won't need your parents' permission to marry."

Ricky couldn't do it—or rather, wouldn't do it. He chickened out at the last minute.

"I can see how much you want to marry me," Stella told him in a fit after he refused to lie.

"We'll wait until I become of legal age," he promised, "then we can get married."

Around Christmas 1959—the same holiday Stella's family gave her a Bible embossed with her name that she would keep with her forever—Stella's mother phoned asking her daughter if she would move to California and live with her and her husband, Bill Street. She promised she could help with the baby and Stella would be able to learn a trade or even get her GED.

Stella agreed to go.

"Ricky tried to talk me into staying and I told him no, I was going down to California with my mother, because it seemed like the only way that I was going to be able to get any support for myself and my daughter. He says, 'I love you and I wanna marry you,' and I said, 'If you love me and want to marry me all that much, I'll see you in California. When I see you in person on that doorstep, I'll know how you feel.'"

Cora Lee came for Stella and Cindy on New Year's Day 1960. She moved them down to her little house in Stanton.

Tough gal that she was, Stella's mother was not the type to talk trash about her husbands. No matter what they did to her, Cora Lee Street had enormous pride. She didn't want her children to feel as though she'd made a mistake in marrying a man. She was always hopeful.

But although her mother never complained, Stella saw evidence of a battering.

"From her waist to her knee and from about her hipbone in the front to just about halfway around in back was nothing but a black mass. Bill had knocked her down on the floor and kicked her with his service shoes on, and they were hard-toed. When I saw the bruise, I got out of her what happened. Mother would tell me a lot of things that she wouldn't tell the other kids because I don't get all bent out of shape like the other kids. I knew there was two sides to the story and I hadn't gotten the whole thing yet. It could have been an entire accident. It could have been intentional, I don't know. I wasn't there."

Instead of coming to California as he had pledged, Ricky Slawson mailed a letter. He threatened that he was going to get custody of Cindy by taking Stella to court and prove she was unfit to raise the girl. Cindy had his name and, therefore, belonged with him. Hell hath no fury like Stella Stephenson, and Ricky should have known it.

"I wrote back to him and told him that he knew that Cindy wasn't his daughter even though she carried his name," she said. The letter went on: *Go ahead and try to prove I'm an unfit mother, try to take my daughter away from me and I'll see you behind bars for 20 long years, because I'll nail you for statutory rape because I was only 15 years old when we started getting together. And I turned 16 a couple months before Cindy was born.*

Ricky never contacted Stella again.

As hard as they had it, there was extraordinary loyalty in the Stephenson family. No one would sell the other out. Punishment was handled by the family, not by outsiders. Cora Lee had taught the girls that "you never, ever air out the family laundry in public!"

They had nothing but each other.

Chapter Fourteen

Early on the afternoon of Friday, June 6, 1986, Bonnie Anderson visited Cindy Hamilton at the two-bedroom apartment Cindy shared with family friend Dee Rogers, on Smith Street in Kent. The girls were getting ready for a night out at Borders, on Central Avenue, for margaritas and tequila shooters. This was the place where Cindy's current boyfriend tended bar.

While at Borders, and barely into their first round of drinks, Cindy got up from her barstool to answer a call. "Dee said my mom's coming over. We have to go home."

"Okay," Bonnie said. "What's going on?"

"Dee wouldn't say. All she said was, 'Your mom's coming over and she wants you here.'" Cindy mused whether it was a family emergency or something of that nature.

"It's either my dad or his parents," she said.

Ten minutes after Cindy and Bonnie returned to the apartment, Stella arrived. She looked as if she hadn't slept all night. She was drawn and worn out.

Stella directed her words toward her daughter. "He's gone. Bruce is dead."

Cindy nearly collapsed. Dee looked equally overwhelmed. The three women took chairs at the dining table in the alcove off the kitchen. Dee poured some liqueurs. Feeling out of place, Bonnie retreated to the living room couch, about fifteen feet from where the other women huddled in shock and grief.

Although she couldn't hear everything being said, a few phrases would register later. "I know what you're thinking. The answer is no," Stella said, her eyes fixed on her daughter's. Cindy didn't say a word; she couldn't. She seemed out of control, grief-stricken.

After about ten minutes, Bonnie, realizing she was an unnecessary interloper in a tragic family affair, hugged the tearful, hysterical Cindy goodbye and headed home.

*

Stan Church, a crew-cut-topped machinist at Foss Shipyards in Seattle, had met Bruce Nickell over the CB radio three years before. He and his wife, Laurie, and their two daughters—Kimmie and Karan—lived in Auburn, not far from the White River Estates mobile-home park that had been the Nickell home before Bruce and Stella moved onto the acreage east of Auburn.

Stan Church and Bruce were close; they would spend hours on their radios, whiling the days away with chatter.

Laurie Church was a solitary woman, and with two daughters and a husband as outgoing as Stan, it was easy for her to stay in the background. Although Stella was flashy, with her penchant for tight jeans and stylish western garb, and Laurie was a conservative homebody, the two women clicked. Soon, whenever Stan and Bruce got together, the ladies would get to talking over a card game, often playing solitaire in tandem.

When Cindy Hamilton and her boyfriend traipsed into Kimmie Church's wedding at Auburn's Presbyterian church, on Saturday, June 7, they were alone.

"Where's Stel?" the mother of the bride asked.

Offering an ambiguous excuse, Cindy implied that Bruce and Stella had something else to do.

However, something was off-kilter. Way off. The Nickells were practically family. Kimmie wanted them to share her special day, as did the rest of her family. Neither Bruce nor Stella would rank something more important than her wedding.

Even worse, the only Nickell presence seemed drunk, though she admitted only to a hangover. It was embarrassing and sad at the same time.

Laurie told Cindy to tell her mother and stepfather to join the family at their home after the reception.

She promised she would.

Later that night, after nearly all the wedding well-wishers had left, Stella finally came calling alone.

"Where's Bruce?" Laurie asked.

"That's what I have to tell you," Stella said, tears dripping from her eyes. "Bruce passed away."

Dizzy with shock, Laurie reached out to hug her friend.

"She told me he had died two days before, but she wasn't going to tell me 'til after the wedding, and after Kim and Dan had gone on their honeymoon," Laurie later recalled. "She didn't want to ruin their day."

Stella gulped a stiff drink and suddenly stood up to leave. "I've got to go . . . I'll talk to you tomorrow."

Stan Church took his best friend's death especially hard. Wracked with grief, he barely said a word for the next three days. It seemed inconceivable that Bruce was gone.

He had seen Bruce on his birthday, June 1. They had talked over coffee at the house, and he had seemed perfectly healthy.

The next morning, Karan cried when Laurie told her that Bruce had died.

"How?" she asked.

Laurie said the doctors didn't know. "Maybe an aneurysm."

"Why didn't Cindy say anything?"

Laurie didn't know. She had assumed Stella had told Cindy to not say anything.

"But why would she bother to show up at the wedding? Wouldn't it have been better not to have shown up?"

Later, when Laurie asked Stella about it, her friend seemed surprised. Stella said she didn't know Cindy had gone to the wedding.

*

Stella and Cindy checked into room 241 at the Orchard Inn in Wenatchee on Monday, June 9, 1986. It was an hour's drive from where Bruce's cousin, Dick Nickell, had chosen the burial site.

Walter Nickell paid for his only son's casket. He asked his daughter-in-law if she had a decent suit for Bruce to be buried in. "No," she told him. "He's gonna be buried in jeans and a sports shirt. That's the way I want it." Walter accepted her wishes, though he had hoped for something a little nicer for his boy.

It was not a time to argue anyway. For Walter, it was a time to cry. He lost his fragile composure in the slumber room at the Jones & Jones Funeral Home. The tears came and wouldn't stop. His son was supposed to outlive him. It hurt to say goodbye. Ruth Nickell didn't cry; she knew her husband could shed enough tears for the both of them.

Stella left Dick Nickell with an uneasy feeling at the funeral home. In the car on the way there, she complained of a headache. "I've got a bad one," she said, "just like the ones Bruce used to give me all the time."

The comment was colored with bitterness from a woman who by all rights should be grieving. Dick Nickell couldn't put it out of his mind.

Jim McCarthy was the only one of the deceased's friends to make it to the funeral. He was big, dark, and boasted of Native American blood, an attribute not lost on Stella Nickell, who, like her mother, prided herself in her heritage. At fifty-four, Jim was a three-time divorcé when he met the Nickells through an Auburn CB radio club in late 1983.

He told people that losing Bruce was the shock of his life. They had so much in common. Big Mac, as he was called on the radio, was the estranged father of two sons. The men shared a fanatical interest in electronics.

Stella's niece, Wilma Mae Stewart, also attended.

A couple of rows of folding chairs had been set up on the lawn before the casket. Stella and Cindy, both dressed in black, occupied two seats in the front row. The widow's face was ashen and her eyes were covered with dark glasses.

It was Stella's daughter, sobbing uncontrollably, who made the greatest impression on Wilma.

"It really struck me, the very well-rehearsed, complicated role that Cynthia Lea was playing," Wilma said later. "Dabbing her eyes with a hanky and no tears struck me as being very phony. I took offense at it, which is why I remember it so well."

Dick and Walter Nickell noticed the same thing.

"Look at Cindy and look at Stella," Dick Nickell whispered to the old man. "Cindy's sitting there bawling her head off, just crying and crying like she can't hardly take it." Stella's lack of emotion struck Dick as suspicious.

Wilma thought her aunt was doing her best to maintain composure, but that there was something disturbing about her cousin Cindy's behavior.

"It was like 'cut, director's gone on break, let's all be ourselves, let's all be natural.' And Cynthia Lea carried on as usual. There would be times when she would be like, 'Wait, I got to put it back on; the director's coming.' She was bouncing between this 'Oh, woe is me, I lost my daddy,' or whatever." Wilma thought her cousin was ecstatic because she was the center of attention. She even sat at the head of the table.

Days after the funeral, neighbor Sandy Scott was out working in the yard when Stella drove up in her green pickup after retrieving her mail. She waved her husband's death certificate in Sandy's direction.

"They said it was emphysema," she said, shaking her head. "He just had a physical with the state. He was told he probably would develop it, but he didn't have it then. Does it happen that fast?"

"Not from what I've heard," Sandy said. She had friends who had developed emphysema, and in both instances it had been a slow and enfeebling disease.

"For the last year and a half, they could sit up on the couch, but they couldn't walk to the bathroom. You don't go to work in the morning and come home and die of emphysema."

Chapter Fifteen

Cora Lee's suggestion to adopt Cynthia in order to allow Stella some teenage fun had apparently been taken to heart, and Stella ran wild in Southern California. She left her baby with her mother whenever she stumbled across some new male distraction. By her own admission, she was a "little promiscuous" then, but she never kept more than one man on a string at a time.

As she had in Seattle, Stella continued seeing older men. Men her own age lacked the maturity she felt she possessed. She, after all, was a mother. A grown woman.

When Stella became pregnant in the summer of 1962, Cora Lee was outraged. She had bailed Stella out of her pregnancy with Cindy. She had put up with Ricky Slawson and his threats to take the little girl. But another baby, another illegitimate birth, was too much. Cora Lee was working on the assembly line at Hughes Aircraft and trying to keep her jobless, wild daughter and granddaughter fed. The state of the house was another matter. She'd recently kicked out Bill Street and as a result, didn't have anyone to help with the mortgage. It didn't matter that this time the paternity was certain, the baby had to be given up for adoption.

The baby's father, a former Air Force enlistee, was five or six years older than Stella. He said he didn't want to get married—even though Stella claimed he had given her an engagement ring—and soon after that she caught her beau in bed with another woman.

With him out the picture, Stella went along with Cora Lee's adoption plans, partly because at eighteen she didn't want another child. Cindy was enough of a handful. But also, if she was ever to find a man decent enough to marry, supporting two kids was asking too much.

Later, Stella would say she held some regret for giving up her baby.

She had thought it was probably the best thing for the child. She knew it wasn't the best thing for her.

For some in the family it would be hard to fathom Cora Lee giving away one of her grandchildren. She had lost two children to tragic childhood accidents and had suffered at least two miscarriages. But according to Stella, it was her mother who had pushed for the adoption.

They kept the arrangement secret. March 10, 1963, was the date her baby boy was born in an Orange County hospital. It was a date she would remember every year. What he looked like, Stella never knew. She never laid eyes on him.

"I could have seen him," she said later. "I chose not to. If I had seen him, I would not have signed the papers. And Mother knew this. She told me it would be best if I didn't see him."

When she returned from the hospital, Stella called Berta, who was still living in Seattle. She told her that her baby had been stillborn. She seemed a bit distant about her loss.

Berta broke down. Her heart ached not only for her sister, but for her mother. Nearly thirty years would pass before Berta would learn the truth. When she did, it left her wondering how well in fact she really did know her closest sibling. She couldn't imagine Stella giving up a baby and not telling her about it.

Though he had been stationed north of the 38th Parallel during the Korean War and was one of only two in his unit of ten to return to the States, Robert Warren "Bob" Strong met his match in Stella Stephenson. He found her abrasive attitude dangerous and appealing. She could alternate between sweet concern and the rage of the most foulmouthed sailor at the drop of a hat.

For Bob, it was lust, if not love, at first sight.

Initially, it was "The Walk" that attracted him. Stella Stephenson would stand straight as a poker, and swing her shoulders a little bit so her chest would swing to and fro and catch the eyes of onlookers. Other women might have thought they knew "The Walk," but they were amateurs compared to Stella's gait. It got her attention.

Bob noticed that Stella's four-year-old daughter mimicked her mother, acting like a miniature Stella, doing her best to walk "The Walk."

Stella also had a way of talking that was different from any woman Bob had known. She was direct and tough. Cora Lee had raised her to be that way.

"She taught us to take care of ourselves and be independent, because she had to work, so she couldn't be there."

The night Cora Lee learned about Bob Strong's intention to marry her daughter, future mother-in-law and son-in-law sat in her car in front of Stella's apartment and talked all night. Cora Lee held hopes that mild-mannered Bob Strong, so respectful and sweet, would balance her daughter and provide some stability for her granddaughter.

Bob and Stella were married on June 3, 1964. The new couple and Stella's daughter moved into a $115-a-month ranch house in Santa Ana. Twenty-foot-high yuccas framed the small patio by the front door and a picture window faced the street. Out back was a detached garage used as a shop, with doors that slid open. Hibiscus blooms and the neighbors' fragrant orange trees competed with the acrid odors of the Orange County Airport just down the street.

Being the old-fashioned type, Bob did not want his wife to work, so Stella stayed home. She remained close to her mother, and even formed a slight friendship with Pat Bilderback, the wife of an alcoholic womanizer who lived across the street. When she needed to shop, Stella left Cindy with her neighbor.

At home, Stella had high expectations: manners were critical. If she caught Cindy with her elbows on the table, the preschooler got a quick, sharp jab with a fork. When she felt it was warranted, her husband got similar jabs too.

Lois Schaefer met the Strongs through Pat Bilderback. An obese woman with minor agoraphobia married to a man twenty-eight years her senior, Lois took an immediate disliking to Stella Strong. She was pushy and defiant. All the men paid attention to her, and she seemed to court it. It wasn't unusual for women to dislike her; Stella rarely had female friends.

Not long after the wedding, Stella Strong was running around and bedding every man in Orange County. At least, that was how Bob Strong saw it.

At first, Stella would just leave the house for destinations unknown. But as time passed and as Bob looked the other way, she grew bolder. Once he caught his wife in a negligee on the couch with another man. Stella said the man was a friend of her cousin's.

"A week later she denied she was ever on the couch in a negligee in the first place," he said. Bob wasn't the type to fight about it. *Let her do what she's doing, and I'll go do what I'm doing,* he thought. *It'll keep the peace.*

One time Stella showed up at her husband's job site, where he was installing cabinets at a doctor's office in Garden Grove. Bob took a break to talk with his wife. While they stood by the side of the car, another construction worker approached and he and Stella engaged in flirtatious conversation.

Bob Strong didn't like what his wife was doing, but by then it had become so familiar. The woman always used sex to get what she wanted. Bob felt it was a trait that ran in her family.

On November 4, 1966, Stella Strong gave birth to a second daughter, Leah Ruth, at Hoag Memorial Hospital in Newport Beach. The sweet baby girl was blue-eyed and blonde, but for some reason never found the place in her mother's heart that her big sister held. Friends suggested the little girl reminded Stella too much of Bob Strong.

Chapter Sixteen

Dee Rogers told friends she visited Stella's place after Bruce died because she didn't want her friend to be alone. The fact that reporters were as thick as the mosquitoes from the run-off below the trailer, and even the national media was pounding on the Nickells' door, unquestionably made her decision to visit all the more enticing.

After what was expected to be a short stop at the FBI offices so Stella could be fingerprinted, they'd be on their way camping for a few days. It was late June 1986. Stella had all the things they needed in the back of the truck. Dee thought camping was a good idea. Stella, who was furious at the media presence outside her home, clearly needed a break.

"Someone is going to have to pay for this!" she told her friend. "You can bet I'm going to jump on the bandwagon and sue somebody for this!"

The next morning, they stopped at Stella's lawyer's office, before heading to the FBI and then on to the campsite in Eastern Washington.

Stella and Dee parked under the Alaskan Way viaduct, Seattle's ugly double-decker thruway that barricades the city from the spectacular waterfront, and hiked up the hill to the Federal Building. Dee was left to read plaques—Fidelity, Bravery, Integrity—in the reception area, while her friend went inside to be inked and printed. When she emerged a short time later, she seemed very concerned, almost frightened, though fear was something Dee Rogers had never associated with Stella or even her daughter, for that matter. Fear didn't run in the family.

"They want me to take a lie detector test," Stella said on the way back to the truck. The idea of a polygraph had never entered Dee Rogers's mind. She was just as incredulous about the whole thing as Stella Nickell.

"Why?"

"I have no idea. But I told them I'd talk to my lawyer."

Stella cracked her truck window and smoked all the way to Stevens Pass. They were heading toward Eastern Washington, on the other side of the mountains. Stella said she and Bruce used to go there. Cindy had been left in charge of Dee's sons and daughter. As much as Dee knew Cindy liked her kids, the prospect was risky. If Cindy was in the mood to take up an offer with a man from the local truck stop, then Dee's kids would have to fend for themselves.

They stayed at the campsite for almost a week, drinking and talking about the FBI and the damned lie detector test. When they grew tired of drinking MacNaughton's, they switched to Wild Turkey. And then they talked some more.

When booze threatened to run dry, Stella hopped in her truck for a liquor store. Dee lolled on their raft and sipped the last of the Wild Turkey.

Stella was gone for quite a while, longer than Dee thought it would take to get to the liquor store and back. Maybe she had run into somebody she knew? Maybe she had gone to see Bruce's folks, who lived barely more than a half hour from town?

Stella never said where she went but she made a similar trip a day or so later. When she returned, she was cool and confident, her old self. Dee, on the other hand, was so drunk she could barely paddle herself to shore. She lay in the river raft on the icy water until Stella bailed her out.

Stella broke out the bottles she had purchased and gave Dee a romance novel she had picked up in town. They were there to get away from the media, but also to have a good time. This was a vacation.

Stella talked about the polygraph and her fear of taking it. "I feel guilty," she said. "I could have done more for him…I wasn't always the best wife."

"Come on, Stella. For Christ's sake, Bruce was a goddamn pampered asshole! He couldn't find the refrigerator unless you pointed him in the direction. He was spoiled rotten!"

"I don't know…" Stella answered. "I also feel responsible because I was the one who bought the Excedrin and brought it into the house. It's my fault. I don't know how it's going to come across on the lie detector."

"Then don't take it. Just don't do it. Talk to your lawyer."

The week eventually came to an end. Although there had been tears over Bruce and she said she was a wreck, Dee thought Stella never appeared to be stressed.

"She was probably one of the coolest people I've ever seen. She carried herself high. She never appeared happy. She didn't appear sad. She just appeared cool, cold, and straight. That was Stella," Dee said later. "She never had any problem going to sleep at night."

Stella would say later that Dee Rogers had been an uninvited guest on the camping trip to Red Rock Mine. Stella had only wanted to be alone, to be with the memory of her late husband.

*

Cora Lee stomped up the hill to the Scotts' place, asking whether Sandy knew when Stella and Dee were to return. Neither woman had heard from Stella in days.

Cora Lee wondered why Stella was away with Dee. It was so out of character, it confused her. "Stella's mad at her for letting Cindy stay with her."

Sandy, who had heard a little of Stella's ire toward Dee during the night she stayed with her, made no comment other than to reassure the woman everything was probably fine.

But Sandy remembered that Stella had told her she didn't trust her old friend Dee.

For the next few days, Cora Lee continued to call Sandy to see if she had heard from Stella.

Always an outsider when it came to her mother and older sister, Leah, almost twenty, hadn't known the seriousness of the Excedrin events in Auburn. Her heart skipped a beat when the FBI caught up with her and requested that she come to their field office in Jackson, Mississippi. They had questions about the cyanide poisoning death of her stepfather.

The agent on the phone tried to calm her. "Don't worry. We always investigate matters like this." Leah was confused by the agents' queries.

"They were asking me kind of odd questions. Did I think he [Bruce] was cheating on my mom? Did my mom cheat on him? Asking me if he ever tried anything with Cindy?"

Leah drew a blank. "I did not live with my mother."

The young woman was trembling when she left, the experience having shaken her. She wondered what had really happened up in Washington—and who was involved. "The way they asked me, I thought they suspected my sister and mom," she said years later.

*

A short time after Bruce Nickell's name appeared in every newspaper in the country as a product-tampering victim, an incensed Cindy called her friend Bonnie Anderson and told her the FBI had been harassing her mother about the Auburn tamperings. They had asked her to take a polygraph, but she had refused.

Bonnie was incredulous. "Cindy, they think that your mom killed Bruce?"

"Yeah, that's what they think! I know she didn't." Cindy didn't beat around the bush. She told Bonnie she was absolutely convinced her mother hadn't killed anyone.

Chapter Seventeen

The photograph album was white vinyl, trimmed with a stripe of gold filigree and a regal script spelling out "Our Family." It was the kind of compendium of memories a mother assembles with great care and love for her children. Two children were listed in the family tree overleaf: Cindy and Leah Ruth. As in most families in which there is attention and enthusiasm for chronicling the joys of childhood, emphasis was placed on the firstborn.

In studio portrait after portrait, a little girl with clusters of brown curls and lovely dark eyes smiled for the camera. The California sun had brought out freckles, and baby teeth had given way to permanent ones. Smile after smile, page after page, until it stopped…

Cynthia Lea had always bruised easily. Her mother and father both said so.

"She had a hell of a lot of bruises on her, but she could even think something hit her and she'd get a bruise; that's how easy it was for Cindy. She didn't necessarily have to be beaten hard to get all of those bruises. I'm not saying that she wasn't," Bob Strong later said.

When Bob come home from work, Stella would sometimes meet him at the door, her voice surging with anger.

"Robert," she said, using his more formal given name as a mother addresses a child in trouble, "You come in here. I want you to punish your daughter. She's in her bedroom now."

Bob went to the bedroom down the hall, but he was torn.

"I mean, the little girl only did what she sees her mother doing—lie, steal, cheat. I couldn't see how it was useful to beat her for something she'd seen her mother do," he said later.

Sometimes he would close the door and tell Cindy to pretend to yelp when he snapped his belt.

Cynthia Lea Strong was a student at Bay View School in Costa Mesa. Her second-grade class picture showed her leaning forward in the third row, straining for the lens to catch her happy smile. Of the twenty-six faces, hers was the only one the camera seemed to notice. The chalkboard read "January 17, 1968."

The fourth-grade class picture also made the family album. She was now in the back row, her smile dimmed and her pose more weary, even grown-up. She was not the same girl.

On January 12, 1969, in tears, Stella Strong made a phone call to her sister Berta. Stella said she had tried everything she could think of to stop Cindy from using her makeup or taking her things. The spanking, as she called it, had been a last resort. And it had left a bruise.

"It was on the leg, because I missed," Stella wept into the phone. "I was just giving her an old-fashioned spanking."

Berta hung up the phone feeling upset. She knew how hard it was to discipline kids, and how she felt when she spanked her own for misbehaving.

When Cindy showed up at school with bruises, a teacher and a nurse questioned her. She said her mother had beaten her with a wooden pole. The Costa Mesa police were notified, Cindy was taken to a hospital and a youth protection center, and Stella Strong was arrested on suspicion of the felonious beating of her daughter. She spent a night in jail and was released on her own recognizance.

Bob Strong confronted his wife about the beating. Stella told him the girl had stolen some crystal earrings and makeup and had given them to another schoolgirl. She had been warned repeatedly to stay out of her mother's personal things. Bob hoped reports of the injuries had been exaggerated.

When he saw the little girl, he knew otherwise.

"It looked like Cindy had been beaten half to death," he recalled.

Years later, Stella's version of what happened was a story of a daughter so desperate for attention that she would turn against her own mother. Stella would not deny that she spanked her, and never denied that there were bruises.

"Cynthia had bruises on her because Cynthia bruises very easy. You can walk up and grab a hold of her on the arm and you will leave your fingerprints."

Her daughter had wanted sympathy.

"She went to the nurses' office complaining that she was sick. And she noticed the bruises on Cindy's butt and she had a couple on the top part of her thigh just below her panty leg. And the nurse asked her what happened, and she said her mother beat her. So the nurse kind of perked up her ears and got to talking to Cindy about it. This was the attention Cindy was looking for. So Cynthia went all out and she said that I had beat her with a stick about the size of a fifty-cent piece and three foot long. It was three foot long because it was meant to go on our doorway. Robert had put some braces in the doorway up against the door frame and that piece of wood hooked in it because that's what I used to do sit-ups with—it held my feet down. Cynthia said that was what I beat her with, was this three-foot-long log that I had in the house."

The day after her release, Stella and Bob went to see Cindy at the center. The little girl, who had survived the handiwork of her mother and the reported three-foot pole well enough to make it to school, was now in tears. But it wasn't the beating that made her cry. She had been hit with the news Bob Strong was not her father. During the admitting process, someone had told the girl that her real last name was Slawson, not Strong.

The child hadn't actually been lied to about her parentage; it was simply a case of her assuming Bob was her daddy and no one having the heart to correct her. She used the name Strong in school.

"And like I say, shit hit the fan as far as Cindy was concerned. She wouldn't even talk to me," Bob said later. "Here's this little kid who finds out that I'm not her real father and she don't even know who he is …"

Life for the Strongs improved somewhat in the weeks immediately following Cindy's return from the children's protection center. The courts put the girl under Bob's supervision and Stella was ordered into group therapy.

Bob Strong went to a couple of the counseling sessions in support of her, but he felt the whole thing was a farce. The therapist let Stella run the meeting—and she was good at it. It was Stella who asked the questions of the group.

One little lady stood and said to Stella, "If you were my mother, I'd be scared shitless of you." "I about cracked up," Bob said later.

Stella enjoyed the classes.

"It taught me a lot about how I could look at Cynthia, and I think that's the reason that I know so well how her mind works."

When Stella's cousin, Bonnie Shields Hickson—Cora Lee's sister Dorothy's daughter—needed a place to figure out what her struggling family was going to do next, Stella readily offered her a place to stay. The first week in May 1970, Stella and Bob went up to Ukiah to move Bonnie, her husband, Wendell, and their three children down to Santa Ana.

On May 15, Bonnie and Wendell made arrangements to have their welfare checks and food stamps transferred from Mendocino to Orange County.

But before the transfer was complete, their plans changed again and the Hicksons decided to head for Texas, where Wendell could likely get work. A car accident in New Mexico, however, forced them to return to Northern California. Back in Mendocino County, they reapplied for welfare.

Orange County, however, didn't get notice of the change in plans. Welfare checks of $119.50 made out to Wendell Hickson were sent to the Strongs' address, the first arriving in September.

Stella Strong cashed them.

Robert Strong told his wife he wanted nothing to do with it. She should send the checks back to where they came from. Stella ignored him.

She later said she did it to feed her kids.

If, in fact, the checks had been used to put food on the table, Bob Strong never saw any evidence of it. Even the neighbors who knew Stella had been cashing them wondered where the money was going.

Neither Cindy, now a fifth grader at Bay View School, nor her little sister Leah, seemed to get enough to eat.

On January 5, 1971, Stella Strong signed over one of the checks to pay a little more than half of what she owed to a Carnation Milk driver. She told her milkman Wendell Hickson had given her permission to countersign the checks.

The following month, the Hicksons paid the Strongs a visit to retrieve belongings they had left behind. Wendell's health had improved, and Bonnie was grateful. Money, however, was still tight.

"If it wasn't for the welfare department," she told Stella, "we never could have made it down here."

"How long have you been back on welfare?" Stella asked.

Bonnie said they had never been off the program. Their case had never been transferred to Orange, because they returned to Ukiah in time to stop it.

Stella told her that checks had been coming to them.

"I hope you've been sending them back," Bonnie said.

Knowing her cousin as she did, Bonnie likely wasn't surprised by Stella's story that she'd had a man forge Wendell's name, then countersigned and cashed the checks. Stella also admitted using the Hicksons' food stamps. She showed Bonnie an ill card she used for the stamps.

Bonnie told her she was going to report her to the welfare department and Stella begged her not to—after all, she was family. "I'm your blood cousin," Stella pleaded.

Two days later, Bonnie made good on her threat and the welfare departments of Mendocino and Orange counties began a joint investigation.

Stella was off God-knows-where when Bob Strong answered Cora Lee's phone call from up in Ukiah, where she now lived.

The old woman was hotter than a Santa Ana sidewalk in August. The family gossip line had leaked some news about Stella.

"Stella better watch her back," Cora Lee seethed. "Bonnie turned her in for welfare fraud and forgery. They're gonna get her good for this one."

When Bob finally told Stella, she seemed to pay it no mind. The threat of an investigation and an arrest just seemed to roll off her back. But that was Stella. She was too tough to let anyone think she was worried.

On the day of her arrest, Stella and her neighbor Pat Bilderback spent the afternoon looking at used cars. Stella was in the market for a car, and she wanted Pat's advice. Where she would come up with the money for a down payment was apparently of no concern, though Bob still wasn't back to work.

When the women returned home, an Orange County investigator was waiting. Bob watched his wife protest and deny her involvement in any wrongdoing.

Then she sat calmly with the investigator at the kitchen table.

"My heart's jumping . . . and she's just sitting there as cool as hell. He just looks at me and looks at her," Bob said later. The investigator was tired of her stories. He knew she had cashed those checks, and he had the affidavits to back it up.

"As far as I'm concerned, you did it. Now, unless you come clean right now and tell me the truth, you're going be put away for a long time," he said.

Stella broke down and cried. She admitted she had done it, and that she had done it alone. "My husband had nothing to do with it," she said, weeping. "He didn't even know about it."

The investigator believed her.

"She knew she was nailed," Bob recalled some years later. "She was making sure that I was clear so that I could take care of the kids. The kids were first, nothing else. She'd lay her life down for her kids."

Stella saw Bob's role differently.

"Him and me agreed ahead of time that he would plead ignorance. I wasn't about to lose my children and have them taken away from us by having Robert go to jail too. I told him to keep his mouth shut," she later explained.

In a plea bargain which Bob Strong thought had taken into consideration her two little girls, Stella Maudine Strong was convicted of a single count of forgery and was sentenced to six months in Orange County Jail.

Cora Lee drove down from Ukiah to help take care of Cindy and Leah while their mother was in jail. Almost immediately Bob started seeing newly single neighbor Pat as the woman of his dreams. She didn't cheat, lie, or steal.

Stella saw what was happening.

By mid-August 1971, she had written the last of three letters to the court, in an attempt to get the judge to take pity on her and release her. She even suggested he could change her probation from three to five years. Whatever it took, she needed out. She worried that Cora Lee was going to take her girls and leave California. Although this might have been a possibility, the truth was that Bob Strong was slipping away.

No man had ever left Stella before. Especially to a dowdy lady like Pat Bilderback.

Bob visited the jail every day and even did Stella's laundry. He made sure the girls saw their mother each Saturday. But the marriage was over. The forgery conviction had been the last straw.

Stella asked Bob if he was dating Pat. He didn't deny it, but he asked her if it was Cora Lee who had been gossiping. Stella scoffed. "Mother wouldn't discuss that with me," she said. "It's my own business."

Later, Stella said she had a "feeling" the two of them had been seeing each other. "It's one of those feelings a woman has inside, you know what's going on." Later, as though she needed to justify why she and Bob hadn't worked out, Stella suggested the split had been mutual.

"He was spineless, no backbone. I loved the man, but he wasn't the right one for me in the long run."

Later, she even attributed part of the reason her marriage failed to the circumstances of Cindy's birth.

"I didn't have a young life, a childhood life. And I felt anger that somebody could do something like that to me like when I was raped. This anger became a part of me. And I took it out on the closest person to me, which happened to be Robert."

Good behavior set Stella free in October 1971, after she had served only four months. By then Bob had asked for a divorce so he and Pat could marry.

Shut out, with no place to go, Stella was furious. *There is no way,* she thought, *that another woman is going to take my place. No way am I going to allow it.*

Bob, who could no longer afford the rent on the house, moved the family into Pat's new place at 234 Victoria in Costa Mesa. He didn't know the best way to handle his wife. He allowed her to move in for a couple of days. Pat, figuring Stella and Bob had plenty to talk over, slept in the workshop.

Stella would never forget her plan for revenge.

"The night I was released from jail I slept with Robert. I was determined to see that no woman would take my husband from me. My way of getting back was action. Taking him to bed was what I did."

Bob saw it all a bit differently. "She figured when she got out she could take me away from any female with no problem."

After seven years, four months, and twenty-one days of marriage, the Strongs officially separated.

*

For her twelfth birthday Cindy asked for a parakeet, and Stella got her one. The girl was overjoyed, and even more excited about spending the day with her mother. But Stella had other plans. After she gave her daughter the bird, she went off somewhere.

A couple of days later, Pat and Bob dumped Stella at the Sunny Acres Motel in Costa Mesa. The situation at Pat's place had been rough. Stella had put the moves on Bob, and a wised-up Pat could no longer risk having the woman in the same house.

Stella called Lois Schaefer and sobbed into the telephone.

"I don't know what I'm going to do. They left me at this motel. Bob doesn't want me…"

Lois felt sorry for the woman. "Bring the girls and come stay with us for a while," Lois said. She later wondered what had made her make that offer. She'd never even liked Stella Strong.

Nevertheless, Stella Strong and her young daughters moved in with Lois and Russell Schaefer, forcing Lois to tread lightly between her best friend, Pat Bilderback, and Stella. The fact that Pat and Bob were now a couple only exacerbated the situation.

Lois had felt sorry for the new couple, but after listening to Stella's side, she felt Stella had been the maligned party.

One afternoon, the Schaefers were discussing food stamps and Lois asked Stella about the application process.

"You should ask Bob," Stella said. "He's the one who did it, and I took the blame because I figured Bob could be out working and take care of the girls and I'd just do the time."

Lois was furious. "How could a man let his wife go to jail for something he did!"

But that wasn't the worst of Stella's lies. She said Bob had sexually abused the girls and that was the reason she didn't want them over at Pat's house.

Lois couldn't believe it. Later, when she asked Cindy if the story was true, the girl denied it.

Cindy and Leah shared a room with the Schaefer children and Stella slept on the living room hide-a-bed.

Stella wasn't the best of guests. Almost immediately, a pattern was established with Stella leaving at night and returning in the morning. When Lois confronted her, Stella was evasive. Since she had no money when she moved in, she paid for nothing. The Schaefers were trying to get by on welfare.

Stella told Lois that she was going to be better off than she and Pat. She didn't like to live down. She wanted to live high. She was going to have things.

The talk hurt Lois.

Yet when the water company threatened to discontinue the Schaefers' service, Stella took care of it. After being out all night, she returned the next day with a receipt from the water district. Lois was so touched she saved the receipt for more than twenty years.

When cookies were all they had to eat, it was Stella who went to the store and returned with enough groceries to fill the cabinets and refrigerator.

Where she went at night, and where she got the money, remained a mystery. Lois called Pat about it. "You know what, Pat, I have a feeling she's either prostituting or she's in drugs. I don't know which."

While Stella was out on one of her night runs, Lois, brushing out Cindy's hair, saw what appeared to be a bite on her shoulder.

"Cindy, what happened to your back?"

"Oh, the dog bit me."

"The dog bit you? Did your mom report it?"

"No, Mom beat it with a wooden spoon."

Lois didn't believe her. The bite was human.

After five weeks of living with Lois, just after Thanksgiving, Stella moved again. Around ten o'clock one night she came to get her girls.

She and a boyfriend had rented a motel room, and she would take Cindy and Leah there. "It's been too much for you and Russell," she explained. "I've decided to get out on my own." Stella woke the girls and told them to pack their things. Lois didn't see them again for a couple of months, until Stella showed up with some man in a Cadillac, looking for her girls' boots. She said she had rented a little apartment up on El Camino in Costa Mesa. Lois Schaefer got on the phone to Pat. She didn't think much of Stella Strong's boyfriends. They looked like bikers. And they were indeed.

For a time following her release from jail, Stella Strong partied with the Hessians, a badass motorcycle gang, rival of the Hells Angels, that had been running around Orange County at the time. She hooked up with Eddie "Butch" Jones.

Eddie Jones was a fiberglass man who spent his days customizing Corvettes and evenings and weekends on his bike with his "old lady," Stella Strong.

Word came from the Hessians that Stella Strong had offered money to someone to kill her ex and his squeeze. Bob Strong called the Costa Mesa police and they promised surveillance. Fortunately, nothing came of the threat. Obviously drunk, Stella called Bob late one evening. She admitted she had, in fact, hired a Hessian to kill him and that no-good woman who had taken her place.

Later, one of the gang members told Bob Strong that Stella's motorcycle-gang boyfriend had been told "they didn't want this damn bitch around here anymore because she was nothing but trouble." She had been kicked out of the gang.

"When the Hessians don't want you around, you know you're pretty bad," Bob later said.

After Butch, Stella settled down with a man named Steve at a rented house on Sungrove. Steve didn't last long. Stella realized he "was not quite right."

Years later, Leah Strong recalled her memories of Steve.

"There was one time I had told Mom about someone touching me and she didn't want to believe me. All I remember is Steve. It was when we lived in California over on Sungrove Street. I remember telling her and she didn't want to believe me; she thought I was lying. She just blew it off."

Stella could not recall any such conversation about Leah being molested.

"I do not recall her telling me, no. I also think that it's possible she remembers this happening because she probably heard Cynthia talking about it. Cynthia tried to tell me some time later that he would not keep his hands off her, and when I asked her why she didn't tell me at the time. And she said no because she didn't want to cause me any trouble. I said, 'I told you from the time you were little, nothing like that causes me any trouble.' I said, 'You are my girls and I will not allow anything to happen to you.'"

Cindy stuck to her story that one of her mom's boyfriends bothered her when she was fourteen:

"He'd, like, want me to sit in his lap, and I didn't like this, and my mother always raised me openly. I mean, I knew about sex, I knew how babies were born, I was not ignorant of any aspects of the human body, and I was very uncomfortable with this man, and I told my mom that I felt that he was making passes at me, and I didn't like it, and she hauled off and she slapped me dead across the face, bounced me off the refrigerator, and called me everything but a white girl, and said that if I hadn't been asking for it. Well, I didn't feel that this was necessary, and I did rebel.

"I told her if she ever, ever hit me again, it would be the last time, and she never did strike me again after that. That was the first time I had ever really stood up to my mother."

Stella then started to punish Cindy and Leah to get back at Bob and Pat. Bob gave Cindy a fish tank, and Cindy told him her mom flushed the fish down the toilet. When he gave her new inner tubes for her bike, Cindy said her mother threw them in the trash.

Bob frequently told Leah how much he loved her beautiful, curly hair.

"Leah went home and said, 'Daddy thinks my hair is pretty'... and she cut it. Stella cut it right at the growth line."

As hard as it would be for Bob to imagine, things worsened.

The Sin-Not was a beer joint off Westminster in Garden Grove. It was a "membership" tavern. Stella hanging around the place was one thing, but Bob and Pat heard she had brought Cindy inside with her.

Later, Bob refused to soften his words. Although Stella denied it, Bob always speculated that Stella had brought Cindy to the bar for one reason.

"To make money," he said. At the time, it seemed Cindy and Stella were headed for the same fate. "Her feet are coming down in her mother's tracks so close that you can't tell there are two sets of tracks."

Bob Strong couldn't handle just sitting by and watching his ex-wife self-destruct and taking Cindy and Leah down the tubes with her.

Besides the men coming and going, school authorities reported that the girls had missed more than a month of school and Stella didn't seem to care. Even the neighbors on Sungrove noticed that the girls were left to their own devices.

Bob filed for custody of Leah, and not surprisingly, Stella became outraged. She had been forced by her mother to give up her son; she was not about to lose her youngest daughter. Stella tried to gather support that she was a fit mother. She went to see Lois Schaefer to make sure she wasn't going to get in her way.

"You better not show up in court to testify against me, or you're gonna pay for it, lady," Stella told her. After she left, Lois called Pat in tears.

"I think I'm gonna get done in, and I want you to know who done it."

The pressure of dealing with Bob and Pat had worn thin, and the only relief Stella saw was to leave.

"I wanted out of California. I had not liked California since the day I set foot in it when I was sixteen years old. I was divorced and I had my two kids; I had nothing to hold me there. One day I just packed up and left."

The first week in November 1973, Stella and the girls drove up to Washington to put some miles between them and Bob Strong, who had petitioned the court for custody of Leah. He would have taken Cindy, too, but he had no blood claim to her.

They stopped at Stella's sister Georgia Mae's place near Tenino, Washington, with sights set on Kent or Auburn.

December in the Pacific Northwest is a far cry from the sunny warmth of Orange County: rain, followed by more of the same. After living out of their car, Stella Strong and her daughters moved into a one-bedroom Kent apartment, though the girls would later remember it as more of a garage or storage building. It was a relatively pleasant time of bonding and closeness for the girls.

Though she was only seven years older, Cindy made sure Leah was dressed and fed before school. Their mother seemed only a visitor.

"My mom would come once in a while in the morning to make sure we had money for lunch. She'd make sure we had groceries and that's about it," Leah recalled years later, still unsure if her mother ever lived with them. It seemed she lived with some man down in a nearby trailer park.

Since Leah didn't have toys to play with, Cindy waited until dark one night and climbed into a Goodwill depository, emerging with armloads of toys. Cindy also set up shipping crates in a field behind a bakery near their apartment to create a playhouse for her little sister.

"We'd build a house, and she'd set a crate down and it would be a couch, set another as a door. She used to do things like that."

Cindy saw that she and Leah never went hungry, even if it meant going to a house next door to ask for something to eat.

No little girl thought her big sister was smarter, prettier, or nicer than Leah Strong did. She was the luckiest little girl in the world with Cindy as her protector. But their time of closeness came to an end. Cindy had fled for California and Leah moved in with her aunt Mary.

Armed with custody papers, Bob and new wife Pat made the trip to Washington to get Leah. When they finally found her, she was at Stella's sister Mary's house in a suburb outside of Seattle.

Mary stood in a state of shock when she answered the door. Stella had told her Bob was dead. Stella was trying to find someone—anyone—to take Leah in.

"If you tell her I told you," Mary said, "I'll deny it."

Her response didn't surprise Bob. The Stephenson sisters, whether they loved one another or hated one another, were fiercely loyal.

"It's like a Mafia, that family. I don't know how else to put it. They'd lay down their life for their own," he said.

Leah returned to Garden Grove, with her mother's promise she would be down to see her in a few weeks. Leah wouldn't see her for nearly four years.

Cindy, running back and forth from Cora Lee's place in Ukiah to foster homes in the Seattle area, never made it down to see her little sister either.

Chapter Eighteen

On a rainy Seattle night in June 1967, Phyllis Cordova nearly died when her car collided with an abutment near the Spokane Street Bridge. She was pitched through the windshield. The soon-to-be divorced mother of four lay in a coma for eleven days. When she awakened, she learned the horror of what happens when flesh presses through glass shards. Her face would never be the same.

By the time she returned to her home in Wenatchee, she was a physical and emotional wreck. Nothing but her singing voice was the same. One night at the Columbia Hotel where she worked, she noticed a man hovering over by the jukebox.

He introduced himself as Bruce Nickell. He was there celebrating his birthday.

The man Phyllis Cordova fell in love with was a loner who liked to drink, sit in bars, shoot pool. Bruce moved from job to job. He told Phyllis he got bored easily. Yet there was also a gentle side. When Phyllis had reconstructive surgery, it was Bruce who stayed with her.

One day he just left Wenatchee for Seattle. He didn't say anything, just left. Eventually, he contacted Phyllis and she moved over too. Bruce was working for the Des Moines water department and living in an apartment near Kent, just behind a bar. It was convenient for a man who drank as much as he did.

In the summer of 1971, Bruce Nickell's alcoholism finally caught up with him. After Phyllis got home from work one evening, Bruce called her from the Country Fair Tavern on Pacific Highway South, having downed an eight-pack of screwdrivers. Phyllis drove out and tried to get him into her car, but he insisted he could drive his pickup just fine. A mile from her duplex, Bruce was stopped by an off-duty officer out with his family.

Bruce was arrested, and since it wasn't his first DWI, he was sentenced to serve four months at Cedar Hills, the county drunk farm near Maple Valley.

Phyllis drove her '64 Ford Galaxy to see her man twice a week. He seemed to be improving.

"He seemed all right. Joking. Playing cards. He made me a beautiful leather-tooled wallet while he was there," she later recalled. He also divulged things she hadn't known.

Bruce said he was sixteen when he discovered he was adopted. He overheard his father talking about it. Bruce became bitter and resentful at the woman who gave him up—whoever she was. Wherever she was.

Phyllis later wondered if Bruce's relationships with women were affected by his mother's abandonment. "I kind of feel that he couldn't continue relationships with women because he was feeling so badly about his birth mother."

Walter and Ruth Nickell gave their son a little thirteen-foot travel trailer they had used on a cross-country vacation, and Bruce was glad to get it. He rented space #52 at the Valley Mobile Home Park on South Central Avenue in Kent. It, too, was convenient. The White Spot Tavern was next door.

Every night after work Bruce Nickell hit the taverns, usually downing a half-dozen beers at a sitting. He generally hung out at a place for a few weeks, got bored with the crowd, and moved on. Since he often got mouthy and physical when he drank, he was sometimes thrown out.

Though their relationship was on and off, Bruce and Phyllis married before a Federal Way justice of the peace in September of 1972.

In January, only four months later, Bruce changed his mind. "I think it's time for us to split the sheets," he said.

Phyllis had no idea it was coming. "Why?"

"I just think it's better. It's time we did."

"I didn't get married to quit," she said.

"I'll meet you after work," Bruce said, not really listening, "and we'll talk about it."

There was another woman on the scene at that time, though Phyllis didn't know it. Her name was Stella Strong. She had just come up from Southern California, and in no time was the talk of the taverns.

It was Bruce Nickell's pattern in dealing with women. He told Phyllis repeatedly she didn't do things the way he wanted. She didn't raise her children right. She was too easy, too soft. Not smart enough. He tore her down.

Stella Strong met Bruce Nickell one afternoon in a tavern in Kent, not far from his little trailer. He walked in and sat down at the bar next to the new girl in town.

"Of course. I'm used to this ..." Stella said later. "I have been all my life. I ignore things like this. I learned to. He ordered a beer and started trying to talk. If he made some remark or asked me a question, I would answer it, and that's all. I was not getting into a conversation with him. And I was about ready to finish my beer and he asked if I wanted another one and I said, 'Nope. I have got to go home. I've got two girls waiting for me.' I got up off the barstool and walked out."

A week later, while her girls were down at her sister Georgia Mae's place, Stella Strong ran into Bruce Nickell again. After that meeting, she told Cindy, "That man is mine, and I'm going to marry him."

Bruce was "perfect-looking" and "he talked very educated, he was intelligent, he didn't make an idiot of himself…" He was tall, slender, and combed his dark hair back from a high forehead. Stella wanted him, and the fact that he was married was only a slight complication.

His heavy drinking didn't dissuade her either. He didn't fit the mold of the alcoholics she had been raised around.

He drank real hard only on weekends.

"He had enough sense to know that it would jeopardize his job, so he would stay sober throughout the week. But Lord, when Friday night came, from the time he hit that door he'd start getting ready to go out, and when we'd go out we'd stay until the bars closed. And then we would start first thing Saturday morning. He knew every bar in South King County that was open at six in the morning."

Stella went along for the ride, her mother's advice playing in her head: *If your husband goes out drinking and he wants you to go with him, go with him. Because then you know where he's at and who he's with.*

By March 1974, Stella and Bruce had moved in together. Stella had found her man, and Bruce found a woman with a temperament to match his own.

Chapter Nineteen

As Paul Webking gathered his wits for SA Jack Cusack's polygraph, Stella Nickell's husband's amended death certificate was issued. Acute cyanide poisoning was now listed as Bruce's cause of death.

As July heated up, Sue Snow's and Bruce Nickell's survivors filed separate lawsuits against Bristol-Myers. Such legal action had been expected. The capsules, despite safety seals and warnings, were simply too easy a mark for a crazed killer—random or otherwise.

Paul had become an effective source for news reporters needing a quick quote on areas concerning product safety. It was not just pain medication capsules that should be banned. He pressed for the discontinuation of all capsules. Drug companies, he said, were more concerned with profits than with public safety.

"There are no need for capsules, period! There is no medical reason for them, and they don't speed up the effects of medication. Tablets work just as quickly."

In July, Hayley was fingerprinted by the FBI. Agents told her that a single latent print found on her bottle remained a mystery. The girl hoped the print would lead to her mother's murderer, and not back to a family member who might have innocently handled the bottle.

When Sue's daughters talked about the mysterious finger-print and suggested a family friend should be printed, since she had been at the house the morning the paramedics came, word got back to Paul, who was in the dark on the subject. Paul spoke to Hayley and asked that she come to him first with any thoughts she had about the case, telling her she could trust him. He liked to be in control.

During this time, the family discussed the lawsuit against Dr. Fligner and the medical examiner's office for negligence. Their lawyers discouraged it. The drug company was at fault.

Yet Paul couldn't help but reiterate the obvious. If Bruce Nickell's death had been autopsied properly, Sue would still be alive.

Chapter Twenty

In 1974, Cynthia Lea Slawson moved into Bob and Pat Strong's home on the corner of Fairview and Trask in Garden Grove. She was more than just a restless teenager. Her mother said she couldn't be handled—Cynthia was incorrigible, deceitful, truant—and put her into a series of foster homes. Cindy figured it was because her mother didn't want her in the way of her own good times. So she'd run away, get returned, assigned another foster home, and execute another escape.

Though only fifteen, the girl had more miles on her than the trucks she hitched rides on to return from Washington to Southern California. Without question, she was following in what Bob Strong knew to be her mother's well-trodden footsteps.

Cindy's time with the Strongs was not peaceful.

Phone calls frequently came in the early morning.

"Do you have a daughter named Cynthia?"

"Yes," Bob Strong would answer, because as far as he was concerned, she was his daughter.

"We found her in an off-limits part of the base. Will you come and get her?" And so he would drive his pickup to Camp Pendleton or El Toro. Sometimes it would be Cindy's voice on the other end of the line.

"Daddy, come and get me. I'm at the Candy Cane Motel." So he would go.

"I didn't think she should be out there doing what she's doing—chasing men. Not boys, men. We're talking Marines. She was basically running around with a bunch of hookers."

As far as the Strongs could tell, Cindy was self-destructing before their eyes. The girl seemed to be on the edge of a breakdown. "I don't want to be like this, but this is the way I was raised. I want to stop, and I can't," Cindy told her stepfather. The words were heartbreakingly familiar.

Stella had said the same thing.

"She used to cry and tell us that she wished she could stop having sex with men frequently," Pat Strong confided years later.

Bob Strong agonized over Stella's influence on her oldest daughter. He had some responsibility in it, of course, but Cindy truly was her mother's daughter. He wondered what was missing in the girl's life.

"It's like the stray dog that comes down the street looking for somebody to care for it. The stray dog will bite you if you try to do anything for it, 'cause he don't trust anybody," he said later.

When he told her she was behaving like Stella, Cindy would lash out in a fit of defensiveness. Her eyes grew cold and full of anger. "I am not my mother."

When the Strongs finally accepted that they had no control over Cindy they turned to their last resort and reported her to the police as a runaway.

The teenager had been gone for several days when the Strongs decided to go over to the hamburger place on Katella and as part of their search, Harbor in Anaheim. The place was a hangout for Marines, and they knew Cindy spent time there. They waited in the truck for their wayward girl to show up.

And she did, looking at least five years older than her fifteen years, wearing hot pants, a vest, and calf-high boots. She looked like a streetwalker.

"Cindy, come over here," Bob called across the parking lot. "I want you to get in the truck."

"No."

"Cindy, I told you I want you to get in the truck. I don't want you just running around."

"I don't want to and I'm not going to."

"I could just throw you in the truck and take you home."

"You do and I'll just crawl out the window and be gone again," she said, turning her back. She was calm. She would only do what she wanted. Bob and Pat's rules were a big joke.

For Bob, the whole business in the parking lot was like talking to Stella. Trying to make Cindy do something she didn't want to only fueled her determination.

Cindy called from some man's apartment the next day, and while she was talking to her stepmother, Pat scribbled a note to a visiting friend. *Go to the pay phone at 7-11 and call the police. Ask for Officer Owenby. Cindy's on the line now. Have them tap the line so they can find out where she's at.*

The police instructed Pat Strong to stay on the phone until they got to Cindy's hideout. She did. "Somebody's at the door," Cindy said, "hold on."

A moment later, an officer got on the line. "We're taking her to Juvenile Hall," he said.

Cindy stayed in detention for a week during mid-February 1975. Authorities attempted to contact Stella, but she apparently had other concerns—mainly, a friend's birthday party.

The only other option was her grandmother, who had already taken Cindy in on many other occasions.

Cora Lee drove all night from Ukiah to get her troubled granddaughter. She didn't even sleep after the Strongs called her to come.

She loved Cindy and wanted to take care of her.

"Cora wanted so much for Cindy to be different than her mother," Bob said. But as Bob saw it, there were differences.

Cindy could be colder than Stella. He didn't worry that some man would really take advantage of the girl; he knew Cindy could handle herself.

"She would be more ruthless. She would be more apt to do something with her own hands. When it comes right down to it, blood and guts, she'll stand toe to toe with you and fight it out."

*

In 1975, Stella, who now used Bruce's last name, wore man-tailored western shirts by day, with the collars always turned up and sleeves rolled in her best tough-girl look. Her blue jeans were boot-cut. At night, she wore spiked heels and skin-tight miniskirts, though other women were wearing skirts mid-knee. Stella did what she wanted and dressed how she wanted.

Bruce and Stella spent the spring and summer months of 1975 and 1976 on weekend camping trips. In June 1975, the couple spent their first overnighter on the beach at Ocean Shores in a camper stocked with a couple of racks of beer. Stella was now nicknamed "Indian," and Bruce was "Bruno." Bruce fished and Stella worked on her tan; it was a happy time.

Stella documented each trip with photographs: "Bruno fishing at Riverside State Park in Spokane." "Bruno fishing on Canyon Rd. outside of Yakima."

Stella could be sentimental, too; she pressed a forget-me-not spray into an envelope she marked "Camping beside a lake."

And on April 12, 1976, "Indian" presented Bruce with an oversize cardboard placard proclaiming him "The World's Greatest Lover."

Stella told people she had fallen for the hard-drinking mechanic from the apple orchards of Eastern Washington. She refused to allow Phyllis Cordova to weasel back into Bruce's life. She told the lady to back off.

Stella had decided to at least try to be solely Bruce's woman. She sent a "Dear John" letter to a trucker named Harry Swanson. Swanson had been head-over-heels in love with Stella when she first hit the Kent tavern scene.

I know you'll understand, she wrote.

Harry Swanson cried when he got the letter. Stella was one incredible woman, and dammit if Bruce wasn't lucky to have her. Swanson tucked the letter into a drawer.

There was little advance notice. Bruce, as he often did, got up with a hangover and his mind made up. He wanted to marry thirty-three-year-old Stella. On September 11, 1976, the couple drove to the Coeur d' Amour Wedding Chapel ("No Appointment Necessary") in Coeur d'Alene, Idaho, just east of Spokane. The bride wore a brown miniskirt and matching vest, set off with a sheer white blouse. White sling-back sandals with three-inch heels made her statuesque. Her forty-two-year-old groom wore a darker-brown leisure suit with a turtleneck.

When Stella and Bruce returned home to their new 1976 Kit Companion, an eight-by-thirty-two trailer on blocks at Valley Mobile Manor, the bride mailed out pretty blue announcement cards: *We would like to tell everyone we have joined hands and become as one...*

In December of the same year, Stella acted as a driver for a tavern friend on a trip to Southern California. She called the Strongs and told them to get Leah ready—she was going to pick her up for a day at either Disneyland or Knott's Berry Farm. The little girl sat by the window waiting for her mother for two days.

Finally, Pat Strong phoned a Costa Mesa motel where Stella had said she'd be staying, only to learn that she'd checked out and gone back to Washington.

Though there seemed to be no time to visit Leah, Stella, Cora Lee, and Cindy celebrated Christmas together a few weeks later. Mothers and daughters gathered in the trailer, faces frozen forever in happy smiles bound for the photo album.

Chapter Twenty-One

Up in the polygraph room on the seventh floor of the Federal Building in Seattle, there was no doubt among the special agents and the examiner, Stella Maudine Nickell was the tamperer.

As the weeks passed, SA Cusack played Stella Nickell's first call to 911 a hundred times. Over and over. What was she saying? How did she say it? Were her responses genuine?

Her voice was calm. Oddly so. There were delays in her responses to the dispatcher.

"I don't know, my husband's gone into some kind of a fit. He's breathing extremely hard, his eyes are rolled back, he told me he was gonna pass out ... I tried to get him on the couch and he hit the floor ..."

She gave the address and told the dispatcher her husband had just turned fifty-three. "Is he conscious?"

"I don't think so, his breathing has slowed down ... I can't see him ... I couldn't get to the phone ... I'm not in the same room he's in. He's in the den."

The dispatcher asked if there was a history of heart problems.

"No, uh, I don't think so. He's had a physical by the state. Works for the state ..."

Works for the state ... just had a physical. Did she go in the other room to file her nails or smoke a cigarette to wait for Bruce to slip closer to death? Maybe she didn't want to watch.

SA Cusack wondered about it all.

But over time the FBI man considered that the tape alone was not enough to discern guilt or otherwise. Why had she made the call? Was it to get emergency help, or was it simply because it was what one would expect a wife to do if their husband collapsed and would make her look innocent?

Was it guilt or concern in Stella's voice? Maybe neither. Based on the tape alone, he could never quite decide.

Airport security manager Gerry McIntyre was happy to comply with a request from the FBI to compile Stella and Cindy's time sheets from hire dates to last shifts worked. By then, both women no longer worked at the airport.

In circling the dates, Gerry made an intriguing discovery: Mother and daughter had missed many of the same days.

"Most of the time when Stella's not coming into work, Cindy's not coming into work too," he said later.

It started to make sense. Up to that point, Cusack had presumed the investigation focused solely on Stella Nickell as the killer.

Could Stella and Cindy have masterminded and executed the crime as a team?

Chapter Twenty-Two

If Bruce Nickell had thought marriage would have reined in his wife, or even slowed her down, he couldn't have been more misguided. Stella continued nuzzling up to any man with a buck for a drink. Friends thought she couldn't help herself. In the spring of 1977, the inevitable occurred and the Nickells separated. Stella told fellow barflies she had rented an apartment in Kent.

Yet true love, or the fact that the couple were well suited for each other, kept them from staying apart for very long. Three months after their split, they reconciled.

By October of the same year, Bruce had moved on to a new job as a mechanic at McDonald Industries, a heavy-equipment rental outfit based in South King County.

As the New Year came, the Nickells struggled to make ends meet while still maintaining their lifestyle of heavy drinking.

Though her oldest daughter would later say Stella gave Bruce an ultimatum—either her or the bottle—it wasn't so simple. Stella not only professed her love for Bruce, she also didn't have anywhere else to go. She told friends her mother reinforced the idea that the wife can't make her husband quit. She had tried to slow him down. But Bruce didn't want to, and more than once they separated. But Stella always came back.

"He kept asking me to come back, and I said, 'I told you, when you slow down and you decide that what you want is a good solid marriage.' I said, 'you've got to slow down on your drinking.' I said, 'I didn't say quit, I'm not asking you to do that. But you've got to slow down.'"

There were other considerations. Stella worried her husband would wreck their truck, hurt himself in a motorcycle accident, or maybe even end up back at Cedar Hills in rehab. It was also a matter of money. Bruce Nickell's drinking cost them $250 a week.

Stella once tried to convert Bruce to becoming an at-home drinker.

"There was one day we were fixing to go out, and I think it was just before his birthday. I had gone uptown to do the shopping during the day on Friday. I had bought him a bottle of Smirnoff. And when he came in and decided to start getting ready to go out, I had made the suggestion, 'Why don't we stay home?' And I gave him this bottle. He says, 'Why don't you fix me a drink?' and he says, 'As soon as I get ready, we'll go out for the evening.' I said, 'Why don't we stay home for the evening?' He says, 'No.' We didn't sit at home and discuss it, but it was kind of discussed throughout the evening. And that's how I came across the fact that he couldn't stand to sit at home and drink. Not even beer," she said some years later.

By the first of the year, 1979, it was time for Bruce to get on the wagon. One evening while drinking at Walt's Inn, he admitted he needed "the cure."

Professional help, Stella told him, was the answer. "I can stand by you, but I can't help you in the ways you need help." Bruce asked her to do whatever she could. Since they didn't have a phone at their trailer, Stella used the bar's pay phone.

"I made some calls, and the easiest one I found was they wanted twenty-seven days as an in-patient, and I knew he wasn't going for that. I knew it in the bottom of my soul. But I relayed the message to him. I said they had some open beds. I said, 'But it's going to require twenty-seven days as an in-patient,' and he said, 'Nope.' I said, 'Okay, you don't want help very bad, do ya?' And dropped the subject."

Bruce guzzled for two weeks solid. He didn't go to work. He took off without a word as to where he was going. Stella would wait a bit, then go after him to find out if he was still alive.

The trail usually ended at Walt's Inn, with a drunken Bruce Nickell at the bar talking with the bartender. Bruce ordered Stella a drink, and without any kind of warning turned and said, "Okay. I'll do it."

"Do what?" she asked.

"I'll become an in-patient."

Stella said she'd make the phone call, but Bruce wanted her to do it immediately. "Make it right now," he said, "because I'm ready for it now." Not about to take the chance that in his stupor Bruce would change his mind, Stella dialed the number for Schick Shadel in Seattle. She spoke with a counselor.

The counselor told her, "I can tell you when he leaves here he will not want to drink, and he will not have any desire for drink and he will not be able to drink."

"That's the words that hooked me," she later recalled. "He says he won't be able to."

Bruce Nickell was admitted to the program the same day his wife made the call. Stella visited every day. Finally, after days of aversion therapy and counseling, Bruce Nickell walked out of the place sober and never drank a drop again.

And although Stella had wished for it, even prayed for it, she couldn't have anticipated the ways their lives would change.

After a while, some would later insist, she didn't like the change.

*

In Ukiah, Cora Lee Rice had fallen for a man she thought would make a terrific husband, her fifth. Stella thought her mother would be better off if this time she just lived with the fellow.

Cindy and her trucker boyfriend lived in Willits, not far from Cora Lee's place. Over the Fourth of July, Stella, Cindy, and Cora Lee gathered for a weekend reunion. Once again, Leah was left out.

Cindy had news to share with her family. She was pregnant.

Stella began to get upset with Cindy and announced she wasn't ready to be a grandmother.

It was just before Christmas 1978 that Cindy, now nineteen, delivered a baby girl in a Ukiah hospital and had a tubal ligation. One kid would be plenty.

Life calmed down for Cindy after the birth of her child. She and her boyfriend rented a small house in Willits. If Cindy had wanted to live the life of a stay-at-home wife and mother, this was her chance.

On February 21, 1979, Cindy wrote her mother about her baby's delivery—by C-section because of an active herpes virus—and to let her know that she was proud of Bruce for quitting the booze.

Also tell him I think it took a lot of courage, she wrote.

There was bad news for Cora Lee, however. Her beau died when a piece of World War II shrapnel moved to his brain. She was heartbroken.

She really loved that man, Cindy wrote.

Cora Lee parked away a pretty dress she had selected for the wedding that never was. She told her daughter Berta that if she never met another man, she'd wear it for her own burial.

A thirteen-year-old with pretty, dark-blond hair and clear blue eyes, Stella's daughter Leah took the bus to Northern California for a two-week visit with her sister and grandmother in the early summer of 1979.

Cindy was living with her baby's father in the little house across the street from a trailer park. She called him her "husband," though as far as Leah knew there had never been a wedding. During at least a portion of her time with her sister, the man was off driving a truck.

Late one night the sisters went out for a drive. Twenty-year-old Cindy parked in front of a tavern and told her sister to go ahead and fall asleep in the car—she was going to be a while.

And she was. Leah and the baby fell asleep. Several hours later, Cindy returned. "Don't tell him about this," she ordered.

Leah promised she wouldn't. She looked up to Cindy, who was pretty, brave, and tough. Leah wanted to be like her. Cindy acted more like a mother than an older sister to Leah.

But Leah wasn't the only one who admired Cindy. Stella also found inspiration in her daughter. Transfixed by the beauty and tranquility of Cindy's aquariums, she set up her own fish tank. She documented each fish and bubble with blurry photographs. In time, she would add two more aquariums to the Nickell household.

Chapter Twenty-Three

When the assignment came across Equifax insurance investigator Lynn Force's desk at his Kent office, the thirty-eight-year-old former naval communications man was only vaguely aware of the Auburn cyanide murders. The Seattle native had worked SIDS, shootings, and drowning cases, but never one like the one on his desk. It was July 18, 1986, when Force got the request from the Minneapolis-based Northwestern National Life.

Stella Nickell's claim was considered contestable because the Northwestern accidental death policy was only six months old when her husband died. She was not under suspicion at this point; it was just a routine examination of the circumstances surrounding her husband's death.

His first task would be to talk with the beneficiary, but that quickly proved to be no easy endeavor. Lynn Force would later estimate he made ten to fifteen calls to the Nickell residence, and though Stella returned many of them, no meeting time seemed convenient. He suggested a meeting at her home, but she said that would be out of the question.

Finally, ten days after he received the request for investigation, Stella agreed to talking on the job at SeaTac.

Stella answered questions about her husband's background and health and signed a medical release Lynn Force said was necessary.

Only after she signed it did she ask what he was going to do
with it. He explained that he'd take it to appropriate medical
facilities, like Harborview, or the family doctor in Auburn, in
order to retrieve information for Northwestern.

Investigator Force had been with Equifax for a total of eight
years, and had seen all kinds of reactions from beneficiaries.
Often, tears fell. Sometimes widows hauled out photographs of
their husbands. Stella was not that way at all. Force explained
that the medical release was only good for Northwestern. In an
effort to spare her from additional contact, he asked a routine
question.

"Are there any other policies?"

"No. He only had this one."

Stella Nickell lit a cigarette as she asked about the policy at
hand. Lynn Force told her it had a $36,000 life amount, with
$100,000 accidental. "The $100,000 is only paid if he dies an
accidental death?" Stella asked.

Lynn Force nodded. "The $36,000 will be paid. The insur-
ance company is investigating now to determine whether he
did die due to accidental means."

Armed with the release forms, Lynn Force moved on to interviews with Bruce Nickell's doctor and the staff at Harborview
Medical Center. Information wasn't sitting quite right, and
after discussing it with his supervisor, he made a call to the FBI.

He told them the amount of insurance he was investigating
was about $136,000. The amount Stella had mentioned had
been smaller.

"She told us Nickell had only one small policy from the
state, and it turns out to be $100,000 plus!"

It was the first week in August when Jack Cusack and Randy Scott headed to Lynn Force's Kent office for a meeting.

Stella now knew about the true value of the policy. Lynn Force had told her.

Chapter Twenty-Four

When Stella and Bruce Nickell moved onto space #212 at the Auburn mobile home park in 1979, they were like most of the other folks there—Bruce was blue collar, a machinist for McDonald Industries, and his wife stayed home to take care of their place. Stella was always the first to admit she hated housework. She had to find other ways to occupy her time and while Bruce was in town, Walt's Inn and her other haunts were out.

Although she had always been uninterested in women as friends, at White River Estates she didn't have much of a choice. She became friendly with Dee Rogers and others because she did not have a car. Tri-Chem "liquid embroidery," the current crafts fad, could only kill so much time.

Days by the pool or in each other's trailers crafting passed slowly. Sometimes babysitting was shared. Dee had children, and she had heard that Stella Nickell often watched her granddaughter.

Fourteen-year-old Jerry Kimble was Bruce and Stella Nickell's paperboy when they met. Problems with his father forced the boy to look elsewhere for a family. Jerry, whose CB handle was Lost Tiger, met the Nickells over the radio. It was a fitting name for a boy whose parents didn't play an active role in his life. Before too long he was calling the Nickells "Dad" and "Mom."

Maybe it was having a surrogate son around in their new home, but Stella kicked off the new year with a new interest—genealogy. She sent away for family birth certificates in January 1980.

Her children were on her mind.

On February 12, 1980, in support of her tenuous relationship with her youngest, Leah, Stella wrote a stinging letter to Pat Strong.

> *You may be Leah's stepmother by marriage, but you are not really any relation to her … You definitely will not be a grandmother by her … the main reason is she doesn't want you to be. You may claim to be her mother (Ha! Ha!) But you never will be as long as I'm alive …*

Stella could not let go of the past. She still held Bob Strong responsible for leaving her after she did her jail time.

So what if Pat, her old friend and neighbor, had been there to pick up the pieces when she was locked up? She wanted Pat to know that what goes around comes around.

If a man will do it once, there is always the chance he will do it again. They are never too old, she wrote.

In the middle of June 1980, Pat Strong answered the phone to Stella Nickell, all sweetness and light, calling to invite Leah to come up to Washington after school let out for the summer.

"I really can't say," Pat answered. "It's up to Bob. He's her father."

"He'll say yes," Stella insisted.

Leah could barely contain her joy when her dad and stepmother agreed to the trip. Though Leah felt Pat had tried to poison her with stories of her mother's past—"she was a biker...she was a bar lizard...a tramp...a crook!"—it had all been in vain. Stella was her mother. And that was enough for the seventh grader. She took a Western Airlines flight after school let out.

A week after her arrival, Bruce and Stella took her youngest daughter on a cruise to Victoria, British Columbia, sponsored by a Seattle country radio station. Stella took photographs that she pasted later into a memory album.

Leah wanted to stay for good but Stella was skeptical about having her daughter remain in Washington.

"We'll go through the summer. If things are starting to work out, then we'll consider going into the school year," Stella said. "But that's going to take you obeying the rules and regulations of this household, not the way your father has raised you."

By the end of July, Stella and Bruce gave in. Leah's return ticket to Orange County was canceled. They'd give parenthood a try.

"We went shopping together, and I loved it. We'd go to the mall at Southcenter. She used to lay out in the sun. She wouldn't go bike riding with me. I could never get her to. She bought me a Radio Shack radio for my bike," Leah recalled several years later.

Stella wanted her to be a friend rather than daughter.

"I tried to do that with both of my daughters. To fit into their life instead of being above them, like a lot of parents are to kids," she once said.

Later that summer, Bruce left for a job at Prudhoe Bay, Alaska. He hated to go, he hated leaving his wife, but at least Stella now had her daughter with her.

Bruce returned from Alaska in September, and Leah Strong enrolled at Olympia Junior High as an eighth grader. She registered as Leah Nickell, because it made her feel that she was part of a family.

Yet, as the weeks passed, Leah began to wonder if, in fact, Bruce really wanted her around. She felt the man was jealous of her mother's attention. He was used to having supper on the table when he got home, and with a young girl in the house other things sometimes became more important.

As far as Leah could see, her mother was the dutiful wife. Not only did she take care of everything at home, she did the banking and paid the bills. Teenager Leah even got used to eating a big breakfast at the crack of dawn, because her mother always fixed one for Bruce.

In California, twenty-one-year-old Cindy's money woes continued. In November 1980, Bruce dispatched a money order for $100, presumably to help Stella's daughter, her "husband," and their toddler get up to Washington for Thanksgiving. The little girl also needed to have her hips x-rayed for a minor hip problem she had at birth.

When Cindy came to Auburn, she and Stella went out drinking, fulfilling a mother's promise to her daughter when she came of age. The following month Cindy needed more money, and Bruce Nickell complied. Via Western Union, he wired $250 to Willits. Stella stored the receipts with some others, including gas charges from Willits to Tacoma, and a deposit for an apartment, totaling $600. Someday, Cindy promised, she'd pay her mother back. Stella insisted on it.

The Nickells were in no position to give any money to anybody. Stella was answering the kind of ads found in the back of the *National Enquirer. Earn $$$ Stuffing Envelopes!*

She even tried to earn a few bucks composing a *Reader's Digest* "Life in These United States" article about one of her girls killing a spider. She just couldn't come up with a winner.

One night after Christmas 1980, Leah returned to the Nickells' trailer with a Polaroid she'd found while babysitting a neighbor's kid.

The photo showed a dining room table piled high with marijuana.

Stella found out about it and sent Leah packing for California.

"This ain't going to happen!" she railed. "You're going back to your father's! That's it!"

Leah cried, but she didn't beg to stay and she didn't ask her mother why the picture had set her off.

"You don't ask questions. When she says something, that's it. You don't ask why," Leah said.

"I explained to her," Stella recounted long after "that this could cost all of us our lives. I said, 'These people don't play games. They get real serious.' And I said, 'Real serious means dead.' I looked at it as basically saving her life, because I told her, I said, 'I would be afraid for you to walk from this trailer to the mailbox and back … because you may never come back.'"

Leah never did return to live with her mother.

*

While Stella continued to develop her skill at Tri-Chem embroidery, in 1982, Cindy Slawson left her "husband," dropped out of beauty college, and met Dave McMurphy, a handsome thirty-year-old native Californian who met her criteria. And she met his too. When they weren't off in the truck together running wood chips, the couple partied at western bars, drinking, dancing, and sometimes using cocaine.

Cindy talked about getting back to beauty college, but Dave never felt she was serious. They moved into a place between Willits and Ukiah and, in time, got to know each other.

Cindy professed great love for her daughter but didn't seem grown-up enough to handle her. Beyond a few weekends and one two-week stretch, during the six months they lived together, she rarely kept her daughter with her. Instead, the baby's father's first wife cared for the little dark-eyed girl.

"Being a mother limited her running around. Her doing whatever she wanted to do whenever she wanted to do it. It tied her down," McMurphy said, explaining Cindy's reluctance to be a mother.

"I tried to get her to have her come live with us. She did for a while, but Cindy couldn't handle her, so she sent her back." The relationship Cindy had with her own mother had problems of its own.

"It was a love-hate situation. Just childhood beatings, abuse, and everything else that she felt very bad about. She hated Stella for things like this. At the same time, she loved her and valued her opinion on things. But I knew it was not a trust situation. No matter what her mother told you, it would be something else behind your back."

Though the Nickells had always been on the edge of financial ruin, or because they were at the brink again, Stella had diamond earrings appraised at Federal Way Jeweler's. They came in at $1,967 and life for the Nickells continued.

The Nickells made friends with fellow CB users such as Jim "Big Mac" McCarthy, Don "Salt Shaker" Webbly, and his wife, Shirley "Sugar Shaker" Webbly.

When the Nickells pulled up to a CB break, they were usually seen sitting very close to each other, like high schoolers on a date. The Webblys found they and the Nickells had more than the radio in common. They also each owned a Honda Goldwing motorcycle.

Shirley, who was Stella's age, was a hard-bitten bottle-blonde whose golden hair truly matched her heart. She needed a friend, as she struggled with a husband who drank as though booze were water. Stella, who had been through the same thing and come out a winner with a dry husband, made the perfect confidante. But Stella was hard to get to know; she didn't seem to let too many inside.

"She puts on a facade of not caring, a very cold lady. When you get to know her, that's not the way she is. I think she had it pretty rough throughout her life, and she puts up a shield. She is a caring, loving person. It's just hard for her to show it," Shirley said later.

148 Gregg Olsen

Chapter Twenty-Five

August 1986 was a month of new beginnings and endings for the principals mired in the Seattle tampering case. SA Ike Nakamoto returned bags of powder that had been taken from the Nickells' home in June. The lab determined the powder was for welding. SA Nakamoto asked if the widow felt up to the polygraph, and again she said she'd check with her doctor. She was still on medication for stress and anxiety.

Things remained decidedly uneasy among Sue's survivors. Though she was hundreds of miles away, Sarah Webb was still a force in the dissension. She could not accept that Paul was not her twin's killer. FBI special agents had not done enough to let family members know that they were completely satisfied that SA Cusack's polygraph exonerated Paul Webking.

And so Sue's daughters and her husband were alone to do battle in the house on N Street. Paul was making moves of his own. He met a flight attendant while at a reunion in Southern California. But he was angry about the girls' lack of trust. Exa Snow did nothing to hide her feelings of hatred, and she snapped back and went toe to toe with her late mother's husband.

He said the girls were a disgrace. They were out having a good time, instead of thinking about their mother. Hayley stood up to Paul. "That's not true," she said. "I grieve." It surprised her that she stood up to him.

He stormed away, slamming the bedroom door. Hayley lay there contemplating how her mother had not deserved any of this. And how she herself was living a life she couldn't have imagined years earlier.

*

Jack Cusack, armed with a photo lineup, was on a search for the pet store that had sold Algae Destroyer—the source of the green crystals—to the tamperer.

In August 1986, he pulled his car into a shabby Renton shopping center near I-405 and parked in front of Fish Gallery & Pets.

He was looking for Thomas Wayne Noonan.

And Tom Noonan was inside, nervously waiting and wondering what it was that he'd done wrong enough to have the FBI looking for him.

By the time Jack Cusack came calling, twenty-four-year-old pet-store manager Noonan was already acutely aware of the cyanide poisonings. Sue had been his banker, the first to give him a car loan, when he was nineteen. Her death had been a shock. Sue was such a nice, approachable lady. Why her? he wondered.

SA Cusack and Noonan went outside to a place near a rockery in front of the store. The FBI agent pulled some photographs from an oversize envelope.

"Do you recognize anyone?"

Tom Noonan studied the black-and-whites for several minutes. The photos were so pitiful, he almost asked who had taken them. It wasn't instant recognition, but there was one that was familiar. He pointed to a woman with glasses and long dark hair. "I don't remember her name," he said. "But she's been in our stores. Did she do something wrong?"

SA Cusack's eyes betrayed his reserved facade.

"His eyes got big … he got really excited," Tom Noonan later said. He had identified Stella Nickell. Cusack thanked him and left a bewildered Tom Noonan to figure out what it was about his customer Stella that could possibly interest the FBI.

Things started to come back for Tom Noonan. And so did the men from the FBI.

In 1979, Tom had started his career at the Renton location of the four-store Fish Gallery & Pets chain. But it was at the Kent East Hill store where he ran into Stella. He worked there for most of the calendar year 1985, before transferring in January 1986 back to Renton.

When SA Cusack again showed up, this time with SA Ron Nichols in tow, to talk about Stella, Tom recalled other details. Visits over the course of the summer and fall would turn up critical case information.

Stella had been a frequent, sometimes weekly, patron of the Fish Gallery. The young man considered her a pleasant, if somewhat pesky, customer. Not overly sophisticated in her taste in fish, she was like a lot of other hobbyists. She wanted fish that looked pretty and didn't die. Stella once confided that she wanted to open her own store someday.

"I hated to talk to her because she would follow me around the store. I like to help customers, but at the same time I don't like to have them monopolize my time."

He remembered a cat bell Stella wore on her purse.

"She'd come in and wear that occasionally. If I was in the back catching fish or something and I heard that, I knew Stella was in the store."

Noonan thought Stella seemed lonely.

"I felt she would go home and there was no one to talk to there."

The talk bothered him, though.

"Sometimes you would get the feeling that there was more to it than just idle conversation," he said, indicating he thought Stella might be hitting on him. "That got scary."

SA Cusack asked if Stella had purchased Algae Destroyer.

Tom Noonan thought long and hard about that one. He said he didn't normally carry it in the store; he preferred stocking liquids. Then he remembered telling Stella that he didn't care for the product when she said liquid Algae-Gon didn't really work for her and she wanted Algae Destroyer.

"Don't worry about it," he recalled her saying. "I'll just go next door and get it." Not wanting to lose a customer, he put in an order for Mrs. Nickell.

"I'd get it, she'd buy some. Others did too. She was one of the primary people I obtained the product for. Twelve would last us maybe two or three weeks, depending on whether Stella was buying the stuff."

Noonan explained that moisture sometimes seeped into the blister-packed tablets, hardening them to the point where they became almost insoluble.

"As a matter of course, I would tell anybody that bought products packaged that way that the only way to get it to work is to crush it up. Add hot water to it."

SA Cusack asked again about the pulverizing procedure he recommended to Stella and other customers. "I can't under-stand; why are you so concerned about that crushing part?"

"It's very important. Are you sure you mentioned it?"

"I told everybody."

SAs Cusack and Nichols now knew how the green material had been mixed into the cyanide. It had been an accident. The tamperer had likely used a contaminated bowl, one they had used to dissolve the crushed green Algae Destroyer tablets when they put the cyanide into the capsules.

Later, when Tom Noonan asked where the investigation was headed, it was Jack Cusack who told him it had stalled. Even though Tom Noonan had identified Stella as buying the product and recalled telling her to crush it to dissolve it in hot water before adding it to her fish tank, that wasn't enough evidence for federal court.

From what the young man could pick up from the tight-lipped investigators who swarmed around the Fish Gallery, Cindy Hamilton was a potential witness of some sort, but she was avoiding the feds at every turn.

"They were very upset that she didn't want to talk to them at all. A lot of them laid it down to emotional distress. Then—boom—she starts singing like a canary."

Chapter Twenty-Six

If Californian Dave McMurphy felt uneasy about going up north to stay with Cindy's mother in the late fall of 1982, it was only because he didn't know where he stood with his girlfriend. He hoped a short separation would bring them closer together. It didn't take long, however, to see that he was foolishly optimistic. By the time he arrived in Auburn, Cindy was dating her baby's father again.

Cindy surprised Dave with a hand-delivered "Dear John" letter the first week in December. She and her little girl were back in Washington to start a new life—a life that didn't include him.

Stella consoled him. She also did her best to get him work by driving him to job appointments in Seattle and Kent. After two weeks of running around, however, it became clear Stella had other plans.

"What I took for casual at first, we'd go out and shoot pool, go into Kent to the bars, and run around... I didn't instigate anything and I really didn't expect something to happen, but it took me by surprise that she got sexually friendly," Dave later said.

The thirty-year-old trucker reveled in the attention. Stella took him out every evening to dinner at the Buzz Inn, then to her waterbed. She paid for everything. She treated him as if he was the only man in the world. She even paid for his truck driver's physical exam.

Stella complained that things weren't so great with Bruce. She was upset that his alcoholism made him a homebody. And though she griped about money, she spent it freely.

"She was happy to be able to go out with somebody she could have a good time with without worrying about if it was going to be a problem or not," he said later.

The only intrusion on the cloudburst of attention occurred when Bruce would call from Alaska. The calls jolted Dave McMurphy back to reality. He was sleeping with someone else's wife in their home. He wasn't proud of it, but Stella was so good at it. He liked being with her.

On November 11, 1982, Bruce made a final cassette recording:

Hello, Babe:

I wasn't really too happy with that little phone conversation we had the other day; that's been working on my mind. I don't know whether it's me in this place or what, but I just get kinda the feeling that something's not right at home ... on the phone the other night, I don't know, it just didn't seem like it was my wife that I was talking to. It felt like I was a stranger ... I don't know, I just ... in the middle of the night I'll wake up and toss and turn and can't get back to sleep. I dug your pictures out and looked through them and all that did was make my nuts ache.

Obviously tired from work and lonely, he said he wanted more than anything else to have a long heart-to-heart with Stella when he came home to her.

... I don't want you getting pissed or upset or ridiculous about anything, or going from one extreme to the other like we have in the past ... It seems like whenever we try to talk, one of us ends up getting mad and throwing a fit ... I don't want any accusations or none of that going on, I just wanna air out some things that's been bugging me and I want you to air out the things that's been bugging you, and if I ask you a question, dammit, I want an honest answer. I don't want any fence-walking or hanky-panky ...

It was going to be hard for both of them, he admitted, and he felt poor communication was their toughest obstacle to overcome.

Stella had had a large family, whereas Bruce had been alone all of his childhood. "I never had anybody to get that close to."

I get to looking at these pictures of yours and thinking about all the good things and it about drives me wild sometimes ... I wish to hell you knew how I missed ya. I wish you knew how much I miss the things we could've had but didn't have. Maybe we will have, I don't know.

On November 21, two days after Stella took Dave in for a driver's exam physical, Bruce picked up his plane tickets at McDonald Industries offices at Prudhoe Bay. His night home was scheduled for Monday of the following week.

"Things will be different now," Stella told her lover. Her husband was coming home and there wasn't room for three in the bed. Dave would be sleeping on the couch now, and eventually, when he got it together, he'd have to find another place to stay.

"It was like two different people. She was one way when he was gone and she just totally did a flip-flop It was like turning off a light switch. It was weird. It was like, 'You weren't even my friend'…"

Since it was no longer appropriate to stay at the Nickells', Dave moved in with Dee for a couple of weeks. He quickly learned that a couple of the ladies of White River Estates had a running competition.

"Stella told me that she and some other ladies were going to see who could get you to bed first," Dee said.

Stella, of course, had won.

Cindy started going out with Dee's estranged husband, and Stella continued cheating on Bruce whenever she could.

It was all too much for Dave McMurphy. He bought a '67 Chevy Bel Air for $350, loaded it up, and burned rubber for California. He couldn't get away fast enough. The man who had been intimate with both mother and daughter figured the women were more alike than they were different. And that scared him.

Stella Nickell's version of what did or didn't happen with Dave, and who slept with whom, is markedly different than the California trucker's. Years later, she maintained there had been no fling with him—or any other man.

"There was nothing between Dave and I, and the reason that he came up… Cynthia wanted to know… if they could stay with us until he found some work. Bruce and I had talked about it, and we said yes. Well, the next thing I know, there's Dave without Cynthia.

"And her and Dave had a few things to discuss. She tried to get across to me, which I kind of grasped her meaning, that Dave and her were no longer together. When we had a chance to talk, I told her that I knew nothing of this. She didn't keep me informed of her life. As far as I knew, Dave had come up to get settled in, try to find a job, try to find a place for them before she come up. I said, 'When I'm left in the dark, what am I supposed to think?'"

Bruce was furious when he discovered all the money his wife had spent while he was freezing his tail off in Alaska. He hadn't worked so hard so she could run around and play pool, drinking with her daughter's lover, no less. Soon after his return home, the Nickells were forced to temporarily ease their financial dilemma with a $1,500 loan from HFC. They listed current debts at $20,401.32, but there were always things to look forward to.

Stella, Bruce, and Cindy cut a pink-and-white frosted cake for her little girl's "Strawberry Shortcake" fourth birthday party. Stella told friends she was glad her granddaughter was where she could keep an eye on her. She frequently made such concern a topic of conversation. She didn't really trust Cindy—not as a mother, anyway.

Once, Stella told a friend she didn't want to be forced to take her granddaughter away from Cindy, but what alternatives did she have?

Others had horror stories of their own. One time Cindy called the Churches to see if her mother was there; she needed her to come up and get her at the motel at Gee Gee's.

Laurie Church's blood boiled when she heard the rest: the little girl "was asleep in the room and spent the night in the room with Cindy and a truck driver."

In April of 1983, Stella and Cindy had it out. It was time for the young woman to get her own place and live her own life. She obviously couldn't live under the Nickells' roof any longer.

Others heard Bruce say he was concerned Cindy would bring drugs into the house, and he didn't want the stuff around.

Jerry Kimble occasionally met Cindy up at Gee Gee's truck stop, where she was a regular. He also got a glimpse of her possible drug use.

"I'd be sitting around, and I'd hear certain things. 'Meet me out back,' or 'It's coming in ...' Or she'd call somebody just to get her little trip for that night. But I was pretty naive about what kind of drugs ..." he said some years later.

Cindy packed up her daughter and lived with Dee Rogers for a while before getting her own place. The split with her parents was bitter at first, but when Cindy needed a sitter, Stella often got the job.

Stella had mixed feelings about her daughter.

"One minute she loved her," her friend Dee recalled. "Next minute she couldn't care less about her. She was a bitch, she was a whore, she was a slut."

"Cindy's just like my mother," Stella once said.

That year, Stella's niece, Wilma Mae, rented a beautiful redbrick apartment in Pasadena, Texas, and enrolled at the University of Houston with plans to become a mechanical engineer. At night, she worked at an upscale nightclub as a cocktail waitress. She started dating a Houston police officer.

When she heard a lawyer was looking for a part-time secretary, she applied for the job.

"If you want somebody that's really good, you'll hire me. If you don't, you'll hire someone off the street," she told the attorney. She got the job on the spot.

About a year later, Wilma married the Houston cop, only to dump him a month after the wedding.

"I left him and sat in a little house for two weeks, no electricity, water. I became suicidal," she later said.

By the end of June, the Nickells did what they had to do to keep afloat. They hired Bill Donais, an Auburn attorney, and filed bankruptcy. A little breathing room was well in order. Casual talk of getting some property and sharing it with Cora Lee also became part of a seemingly brighter, optimistic future.

By late fall Bruce and Stella had picked out a beautiful spot, five acres off of Lake Moneysmith Road east of Auburn. There was even a spot for a duck pond.

Friends chuckled at how perfect it all seemed.

*

What an entrance the girl in the bathing suit had made! The man at the bar couldn't help but notice Stella's daughter when she sauntered into Gee Gee's truck stop one night in the summer of 1983. He was a trucker from New Jersey named Pepper Hamilton. He asked her if she'd like to come back later for a few drinks; she promised she would.

And so it went. Over the next few months, whenever the six-four, 260-pound behemoth of a man returned to the Northwest, he'd call Cindy for a date. By the following spring, Hamilton decided to make a permanent move to the Seattle area. He took a job at a Tacoma trucking firm, and he, Cindy, and her little girl moved into a town house in Kent.

Even though Pepper Hamilton's CB handle was "Running Scared," it was his girlfriend who did most of the running.

Before daylight one morning, the trucker returned from a long haul earlier than scheduled to find the town house empty. He drove down to Gee Gee's and, without really even trying, found her car but no Cindy.

He left a note: *When you get back to your car, do you mind coming to pick me up?* When Cindy caught up to him, she had a ready excuse.

"It was an old friend, we went over to the islands ..."

Pepper knew better.

"I'm not jealous," he said some years later. "I'm on the road and do what I want to do. Why should I tell someone else who I'm living with what in the hell they should do?"

Besides, he later said, the girl just couldn't help herself. "She's got a fetish for truck drivers."

While stepdaughter Cindy was exploring her possibilities at the truck stop, Bruce Nickell was laid off from McDonald Industries in the spring of 1984. When it became clear he was not going to be asked back, Bruce, devastated and depressed, filed for unemployment on April 2.

Stella took a job running a sewing machine, piecing goose-down jackets, comforters, and slippers at the Eddie Bauer factory in Kent. Mother and daughter declared a truce, and soon Cindy came to work there too.

Cindy told her mother that she and Pepper Hamilton were going to get married although he had once had a drug problem. "If I ever found that he was back on the drugs again I would leave him," she said.

"How can you say that when you're on them yourself?"

"I'm talking about the hard stuff."

Stella knew that, to Cindy, "hard stuff" meant anything using a needle. She doubted the marriage would work; her daughter wasn't marriage material.

"Cynthia wants somebody to toe the line she lays down. But she doesn't want somebody she can run over the top of. And she wants everything her way; she wants somebody who makes good money so she can keep herself in style. Her temperament has a lot to do with a lot of things. If Cynthia thinks one little thing is unjustifiable, she goes off the deep end about it. And she can rant and rave for hours."

Chapter Twenty-Seven

Lake Holmes Road wound through leggy, sun-starved alders and the tight pyramids of Douglas fir and West Coast cedar just above the Green River like the wild loops of an amusement park ride. Green was everywhere. And at the top of the wild ride was a plateau of farmland and new subdivisions.

It was paradise, and despite continuing financial woes, Stella and Bruce Nickell moved onto their five acres at 17807 S.E. 346th in Auburn in May 1984. Jim McCarthy was on hand to move the trailer from White River Estates and set up the blocks on the Nickells' little slice of heaven.

It was a beautiful spot in the country, the kind of place where the frogs chirp so loudly at nightfall that windows have to be secured to hear the television. Stella made a checklist of things for Bruce to do and went into action herself. She talked about cattle, maybe a duck pond, and, of course, her own mother.

Cora Lee had made it all possible. Her life savings of $20,000 had been the money used for the property deal. When she arrived from Ukiah, she'd have her own trailer set on the property. Bruce and Stella would be there to help her in her old age. If the other Stephenson kids were jealous, that was too bad.

The Nickell property was a bona fide mud pie in late September, so Stella arranged to have Cindy's wedding at Stan and Laurie Church's place. She didn't want the wedding ruined by muddy shoes and short tempers. Stella did most of the work—from inviting guests to arranging the seating. All the bride and groom had to do was say "I do."

The words were easy enough to say, of course, but Pepper knew the marriage was an impending fiasco. Trucking kept him on the road twenty-four hours a day, seven days a week, and a woman like Cindy didn't seem to like to be alone. Even worse, he doubted she really loved him anyway. She was looking for support, mostly money.

Stella had had her own idea why Pepper Hamilton consented to marry her daughter. She'd badgered him into it.

"It's very possible that he done it to get me to shut my mouth," she said later.

The nuptials were simple, as homey as a parlor wedding in a big old house could be. The only contemporary touch was the wedding music. Cindy chose "Drive" by The Cars.

Karan Church pulled her mother aside when the song was played.

"Mom, listen to the words! Cindy's playing a one-night-stand song for her wedding!"

The bride wore a spray of tiny white flowers in her hair. Her wedding dress had white lace sleeves and a medieval lace-up bodice that gripped her so tightly, it did little to flatter her ample figure.

Stella wore a flashy dare-to-be-ignored red dress with twin slits to the thigh on her daughter's wedding day. Bruce dressed in his best brown leisure suit and shirt, cuffs rolled back and collar wings stretched out.

Jerry Kimble, in his Air Force uniform, kept a quiet profile, talking mostly with Bruce and Stella and Jim McCarthy.

Dee Rogers was also among the invited. Her recollections focused not on the ceremony, but on something she later claimed the mother of the bride had told her.

It was about Jim McCarthy. "Stella stood there and pointed Jim out to me. She flat told me that she was dinkin' Jim. Now, I'm not saying they carried on a continual affair," Dee later said. "She wanted to be free to be able to go with Jim. I think she felt that if she was free, then she could have Jim."

*

During the second week of October 1984, Bruce finally got a job, albeit a temporary one, with the State Department of Transportation. Though things with her mother seemed to be going better since the end of her stepfather's long stretch of unemployment, it was not so with Cindy.

Just a little over two months after the wedding, Pepper Hamilton came home to an empty refrigerator and a letter from his wife. *I can't handle this life, there's no money. I put your things in storage. Your dog is in the pound...* In a way, Pepper felt relieved. Cindy was great at a lot of things, but being a wife wasn't one of them.

Cindy moved in with Dee and her children. It was New Year's Eve, and though Dee had trouble keeping up with her younger friend, it was party time again. Cindy was back looking for someone new at Gee Gee's.

Cindy had stayed with Dee off and on since she left the Nickells' in April 1983. Originally, the arrangement had come about when Stella asked her old WRE neighbor if she'd help Cindy out with a place to stay. Stella told Dee that Bruce was worried that Cindy wasn't taking care of her little girl.

Dee had gone through another marriage by the time Cindy and her child came calling again the last day of 1984. Dee didn't mind the intrusion. The longer Cindy stayed with her, the more she became a part of the family.

Dee had a single rule: "Never bring anyone home to sleep. If you want to sleaze, you call me and I'll take care of [Cindy's daughter]. Have your ass home by five a.m. I leave at five ten."

Since Cindy had difficulty holding down a job, the burden of the bills fell on Dee Rogers's shoulders. Cindy handled the household chores and often had dinner ready. For a time, it worked out.

Cindy kept a datebook in 1985. It was the kind with a soapy nude hunk on the cover, and endless notations of the dates with truckers she kept over the winter and spring months. When a man stayed the night with her, like a schoolgirl, she'd describe it in the datebook. When she told a man she loved him, she also wrote it down.

She had her dates with the courts, too: her divorce, a speeding ticket, a conviction for the unlawful issue of a bank check. A DWI and a night in jail in late April 1985 might have slowed her down a bit. But if it did, it wasn't for long. Cindy kept right on doing whatever it was that was going to make her happy.

Katy Hurt, an attractive brunette with a track record much like the woman who would become her close friend and roommate, was working swing shift as a cashier at the 7-Eleven on R Street in Auburn when a woman came in and asked for some quarters.

It was mid-spring 1985.

"We don't sell rolls of quarters, and if we did you can't have any!"

As the woman walked out of the store, she called, "What a scrawny little bitch!" She got into a lime-green Chevelle and pulled away.

The next day, who should show up to be trained for the graveyard shift? The same woman. Her name was Cindy Hamilton.

"You're the bitch who wouldn't give me any quarters," she said.

"Yeah."

"I couldn't believe it," Cindy said, laughing. "You were so little and had the guts to speak to me like that."

Katy immediately liked Cindy's confidence. She was so direct about saying what was on her mind.

Over the course of the next few weeks, the two talked at shift change. They found they had plenty in common. Both were the single mothers of daughters. Both were poor.

Even though she lived in low-income apartments and had a rent payment of only $120 a month, Katy was having financial problems of her own. She suggested Cindy and her daughter move in to share the expenses.

In the late spring of 1985, Cindy put her things in storage and she and her little girl moved into Katy's two-bedroom River Terrace apartment on 31st in Auburn. When Cindy was home, she slept on the couch.

Katy liked to party as much as Cindy did. Whenever they had the chance, which was often, the two went drinking at the Eagles Nest in Auburn.

"She didn't bring a lot of guys around the apartment. I didn't see a lot of the guys she dated, I just heard about it. She pretty much kept it away from her house, away from her girl," Katy recalled.

Shortly after moving in with Katy, Cindy made the peculiar decision to move into the Auburn Travelodge.

She said she needed some time to get away.

At the motel and later, while living with a man, Cindy entrusted her daughter's care to another person, Katy Hurt. Like so many things, it was a repeat of what Stella had done to her. Luckily for Cindy's little girl, Katy was an excellent surrogate parent. She thought the child was sweet, quiet, and a bit of a loner. She never asked for anything.

"She kind of reminded me of the perfect child. I don't ever remember Cindy getting angry with her. [The little girl] did what she was told."

Cindy had problems she needed to deal with and compared to Katy's they were extreme. Her mother, her sister, her daughter seemed to be caught up in it.

She told Katy her mother said she had been a rape baby.

"Why did she tell Cindy that?" Katy wondered later. "Can you imagine the guilt that put Cindy through?"

There was also talk of abuse. Cindy claimed to Katy that she had worked the streets as a prostitute when she was a teen. She even admitted she was scared she'd abuse her own child.

Cindy seldom spoke of her little sister, but when she did, it led Katy to suggest, years later, that Stella had been more partial to her youngest daughter.

Then there was Stella herself.

"I recollect Cindy making the comment that she felt like she was in competition with her mother. And that's sad. Competition with your mother, come on!"

Competition or not, mother and daughter still seemed close. That same spring, Cindy stayed at her mother's trailer for a few days, even cleaning the place top to bottom. When Bruce needed a house sitter while he and Stella attended his parents' sixty-fifth wedding anniversary, he called on Cindy.

After Cindy's little girl's summer vacation from school concluded, Cora Lee finally moved onto the acreage in Auburn. Cindy was among the family members who helped her grandmother get settled into her single wide trailer.

Chapter Twenty-Eight

Casual fraternity among SeaTac Airport workers develops surprisingly fast. Rampers, baggage handlers, ticket agents, even foodservice folks pass through the security scanners, each with a hello for the lowest rung of the totem pole—PDSs, or Pre-Departure Screeners.

Even the Port of Seattle's janitorial staff made more money.

But when Stella Nickell went to work in 1985, she had no real skills other than a polite, respectful demeanor. That was enough to get her the screener job at Wells Fargo Security, the company holding a contract servicing Alaska, Horizon Air, Thai, and Continental.

Since turnover was an astonishing sixty to eighty percent, Stella had a chance to move up, and she planned to.

The job, which paid about four dollars an hour, was hardly career material. The hours were long, and when no flights were leaving, it was dull. Employees later remembered Stella Nickell as aloof, with scarcely two words for anyone she didn't know. She wasn't particularly likeable. Stella's speech to airport passengers had a cool deliberateness about it. She ended each word with a decisive pause. Everything was a command.

"Please. Put. Your. Items. On. The. Tray."

To the other employees, she was the type of lady who bragged she carried a .38 in her purse, and no one doubted it was true.

*

Cindy Hamilton returned to Katy Hurt's tiny apartment with a perplexed, bewildered look on her face. Katy noticed it right away.

Cindy had just come from visiting her mother. She took a chair at the kitchen table, and Katy stood next to her.

"Cindy, what's the matter?"

"Nothing."

There was silence. Finally, Cindy spoke again.

"Katy, you aren't gonna believe what my mom asked me. She asked me how much cocaine it would take to kill a person."

"What did you say?"

"I told her it depended on the weight of the person." Although Bruce Nickell's name was never mentioned in conjunction with the cocaine, the implication was that Stella had asked the question with regard to him. "Your mom wouldn't really do something like that," Katy said. "She's just asking about it, isn't she?"

"Yeah, I guess," Cindy answered, seemingly far away in thought.

*

The Wells Fargo employees operating the scanners at SeaTac were nearly without exception "have-nots" reveling in the power to tell the "haves" what to do.

"Move over here, ma'am."

"No, I said over *here*!"

"I want you to open your luggage."

"Sir, you'll have to take off your watch!"

Air travel was for businessmen and for those lucky few who could afford a vacation somewhere other than in an RV along some Western Washington river. Earning only $107 a week left no money for the luxury of an airplane ticket.

For the most part, the workers were down-and-outers, or people who liked the pseudopower of a uniform. Some were starting over.

Bonnie Anderson, a lively, round woman who looked younger than her thirty-two years, was forced to take the job when nothing better could be found. The single mother had worked steadily for more than a decade for Washington Natural Gas. She had worked her way up from clerk to a good job in the utility's engineering division. She quit to become an insurance agent, a move she quickly found to be the biggest mistake of her life.

By the time she took a job at Wells Fargo in November 1985, she had moved in with her mother, run through her company stock and most of her pension. She was desperate, and desperation, for a woman such as she, was completely foreign.

Stella was standoffish toward new hires like Bonnie. But in time she found it comfortable to talk with Bonnie about her life, her marriage, and her daughters.

"Before he quit drinking," Stella said of her husband while the women were scanning luggage, "we used to go out and have a lot of fun, we used to go dancing, we used to go to bars. I'd get dressed up! Then he quit drinking and he never wants to go out anymore, we never do anything."

She said her husband couldn't fathom her need for a break from the stark boredom of sitting around the house night after night. The repetitiousness of the Nickells' lives was draining her—listening to him chatter on the CB while she retreated with a book. Sometimes, Stella said, she just had to do what she had to do.

Stella told Bonnie that one night she dressed in a tight, low-cut blouse and a miniskirt, and put on a blonde wig to go out and party.

She had a great time, but Bruce was furious when he found out what she had done. Stella said she just blew him off.

*

By early winter of 1985, Cindy had joined her mother at the airport. If Stella seemed cool and indifferent, Bonnie Anderson found Cindy to be her mother's opposite. Cindy, an outrageous flirt, sucked in the attention. Bonnie, for one, was happy to be selected as a friend.

"Here I am, this short little fat person, and you know, this gorgeous girl who was so much fun to be with and she made me feel like she was having fun being with me. Like I was someone that she wanted to pal around with."

There was something about Stella's daughter, and even years later Bonnie would fail at describing exactly what it had been, but she felt the young woman could—should—have been more than a luggage scanner at SeaTac.

"She had so much potential for making the world sit up and take notice of her."

The Wells Fargo employees had other things to talk about besides Stella and Cindy. One subject that became the buzz of the concourse was employees Jim and Jeanne Rice's plan to establish a private bodyguard business "for rich people in Mexico." Word was, there was a lot of money in it. Others dismissed the plan as far-fetched and ill-conceived.

Some employees noted that despite the Rices' shortcomings, Stella talked of joining them in their bodyguard venture.

"What about your husband?" Bonnie asked.

"I'll just go. I'll just leave."

One morning, Bonnie talked with Stella as she filled out paperwork. Stella said she was doing it to get her own credit and to get her own insurance card.

When Stella was well established in her job, she used her MasterCard to purchase $20,000 worth of All American life insurance. Five days later she received a letter from the ITI School, stating she was in default of a student loan. Stella Nickell never even finished the class she started five years before. She owed $1,019.

The next month, she filled out a second group term insurance application, another $20,000 from All American Life.

Cindy, who once more had returned to live with Dee Rogers and her children, told Katy Hurt of the bodyguard plan she and her mother had discussed at SeaTac. Stella had been pushing it as a way to make some real money. Cindy wasn't convinced.

"I don't think I could do a job like that—actually having to pull out your gun and shoot somebody. You think your mom or you could really do something like that?" Katy asked.

"I think my mom could. I think there's a possibility I could if somebody was shooting at me."

"Yeah, but sometimes they don't shoot at you, and you have to make the first move to shoot to protect your people's kids."

"Yeah ... I don't know."

"Why would your mom want to do that?"

"She's bored with her life."

Chapter Twenty-Nine

Jack Cusack's mind overflowed with thoughts about the cyanide poisoning case surrounding Stella Nickell and her daughter Cindy Hamilton. Around and around, the images of the women from South King County circled in his head. Smart. Tough. Wary. Crass. Funny. After meeting more than a few, the special agent couldn't deny the women of White River Estates were a formidable force.

And in the vortex of it all was Stella, a woman who'd put herself in the middle a major U.S. government investigation.

On September 4, 1986, insurance advisers at the state offices in Olympia learned Equifax was investigating Stella Nickell's claim. The information wasn't of particular concern. Accidental deaths were always investigated. But there was other news: the FBI was also looking into the possibility that Nickell was the tamperer.

Bruce Nickell's wife, however, continued to call the State Employees Insurance Board (SEIB) for more information on when she could expect her money.

On September 26, Stella phoned and left a message for Sandy Sorby, an insurance adviser whom she had met briefly in July. She got a call back the following Monday from Pam Stegenga, who was now handling the claim.

"The final report on the investigation is due in the first week in October," Pam Stegenga told the widow. "I'll have the information for you then."

Stella thanked her for her help. It had been three months
since her husband's death. The Olympia women, both in their
mid-thirties, felt sorry for the widow. They thought she seemed
lost and sad—an unlikely perpetrator in the FBI investigation.

Yet it was information relayed by Sandy Sorby that added
fuel to the FBI case. The state employee told federal agents that
on July 7, Stella arrived at the SEIB offices on Evergreen Park
Drive in Olympia to file a claim on her husband's life insurance.
She had been expected. Dick Johnson, Bruce Nickell's boss,
had phoned ahead on July 2 with the shocking news that Bruce
had been a cyanide-poisoning victim.

Stella gave Sandy a copy of an amended death certificate,
pointing out how her husband's original autopsy had been in
error, and that he had been killed by cyanide.

From her briefcase, she spread out some newspaper clippings.

"Do you want to go through them and pick out what you
need? Or do you want copies of each one?"

There were dozens. Maybe even a hundred.

Sandy Sorby didn't look at them. "No Just give me a couple
of them." It made her nervous, standing there with the surviving
spouse of the cyanide victim.

Stella had filed her claim after the amended death certificate
was ready. She had waited until the papers were in order.

The information was interesting, maybe even significant, to
the FBI. Jack Cusack and Ron Nichols both felt they knew why.

"Stella Nickell knew all along that cyanide was the cause of
death, and she waited for the authorities to catch up with her,
so she could claim that $100,000 accidental-death benefit,"
Cusack said. *With her briefcase full of clippings, she was just a
lady out to take care of a little business,* Cusack thought.

Even after talking with the FBI, Sandy Sorby was confident Stella Nickell would be dropped as a suspect. The sad-looking widow just didn't seem like a killer.

About damn time.

Stella Nickell did what the FBI thought she'd do. She called the Seattle Field Office and said she'd come in for an interview in mid-November 1986.

Jack Cusack took in some air with the news. Relief. He felt he was finally going to uncover the truth.

SA Cusack and SA Ron Nichols prepped for the big interview. Neither knew what the woman would say during the interview or if she'd finally consent to a polygraph.

In case she did, they had to be ready.

First, they planned to walk her through the chronology of the couple years prior to her husband's death.

What did she have to say about Bruce?

Her marriage?

The insurance?

Their money problems?

And, most importantly, what was she going to say about the bottles she claimed to have purchased at two different times, in two different places?

The questions, the approach, even the seating arrangement in the interview room were carefully planned. Both men knew that when interviewing a suspect, there seldom is a second chance for follow-up.

While they waited for the big day, SA Cusack continued to interview those close to Stella.

Jerry Kimble was another who found himself sitting across from the FBI. The twenty-two-year-old had been close with the Nickells when they lived at White River Estates Jerry was unshakeable. Nothing could sway his belief that Stella had been a victim of the whole thing. The warm-hearted woman who had befriended him when he was her paperboy could not have hurt anyone. It wasn't who she was.

"Stella is the most intelligent woman I've met in my life," he told the agent. "I don't know if it's just in her nature, her tarot cards, Ouija board, telepathy, or what. But when she wanted to talk to me ... something would say to me 'call Stella.' I'd call her and she'd say, 'As a matter of fact, I did want to talk to you.'"

Jerry felt that even SA Cusack believed Stella could be innocent.

"The way he states it and the way he feels are two different things," he said. "The way he states it they got her cold turkey, that's how they are. I get the indication that they don't know a hundred percent for sure that she did it. But they tell me, 'All the evidence is there.'"

Chapter Thirty

By default, Dee Rogers had become a mother figure to both Cindy and her daughter. But, as it had been during the times they had lived together previously, it seemed it was Cindy who needed the most care.

"She would have days when she was so depressed, then she'd be on such a high—giggling, laughing, wanting to go do this and that—then crash. Then she wouldn't get out of bed for two days," Dee recalled.

The woman was trying to grow up, Dee rationalized, but just didn't have a clue how to go about it. She certainly wasn't able to deal with a small child.

"I think she saw some of her mom in herself, and it scared the hell out of her," Dee Rogers said. When it looked as though Cindy's daughter was going to be Dee Rogers's sole responsibility, she laid down the law.

"Cindy, I cannot raise your daughter."

"It'll only be for a little while. I'm going to send her down to live with her dad." She made good on her promise. By early spring 1986, the little girl had gone; she was out of sight, out of mind. All Cindy seemed to care about was Cindy. It infuriated Dee. "What would it take for you to sit down and write your daughter a letter?"

Each time Cindy promised she would.

Stella's sister Berta flew to Seattle to celebrate their mother's sixty-ninth birthday on March 17, and her own, on the twenty-fifth. Stella picked up her sister after her shift at the concourse.

Berta stayed with Cora Lee and saw the Nickells over the course of the week. She liked Bruce, whom she had never met before.

Later, she would say that Stella seemed happy too.

When she returned home, she told her husband about the great relationship Stella and Bruce shared. If there had been any financial or personal problems, she didn't see any.

"That's what marriage should be," she said.

On April 15, 1986, A.J. Rider and her husband, Jim, arrived from Yakima and moved in with the Nickells. By Jim Rider's birthday, a week later, he and A.J. were working for the security company.

Things were looking up.

Initially Stella and A.J. shared the same work schedule, which made it especially easy for their commute to the airport. On the days Cindy went to work, they'd pick her up too. After a short time, A.J.'s schedule changed to Tuesdays, Wednesdays, Thursdays off. The days were ten hours long, then three days off.

A.J.'s daughter, Barbie, a first grader, went to Cora Lee's after school until her mother and Stella got home. Occasionally, Stella watched Barbie on her day off, but she made it clear she'd rather do other things.

When the Riders got home, off they'd go with Bruce on the motorcycles. Bruce seemed glad to have them there.

Wilma Mae Stewart did not like her first cousin Cindy. And though she was smarter and more beautiful, in some ways she felt inferior. Cindy was their grandmother's favorite, and Wilma wanted to be. Neither did she appreciate the way Cindy treated Aunt Stella, Uncle Bruce, and her own little girl.

"I did not like the fact that she used her mom for babysitting. She lied to them. They helped her with some schooling with promises of paying back, and that never happened," Wilma said later.

Cindy talked about her cousin too. When she did, it was also laced with bitterness.

"Stella couldn't raise her own children, but she took Wilma in for a while. Stella and Wilma had a special relationship. There was jealousy from Cindy that Wilma got the respect and love Cindy wanted from her mother," Dee Rogers said.

Wilma Stewart had always dreamed of going to England, and in the middle of May 1986, she was on her way. She had saved enough money from her job as an assistant in a Houston law office and got her first passport. She was deep into her travel preparations when Aunt Stella called late one night.

"Uncle Bruce and I are having some problems. I'm thinking about leaving him."

Wilma suggested her favorite aunt should come to Texas.

"You can live with me."

"Well, I may," Stella answered.

Wilma liked the idea. She was lonely in Houston and her aunt had always been a lot of fun. She wanted to be closer with Aunt Stella.

But there was a problem with the timing.

"Let me tell you this," Wilma said, "if you leave Uncle Bruce, you'll have to do it now or you'll have to do it after I come back from England. I'm not leaving that door unlocked and I'm not leaving the key under the mat."

"If you see me, you'll see me; if you don't, you won't," Stella said.

Wilma didn't question her aunt. She figured she would tell her all about it when she got down to Texas. The idea her aunt might have grown weary of catering to her uncle didn't surprise Wilma in the least.

"We're very much alike," Wilma recalled later. "We have a tendency to wear the pants in the family. We call the shots. All the women in our family are very dominating. Bruce goes to work, comes home, gives her the check. He expected the bills to be paid. My aunt Stella spoiled him."

By May 23, there had been no sightings of Aunt Stella and Wilma left for England, as planned.

Chapter Thirty-One

Dee Rogers was a decent woman, but even by her own admission she was no saint. She couldn't keep up with Cindy's mood swings. The young woman's ups and downs became more pronounced. It was man after man, high after low. It didn't seem to improve, even with the responsibility of motherhood relinquished altogether to someone else.

By October 1986, Cindy was showing the stress of the FBI investigation. She was drinking harder than usual, and fooling around at Gee Gee's.

"What's your problem?" Dee asked after what had become another all-too-familiar argument. "I don't even like you anymore!"

"You want to know why I'm doing this? You want to know why I'm so bitchy?"

"Why don't you just fucking tell me?"

"My mom killed my dad," she finally blurted out.

"What in the fuck are you talking about?"

And so, for the first time, Cindy told her story.

"She talked about how they had been working together, about the poisoning, things on the property ... how Stella had talked about her father's death," Dee recalled.

Cindy cried and rambled topic after topic:

"My mother was having an affair with Jim McCarthy ...

"My mother wanted to buy some heroin ...

"I thought she wanted to be a drug dealer ... then I knew otherwise ...

"My mother talked about putting drugs in his iced tea ...

"She said it would be easy to reenact the Tylenol murders ..."

Cindy said she'd seen some white powder in a small Tupperware container in the airport locker she and her mother shared. It happened just before Bruce died.

"I think it was cyanide," she said.

Cindy was now in high gear, spouting off more atrocities planned by her mother against her husband.

Dee knew what had to be done.

"Cindy, you have to tell the FBI."

"I can't ..." Cindy cried. "What about Grandmother? What ..."

"You have to. I know you, and you cannot live with it. You have to make it right. You have to."

"I can't."

"You will."

Cindy had been building a groundswell of anger for weeks. She had been testy with everyone. Especially with her mother. She told Dee Rogers she "popped" her mom with her fist in front of Walt's Inn one night.

Stella later told a different version of what happened between mother and daughter.

"There was no physical contact. The only time that Cynthia and I ever had an altercation in public is when Cynthia thought I was too drunk to drive home and she went out and took the coil wire off my truck.

"I would never hit Cynthia in public. I really don't think Cynthia would hit me. She knows she's bigger than I am, but she's not real sure whether she can whip me or not. And she knows being my daughter, if she were gonna hit me, she'd have to whip me. Because I'd bring her down a peg or two."

A day or two later, Dee Rogers made a phone call to the FBI from her office at Lincoln Mutual in Bellevue.

"I called Randy Scott and had him meet me in Bellevue at my job. I said to him, 'I think Stella killed Bruce.'" The agent wanted to know why she thought so.

"I told him that I had a conversation with Cindy and there was a lot of emotion and she wasn't ready to talk. I would talk to her some more and try to persuade her to talk to him."

While Dee was waiting for Cindy to come forward herself, Stella was methodically but politely doing her best to collect on her late husband's insurance policies. She was, she said, entitled to it. She spoke with the SEIB's Pam Stegenga on October 10, but the insurance adviser told her she'd have to get back to her.

An SEIB supervisor called Northwestern Mutual on October 14 and learned the FBI was still investigating. The Equifax report was complete, but the FBI's was still pending. There would be no payout until Mrs. Nickell was released as a suspect. The report might be ready by the end of the month.

Pam Stegenga phoned Stella back the same day and relayed the essence of the news. "Does it always take this long?" the widow asked.

Pam told her that sometimes it did.

*

Cindy Hamilton was walking a thin line. She continued to see her mother, but she had let a hungry cat out of the bag, and with the FBI involved, it was dinnertime.

When she returned from visiting with her mother, she told stories about the insurance and what Stella had promised they'd do when the money was released.

Dee thought that Stella was trying to buy her daughter's silence. The two had even gone out looking for property for the site of their much-dreamed-of tropical-fish store.

"Cindy went along for the ride; she didn't want to tip her off as to what she was doing. It was kind of like making her sick to do it, but she was trying to play middle of the road."

*

As Cindy planned her betrayal of her mother, another Auburn daughter struggled with the loss of her mother. On October 26, 1986, Hayley Snow crawled onto her bed in the room her mother had helped her decorate. She missed her mommy.

Paul was going through adjustments of his own. But he didn't do it alone. He was still seeing a pretty flight attendant.

The first Sunday in November, Paul and his girlfriend took in a concert. The fleeting sight of the couple off to have a good time only reminded Hayley of the time her mother and Paul saw The Judds perform, shortly before her death. They had come home laughing, joking.

"Why can't she be here?" Hayley asked herself. In a few days, it would be five months since her world turned upside down. Sarah Webb wouldn't let her suspicions lapse. The polygraph results still meant nothing.

"He did it," she said. "He killed her ... I don't know how, but he did." She pointed out how Paul had ditched Hawaiian shirts and shorts for a more professional look. He was spending money right and left. And now he had this girlfriend.

"Sue hasn't been dead half a year!" she said.

*

Like Wilma Mae Stewart, Jerry Kimble didn't care much for Cindy. What she told him shortly after he returned to Auburn after being discharged from the Air Force that November made his growing disdain even more enduring.

Cindy invited Jerry to go out drinking. They hit the usual spots, with Cindy leading the way as she always did. She knew everybody, and everybody knew her. Though Jerry had been away, it was evident his "sister" hadn't grown up much. The two of them and a bottle of tequila ended up alone at the Nickell place around 1:00 a.m. If Stella had been there, the conversation surely would have taken a different, more polite turn.

Cindy said her mother was the killer.

Jerry didn't believe her. Was she drunk, or just spiteful? Maybe a combination of both? Whatever her problem, she was talking crazy.

"What makes you say that?"

Cindy said her mother had confided plans of killing Bruce while they worked at the airport and talked of overdosing him with cocaine. She wanted information on drugs, but Cindy didn't know anything.

"Mom even read up on poisons."

Jerry thought it was crazy talk and told Cindy so.

Cindy continued to make her case against her mother. The young man had no choice but to listen. No one argues with Cindy. Like mother, like daughter.

And around the time her mother was reading a book about poisons, Cindy claimed Stella gave her a small bag of "white powder to get rid of."

Though she never used the word "cyanide" when relating the incident, Jerry Kimble felt the implication was clear. Jerry also recalled that Cindy also told a tale concerning tarot cards.

"Stella was into tarot cards and stuff like that. Them two [Stella and Cindy] set down at the house one night and were talking about poisons. How this one worked, how this drug worked, and what would this drug do and so and so. This is a conversation Cindy and Stella had. She had brought up all the stuff they had talked about, the different poisons, drugs, all that stuff. They were asking [the tarot cards] questions."

There was more proof, Stella's daughter insisted. She told Jerry that the authorities had found an algaecide inadvertently mixed in with the cyanide used in the tamperings. Her mother used that very brand.

How could Cindy have known that? Had Stella told her? Had the FBI leaked it to her in hopes that the information would push her over to the government's side? Or could it have been learned through the Kent gossip mill? Dee Rogers had a pet-supply-wholesaler friend who might have passed on information. FBI agents had been all over town, asking enough questions so that a reasonably bright person could fill in the blanks.

Cindy said the Excedrin capsules found in the bathroom also pointed to her mother being the killer. "Mom never kept any medicines in the bathroom, especially aspirin," she reminded Jerry.

Jerry had been drinking all night, but he wasn't drunk enough to believe a word of it. He was angry, and it seemed clear to Cindy that he didn't buy into what she was saying. Cindy got mad at him, and told him off.

"Well, you can believe what you want to believe."

Thereafter, Jerry wondered about Cindy's motivation for telling him all this. Was Cindy setting him up to go against Stella? The whole idea of Cindy's claiming ignorance of various drugs was a joke. "Cindy knew very well what drugs are, but I didn't put two and two together then," he said.

And while Cindy was stabbing her mother in the back, Stella's heart was being won by her former—and now current again—lover, Harry Swanson.

The man from Chimacum didn't want to move too fast with Stella, but he didn't want to wait too long and lose her again. Now he had a plan. He shelled out a thousand dollars for a diamond engagement ring.

Harry and Stella were eating at Ivar's, a fish-and-chip place on Seattle's waterfront, when he finally summoned the courage to propose to Stella.

Stella became teary-eyed and gladly accepted.

*

"I know," said Stella Nickell when Jerry Kimble drove out to the property to tell her about all the "evidence" Cindy had insisted proved her guilt. Stella completely dismissed it. It was bullshit. There had been no white powder, no discussions of drugs, no books on poisons.

When he told her government chemists had detected traces of an algaecide mixed into the cyanide, Stella told Jerry that everybody used an algaecide in their tanks. It was available at any pet store.

"I don't know why they're doing this to you," Jerry said. "I don't believe you did it."

Federal agents returned to White River Estates, where Jerry was once again living with his folks. One agent asked him about his conversation with Stella, though from the questions fired at him, Jerry felt the FBI already knew what had been discussed. He wondered if the Nickells' mobile home had been bugged. The agent's timing, knowledge of his visit, and the conversation pointed to such a conclusion.

"It might be a good idea for you to stay away from the situation," the agent told the young man. Jerry took it as more of a threat than a suggestion.

The way he saw it, the FBI had grown weary of losing cases like this. With the Auburn cyanide poisonings, they finally had a chance to make a case against somebody on a product-tampering charge.

But Jerry didn't care. He continued to see Stella. He loved her so much.

Plus, he knew she was innocent. When he heard she agreed to sit across from FBI polygrapher Jack Cusack, Jerry didn't worry one damn bit.

Chapter Thirty-Two

It was the interview of a lifetime and both special agents, Jack Cusack and Ron Nichols, knew it. Stella Maudine Nickell was on the way. At about 10:00 a.m., November 18, 1986, the FBI agents looked out of a seventh-floor window of the Federal Building in time to watch the prime suspect walk across First and Madison flanked by the federal agents who had "chauffeured" her from rural Auburn.

While Stella, all puffed up and happy-acting, cooled her heels in the waiting room, SA Cusack met with an agent and learned that during the drive in she had seemed confident and friendly, even chatting about her tropical-fish hobby.

The special agents greeted her and seated her with her back to the door at a huge conference table.

In this initial encounter, SA Cusack saw her as a woman who had decided she didn't have to give up the battle to age. She was a vision of extremes—her hair a startling inky black, her lips a deep red. Her second-skin jeans were tucked into cowboy boots, and she wore a fringed buckskin jacket. When she moved her purse, the bell attached to it tinkled.

There was a bell, after all. Tom Noonan had in fact identified the suspect with this oddest of details.

"I'm glad to be here," Stella said. "Just glad to do anything I can to help with the investigation."

Jack Cusack sat directly across from Stella, with Ron Nichols on his left. Both men tried to put her at ease without undermining the seriousness of the interview. SA Cusack asked her if she'd sign a document waiving her rights and indicating she was there of her own free will. With zero hesitation, Stella complied.

For the next hour and a half, Bruce Nickell's widow stuck to her original story that she had purchased the two bottles of tainted Excedrin at two different times, at two different stores. The agents had fully expected she would have reconsidered the odds of that happening and changed her statement.

"I'm absolutely certain," she said, her direct gaze adding to her emphasis.

"Did you try to resuscitate Bruce with mouth-to-mouth while you were waiting for the aid car?"

"No. I do not know CPR. Besides, he was still breathing when they showed up."

Throughout the interview, she remained direct and responsive to the questions. She spoke with conviction. When asked about insurance, Stella said her husband had the one policy from his work. It was valued at around "$25,000 or $35,000."

"Any other policies?"

"No."

The agents ran through Bruce's life right up to his death at Harborview. There was little, if any, deviation from the original story she had given to SA Ike Nakamoto in June. She did say, however, that she had suspected Bruce of seeing a prostitute in the weeks before his death. She even confronted him, but he had denied it.

SA Nichols asked about her tropical-fish hobby, and the woman seemed to brighten. She and her husband both enjoyed fish.

Bruce liked fancy guppies.

When he asked about any algae problems, however, the slight smile left her face. "I've heard about that... I don't use that product."

"What product?"

She tightened up and said nothing more on the subject.

As the interview drew to a close, SA Cusack leaned forward.

"Hey, Stella, we appreciate you coming down here today to help us cover some of these areas we've discussed. Are there any questions you'd like to ask us?"

She couldn't think of any.

"Would you be willing to help us some more?"

"Anything I can do," she said.

"Stella, we'd like you to take a polygraph this morning."

"What?" Her composure wavered. "What are you trying to do? I loved my husband. Are you trying to drag me through it all over again?" Tears fell. "I came here to help ... and you're doing this to me?"

"A polygraph would help us put some of these questions behind us. It would help move the investigation forward."

She continued her sobs, insisting she couldn't go through such an ordeal.

"I can't believe you want to drag me through this again!"

"But it would be less traumatic than what you've already done here today. We've already talked about Bruce's death," SA Cusack said, trying to calm her. "I'd just like to ask you two questions. You'll know what those questions are beforehand. All I'll ask are two questions."

Stella dabbed her tears and said she just couldn't go through it without her doctor's permission.

"If your doctor says it's all right?"

"I'll do it."

SA Cusack pressed her. "There's a phone right here. Why don't you call him?"

Stella shook her head but held his gaze steady.

"Oh, no," she said, "I couldn't do that. I want to see him in person."

The FBI agent wouldn't give up. Like a salesman overcoming objections, he tried one more time.

"If he says it's okay, and your attorney says it's okay, will you consent to the polygraph?"

Stella, surprisingly, promised she would.

At that moment, SA Cusack thought Stella Nickell might have said just about anything to get the hell out of the FBI's office, but she couldn't really leave, she had to wait for her ride. An FBI agent was dispatched to retrieve the car from the garage down on First Avenue.

To his way of thinking, Stella had been a woman on a mission that morning. She had wanted to see where the investigation was going, how much information the FBI actually had about her, and, if she could, throw them off the track.

Yet if that had been her intention, she had failed. Miserably so.

"Well, Nichols," SA Cusack said, "I don't think Stella has any idea how she incriminated herself."

That afternoon, just hours after Stella left, SAs Cusack and Nichols learned Equifax insurance investigator Lynn Force had done it again. He had sent over a packet of information proving that Stella had sent correspondence to All American Life concerning *two* policies.

Lynn had been shocked by the discovery. It had been only four months since he had talked to Stella at the airport, and at that time she had denied the existence of any other policies.

The insurance investigator believed Stella had "assumed that since these were two small polices of $20,000 each, there probably would be no investigation. The total coverage on her husband's life was now $175,000 plus.

"Here she was telling us this morning that she had only one policy on Bruce, after she had sent a letter a week ago," SA Cusack said.

She had such bad luck when it came to insurance.

First there had been Bruce Nickell's failure to take the physical for the $25,000 supplemental life for which he had applied. Then there was the "clerical error" that had cost her the MasterCard policy through All American, as she had told the FBI back in June.

As SAs Cusack and Nichols both knew, Stella said Bruce had been covered by a single "small policy from the state" during the November interview. Nothing else.

And now there was proof she had been lying. Her stories were unraveling.

All American Life had received two separate letters from Stella, both written on October 20, both accompanied by specification schedules and death certificates. It was clear she knew there were two policies totaling $40,000.

The first one referred to policy no. 200387, which had been applied for on September 5, 1985:

Dear Sir,

*I am writing in reference to a claim on the death of my
husband, Bruce Nickell. I am not sure how to do this because I
have never had to send a claim before. I called the 800 number
and was told to send a certified copy of the death certificate,
so I have enclosed one and a copy of the policy. Thank you.*

Very sincerely, Stella Nickell

The second letter referred to policy no. 247301, for which she
had applied October 14, 1985:

To whom it may concern,

*I am writing in reference to the claim on my insurance policy
for my husband Bruce Nickell's death. Bruce died June 5th,
1986. I do not know how to go about this as I have never
placed a claim before. I am enclosing a certified copy of the
death certificate and a copy of the policy. This is what I was
told I needed to send when I called. Thank you.*

Very sincerely, Stella Nickell.

There was also the claimant's statement filled out by her and
witnessed by boyfriend Harry Swanson and her daughter Cindy
Hamilton. It was dated November 12, 1986—less than a week
before the interview. It was further proof that Stella Nickell had
sought the money from two more policies. She wrote: "Both
policies are the same."

And while Stella's motives seemed clear, her daughter's feelings professed to pal Dee Rogers seemed at odds with her witnessing the signature. What was Cindy doing? Trying to go with the flow? Making a play for the best deal? If her mother could beat this, she'd get the money. If she didn't, there might be other payoffs.

*

On Thursday, November 20, two days after storming out of the FBI office, Stella phoned Pam Stegenga at the employee insurance bureau in Olympia, who picked up a call from a very persistent Stella Nickell with questions about getting her money.

Stella seemed surprised when Pam told her the investigation was still pending.

"I was downtown the day before yesterday talking with the FBI, and it's my understanding the investigation is over," she said.

She rattled off the names of two agents she had met with but did not mention Cusack or Nichols.

Pam promised to make some inquiries of the carrier and get back to the widow right away. She called Northwestern, who informed her the FBI told Equifax "they could not rule out the spouse as a suspect yet." Northwestern was reviewing the Nickell file, and after an upcoming meeting with the FBI, promised to send a letter to the widow.

"Assure Mrs. Nickell that the claim is being worked on," the benefits adviser was told. Passing on such assurance was something Pam didn't quite feel up to.

The next day, an SEIB assistant manager called Stella and told her the state had no control over the investigation or the payment of the claim, and, in fact, she should cease from calling SEIB. Northwestern would deal with her directly.

Pam felt relieved that she would not have to talk with the widow again. She dreaded Stella asking point-blank: "What is going on? What do they think happened?"

Stella Nickell's shopping habits bore further scrutiny in the days after her FBI interview.

During the course of the interview, the suspected tamperer had denied shopping at Pay 'N Save North, where one of the tampered bottles had been recovered.

"I don't like the way that store is laid out."

She said the store located in south Auburn was more to her liking.

SA Jack Cusack couldn't understand why she'd deny that, when it was so easily disproved. When her subpoenaed checks came back, seven written in 1986 were made out to Pay 'N Save North.

None had been written to the south store.

Chapter Thirty-Three

Cindy and Dee had become shadows of their former carefree, boisterous selves as they continued to visit the taverns around Kent in December of 1986. The bar scene was no longer beers, boys, and foosball, but one long confab in the back of the bar. All they could talk about was Stella and the FBI, with a special emphasis on how Stella would retaliate for their outrageous betrayal.

Neither considered her likely to make a frontal attack. Maybe she'd go after the children? Dee grew so paranoid, she phoned her first husband in New York and told him about the cyanide murders. Would he take all three children if Stella got it in her mind Dee had gone to the FBI? Even though only the two eldest were his children, he agreed.

At home, Cindy became frantic if the kids were ten minutes late.

Cindy feared her mother would go after her daughter down in California. Or maybe she'd even try to kill them.

"If you die in an accident," Dee Rogers moaned, "what does she have? She's got me on hearsay. She'll get off scot-free with all the insurance money."

As the holidays approached, Dee's sense of humor reemerged.

"If we get cookies from your mom for Christmas, they're going down the toilet."

*

While SA Randy Scott was working with Pam Stegenga at the State Employees Insurance Board, gauging Stella's inquiries into her husband's life insurance, the suspected tamperer continued to flip-flop on her pledge to take a polygraph. There was always an excuse. Her doctor didn't think she was ready. Her lawyer didn't think it was a good idea. But by mid-December all of that changed.

Jack Cusack was at home having dinner when the FBI switchboard relayed the message that Mrs. Nickell was on the line and wanted to talk.

"Give me a second to get to my office and patch her over," he said, and went down the hall and shut the double doors to his office.

"Mr. Cusack?" Stella asked when he picked up the line. She seemed confused by the delay.

"Yes, Stella. This is Jack Cusack. What can I do for you?"

"I want to take that polygraph," she said. "This has dragged on … too long…"

Jack Cusack told her it was a good idea.

Her speech was odd. She slurred her words slightly. At their interview in November, Stella's words had been clipped and deliberate.

"I'll even take that truth syrup if you want me to," she said. "I don't have nothing to hide."

"That won't be necessary," he said. They talked for a moment more, and she hung up. The SA leaned back in his chair, both excited and amused.

Truth syrup?

*

Harry Swanson could never forget the morning of December 15, 1986. The air was icy outside, but inside the mobile home everything was warm and wonderful. Stella woke up, beaming.

"Babe," she said, "I'm ready to get this thing off my back! I'm gonna do the polygraph today!"

Her mood was so positive, so upbeat, one would have thought that Stella was off to Olympia to pick up the first of twenty annual state lottery checks. She called Laurie Church to tell her she was on her way to be polygraphed. The news surprised Laurie since Stella had told her repeatedly she'd never take the exam because her attorney told her the tests were unreliable.

"The goddamn FBI keeps hounding me, and this is the only way out of it."

At the Seattle FBI office, preparations had been made. Every detail had been readied. Evidence charts were organized in case she talked or argued. In the event Stella confessed, an assistant U.S. attorney would be on hand to offer a deal: no death penalty if she talked. Ron Nichols was also there, but this was Jack Cusack's show.

"I feel like I'm walking into the lion's den," Stella said with a half smile in the hallway on the way to the polygraph room.

Stella had two sides, and on this day both might reveal themselves. She tried to be what SA Cusack considered the charming "win-you-over Stella," but she slipped toward the "you-aren't-going-to-make-me-do-anything-I-don't-want-to Stella."

She studied the examinee's chair. It was black and intimidating, with large, padded sides where the occupant could rest their arms when attached to the sensors. Though Cusack and Nichols were there to greet her, the chair might have been all she saw. The white aggregate walls of the room were devoid of pictures, devoid of distractions. Window blinds were drawn.

As Stella took her seat, SA Cusack explained the polygraph. He was cordial yet professional. He told her he viewed all people as bilingual.

"There's what's audible, of course, and what comes from the heart. The polygraph measures what comes from the heart."

Stella took it all in, and though invited to ask questions, she had few. He told her the sequence of events: they'd talk, then he would conduct a pretest to show her that polygraphs really do work, and finally, they would do the exam itself.

First, the questions were qualified.

"When I ask about the cyanide," he said, "I'm talking about the potassium cyanide from this case. I'm talking about the cyanide that killed Bruce and Sue. I'm not asking about cyanide from ten years ago. Do you understand?"

She nodded.

"When I ask about tampering with capsules, I'm talking about the capsules in this case. I want to make sure that you are comfortable with all the questions. We can't have any confusion here."

Again, she nodded.

With components in place, the FBI agent asked Stella to select a number, write it down on a slip of paper, and place it under her arm. She was told to answer "no" to each of his questions, even when he came to the number she wrote down.

"I'll be able to tell you what number you wrote," he told her.

And so he did. Charts indicated at which point Stella lied; it also showed how her heart had raced as SA Cusack got closer to the number.

Then it was time for the real thing. The case agent asked a total of ten questions concerning aspects of the Seamurs case. "Regarding the capsules, did you put any potassium cyanide in any of those capsules?"

"No."

"Did you cause the death of Sue Snow?"

"No."

The serious look on Jack Cusack's face never indicated one way or another what the test results were indicating. He swung his chair around to the big black chair Stella occupied so silently. He spoke in a low, barely audible voice.

"Hey, Stella, it's over. I just want you to listen to me for a few minutes."

She looked up but stayed silent.

"I know that if you could change things, Bruce would still be alive. But you can't, Stella; you're here today and we're going to work with you. You need help. Maybe we can arrange for the help you need," Cusack said, his voice still low. "First, you have to tell us in your own words why you killed Bruce and Sue Snow."

Stella's eyes were dark. Her lips tightened like a twisted rubber band. "Are you accusing me of killing my husband?"

"Absolutely. I know you did it. And you know you did it. Let's work it out here."

Ron Nichols stepped in to go over the evidence the FBI had gathered during Seamurs, all showing she was the killer—the bottles, the algaecide, the insurance.

Stella sat and listened.

She's trying to see if we have enough to prove she's guilty, Cusack thought.

"This is going to be hard on your family, your mother. Do you really want to put them through this?"

Stella looked up. "I want to see my attorney."

Her vocal pattern was odd. Her words seemed choppy, as though she were speaking in a different dialect.

I. Want. To. See. My. Attorney.

Stella's attorney, Bill Donais, who had been waiting outside the room, didn't seem to know how to handle what was happening with his client. He decided it was best they left.

The FBI polygrapher with the silver hair and the dark eyebrows knew then that getting a confession out of her was not going to happen.

Later, Jack Cusack described Stella during the closing moments of the polygraph: "She looked like a female bank teller sitting there watching a video replay of her stealing money out of the till when she has been emphatically denying it for weeks. She looked like a broken-spirited young girl in a forty-two-year-old's body."

Stella was totally dejected and deflated when she and her lawyer, Bill Donais, arrived at Andy's Diner to meet Harry Swanson.

"Boy, they came in with sad faces. She said she passed three tests and they rigged it and she failed the last one. They heard the papers being crumbled and thrown in the wastebasket or something. Her lawyer said, 'I can see where this is going, come on, Stella, we're leaving,'" Harry Swanson recalled.

Stella was never quite the same after that trip to the Federal Building. She kept saying she wasn't a killer and she was being set up.

"It's me they are gonna nail," she told Harry. "They have to have somebody, and I fit right in."

That same evening, an upset Stella and Harry showed up at the Churches'.

"I have never been so disgusted with people my whole life," Stella said, claiming that Special Agent Cusack had "failed" her on the polygraph. She seemed convinced some kind of "hanky-panky" had gone on.

"I did a test, and another test, and Mr. Donais was in the outside office and he wanted to see the test and they lost it. From one office to another with a connecting door, they lost it." This was not true.

"They kept saying, 'You might as well tell us the truth— you're guilty. Come on, Mrs. Nickell.'"

"She was shaking and crying, they got her so damn frazzled. And Stella don't get frazzled," Laurie Church said some years later.

Cindy Hamilton was waiting for Dee Rogers when she came home after working another ten-hour day. "She failed the fucking polygraph!" Cindy said, barely waiting for Dee to get in the door.

Her mother had called her with the news at the gas/minimart where she worked.

"She fucking failed it!"

Chapter Thirty-Four

The holiday season following the passing of a loved one is usually the most difficult time for survivors. Hayley Snow's thoughts were on her mother, reminiscing about the Christmases they'd always had. Sue liked to decorate a great big tree in a single color, all pink or rose, her favorite shades. That year the house held no pink decorations. No shimmering tree. No cute stockings. Christmas presents were in a forlorn heap on the living room floor.

It was not a happy time for Hayley, but an excruciatingly sad and confusing one.

Paul announced plans to marry the flight attendant. Her mother was dead, her sister was away at school, her aunt... everyone was out of touch. She was in the house that had been her home, but it didn't feel like it anymore. And while it was true that Connie Snow, her biological, her real, father, was only a few miles away and she could have moved in with him, she had elected to stay. Leaving Paul would mean leaving her mother's memory. Her mother's house. *Her house.*

Aunt Sarah continued her "Paul is the killer" chant, but Hayley didn't really believe it. At least, not all the time. The fact that Paul was marrying Sheri so soon after her mother's death, well, that really troubled her.

Had he known her before Mommy died?

Did she know?

What if…

*

Stella Nickell looked like ten miles of washed-out road when she drove up neighbor Sandy Scott's rutted driveway on December 22, 1986. She was pale, her hair a mess, and befuddled about something. That got Sandy's attention. Stella was not the kind of person to be unhinged about anything.

"They said I lied."

Sandy gave her neighbor a blank look. "Lied? About what?"

Stella shook her head in disgust and disbelief.

"About taking the pills out of the same bottle as Bruce," she said.

"Sandy looked perplexed. "What did her taking capsules out of the same bottle as Bruce have to do with how Bruce died?"

"They asked me if I took pills out of the same bottle that Bruce had, and I said no. They said I lied."

Her story didn't make sense to Sandy.

"Stella, you did say you took some of those," she said.

"I did?" Stella looked blank, totally blank.

"Yeah, when we were sitting there with that FBI agent you said you had taken some out of the same bottle. When I came home, I said to Scotty, 'My God, can you believe Stella took capsules that could have had cyanide in them? Can you believe the luck of the draw that she would take capsules out of that bottle and not die?'"

Sandy reminded Stella that she had told her the night before the FBI came that she had a backache from all the driving after the funeral. She had said she took some Excedrin.

"I did?" Stella repeated. Then, oddly, she shook it off and seemed to accept that she had made an error on the polygraph answer she gave.

"They tried to make me confess. Of course, I'm not going to confess to something I didn't do. I'm telling you, Sandy, I was set up. I don't know how, but I was. That polygraph was a fake!"

Sandy was surprised by the conversation. Stella had told her that she wasn't going to take the polygraph. She wondered why she had changed her mind.

It was around that time when Stella and Cindy met for the last time. Cindy came to collect her dog. Stella later told her version of what happened.

"She was kinda standoffish and she flipped out when I told her I was thinking of going down and seeing [Cindy's daughter] over Christmas."

Stella wanted to tell her that Bruce had died. Curiously, Cindy didn't want her to know, even though it had happened more than six months earlier.

"I think she has a right to know about her grandpa."

"You stay away from my daughter."

"She's also my granddaughter."

"I will tell her when I think the time is right. I'll tell her myself."

"Well, I was just trying to help, because you haven't had any experience in this. If you tell her the wrong way, it's gonna scar her the rest of her life."

"You haven't had any experience in this, either."

"No, but I'm a little bit older. I basically know how to break it to [the girl] so it doesn't scar her for life."

"I'll tell her myself. If I don't do it right, we'll just have to get over it."

"That's not the way to do it. You have to be careful with her; you can't tell her over the phone, you've got to be there face to face with her."

Cindy stormed out of her mother's trailer and never came back.

For Christmas, Stella and Harry drove east of the mountains to Wilma Stewart's place in Pasco. Dee and Cindy went to celebrate with friends north of Seattle. Being separated by a major mountain range was about right.

There was no turning back for mother or daughter.

Chapter Thirty-Five

The rural neighborhood off Lake Moneysmith Road was the kind of place where an FBI surveillance team would have been embarrassingly conspicuous. Even the most resourceful agent would have been hard-pressed to find a place to park that could go unnoticed.

Jack Cusack needed an extra pair of eyes, and it was Sandy Scott's name that surfaced on an FD 302 report as the neighbor who had been at the Nickells' when the FBI came out. With her husband, Harold, a police officer, Sandy seemed a safe bet.

But then again, Jack Cusack couldn't be sure. Who was to say how deep Sandy and Stella's relationship ran? If she was Stella's confidante, would she tell her that the FBI had sought her help in making the case?

Jack Cusack worried needlessly.

Sandy Scott felt relief when the FBI knocked on the door of her mobile home. Stella Nickell's visit after the polygraph had rattled her. She didn't want to believe Stella was guilty, but she could not ignore what Stella had said: how she'd lied about taking the capsules after Bruce's death.

If Jack Cusack hadn't come calling, Sandy Scott would have called the FBI anyway.

Over the next few hours, Sandy recounted her recollections of the Nickells and the comings and goings from their place down the road.

She remembered the phone call Stella made after returning from Eastern Washington.

"She called me fairly early in the evening and asked me to call the neighbors and let them know Bruce had died. Normally, it's done before the funeral. But this was after."

"After the funeral?"

"That's what she said."

"What did she do after she got back from the hospital after Bruce died?" SA Cusack asked. "Did she have someone come over?"

Sandy didn't know. "But I did see her take a walk where she and Bruce used to go ... down the trail behind their mobile."

She told the agent Stella was concerned about Cindy's whereabouts.

"We know exactly where she is but that information is confidential," SA Cusack said.

The FBI agent then asked if the name Jim McCarthy meant anything.

She said it did. In fact, she had wondered if there had been some kind of affair going on between Mac and Stella. He had been a regular visitor on the property, often arriving when Bruce was away at work.

"Stella said Mac's wife suspected them of having an affair, but that she was a 'very uptight person.'"

Sandy never saw his car there overnight, but she wasn't looking for it, either.

Once Sandy had made up her mind that she'd help the FBI out, she felt free to record her recollections in a log she kept. The Seamurs case agent encouraged her to call with any information or questions, and so she did.

A few days later, Sandy called SA Cusack about a conversation during which Stella had told her that she was taking financial management and investment courses out at Green River Community College.

"Just thought you'd want to know."

Sandy Scott had definitely been the right one to seek out for help. She seemed to be working the case as hard as an FBI first office agent. *Investment courses?*

Stella, it seemed, was planning on coming into some money.

*

No two people write in exactly the same manner. Each person's writing contains singular distinctions, which develop as an individual matures. Federal investigators had asserted that Stella Nickell's motives had been greed. She murdered for the insurance money. If, in fact, that truly was the case, then the insurance applications were of critical evidentiary interest.

If Stella had forged her husband's name, the answer would be right there, undisguised by the blue ink of her pen.

It was Lee Waggoner, a ten-year veteran document-examiner in the FBI's forensic lab in Washington, D.C., who provided the information the FBI had been seeking. And it was no easy job.

Lee had spent endless hours sifting through thousands of documents, looking for signs of outright tracing or the hesitant strokes of a person attempting another's penmanship.

It was known that for most of the Nickells' administrative business, from credit applications to employment questionnaires, Stella filled out the documents. Often, Bruce would provide his signature. Sometimes, however, he did not.

The document most critically assessed was the September 5, 1985, All American Life application.

Though the agent, whose only tools were good lighting, document magnification, and years of study, couldn't establish exactly who had written the "Bruce" portion of the signature, he was certain it had not been Bruce Nickell.

The "Nickell" portion was freely written with a majority of characteristics consistent with Stella's handwriting. Three slight variations mimicked the samples known to have been written by Bruce Nickell. "Nickell" was written by Stella.

The All American Life application from October of 1985, by contrast, left little ambiguity. What purported to be Bruce's signature had unquestionably been forged by his wife, Stella.

Chapter Thirty-Six

As the pace of investigation stepped up, Stella Nickell began to show signs that she thought she might be arrested. She was putting things away. Organizing. Would-be boyfriend Harry Swanson returned to the property one afternoon to find Stella hovering over the smoking burn barrel behind the mobile home.

He watched her drop nude Polaroids into the flames, one by one. Harry recognized many of them from an X-rated album he had seen stored in a bedroom drawer. Most were of Stella in her younger days, though some were of Bruce in various states of arousal. Stella allowed herself to keep two of Bruce, and later stored them in a green plastic jewelry box.

She cried as she dropped those remembrances into the cauldron. "I'm gonna be the fall guy ... who else can they get but me?"

Stella had no idea just how many people were monitoring her every move. Whenever she spoke with Stella—or remembered anything that she considered potentially helpful—Sandy Scott phoned Jack Cusack. He'd make notes and request additional information as needed.

He asked Sandy to try to get Stella talking about her algaecide. He wanted to avoid having to get another search warrant to find out what she used in her aquarium.

On January 18, Sandy left her son with her husband and hiked down to the Nickells' mobile home for coffee and any incriminating information.

When she had the chance, she brought up the algaecide. "What kind do you use?"

Stella said she didn't use any, but she had bought a liquid called Algac-Gon. "I'll show you," she said as she pulled a small bottle from her aquarium supplies.

Stella explained that she had purchased the product before she got her algae-eating bottom fish. The bottle, she claimed, had never been opened.

"I don't like to use chemicals in my tank."

Sandy covertly studied the bottle, trying to memorize its batch code—0400500—in case the FBI wanted the number.

During Sandy's visit, Stella spoke of fights she and Bruce had had about money, though they were nothing any other couple didn't go through.

Bruce had been worried about his job and would often come home agitated. Stella wondered if stress was causing the headaches he had just before his death.

The minute she got home, Sandy took her place on the sofa and pulled her FBI log from an end-table drawer. She had a lot to write down.

Could it cause headaches? she wrote of the bottle of algaecide in a note for her next conversation with Cusack. *Could Stella have given her husband some of that liquid? Is that why he was so strange the last time I saw him?*

Sandy Scott recalled the last time she had seen Bruce Nickell alive. She thought it had been on the evening before he died.

She was down at the Nickells' picking up paperwork for the neighborhood road committee.

"Bruce was sitting in the family room; he didn't even acknowledge me when I walked into the room. He stared straight at the TV. He did not move a muscle. My thought was they had had a fight. Stella was acting like it was the normal way he acted."

Sandy wondered if he had already been poisoned somehow.

"It was almost like his eyes never blinked," she said. "His hands were on the arms of the chair. He didn't move a muscle."

Chapter Thirty-Seven

Even with insurance policies, forgeries, a failed polygraph, and the apparent lies, the FBI still didn't have a case—not one that would indict Stella Nickell under the federal law passed after Chicago's poisonings as the nation's first product-tampering case. Joanne Maida, the assistant U.S. attorney assigned to prosecute the case, kept calling for more evidence—evidence that plainly didn't exist.

Cusack, Nichols, and the others at the FBI needed a stroke of luck.

That luck came with a phone call from Dee Rogers, a day or two after Cindy broke down to her about Stella, before the polygraph confirmed their darkest thoughts. The real luck came when Cindy decided to also come forward.

Jack Cusack and Randy Scott had a meeting to strategize before going to see Cindy and Dee. Cusack, who had spent the better part of his career orchestrating interviews, needed to make sure he and Scott were on the same wavelength. Though neither knew what to expect, both knew one possible scenario was that Stella's daughter would freeze up and say nothing.

Finally, the two agents and two women gathered around a dining table in the alcove of a dimly lit restaurant. Over the course of the next couple hours, a story unfolded that seemed bizarre enough to be true. Cindy said her mother had killed Bruce because she was bored with him and wanted more excitement in her life. She killed him because she didn't want to lose "half of everything she had worked so hard to get" in a divorce.

Stella also planned to open a fish store. Cindy said the plan called for her to handle the care of the fish and breeding, about which she said she was quite knowledgeable. Her mother would manage the in-store operation. The notion of killing one's husband for a fish store was not particularly shocking to Jack Cusack. Over the years he had heard people say they had killed for far less.

Of course, the FBI wanted to know how it was that Cindy knew Stella was going to kill Bruce. She said her mother had told her she had been having an affair for more than a year with Bruce's buddy Jim McCarthy.

"He has Indian blood, and that's a big deal for my mom. She said she was in love with him. She wanted to marry him, but he wouldn't leave his wife. He was always over at the house on my mom's days off from work—when my dad was gone."

Neither of the women seated at the dinette table could prove it, but they felt Jim McCarthy was one of the underlying reasons for the whole plot. They pointed out that he had a darkroom setup, which they knew sometimes contained cyanide.

"My mother told me cyanide is used in photography."

"How did she know that?"

"She researched it at the library."

"Which one?"

"I don't know … She went to all sorts of libraries, bookstores. That's the kind of woman she is."

Cindy claimed her mother saved empty capsules and kept them near her fish tanks. She also used capsules or tablets to kill algae—until Cindy suggested she switch to a liquid algaecide.

Cindy said the conversations, which came and went, heated up again around Christmas 1985 and the new year, while scanning carry-on luggage at SeaTac. Her mother kept telling her, "We could have so much fun with Bruce out of the way. With his insurance, we'd have the money to open a fish store."

"Did you really think your mother was going to kill Bruce?" SA Cusack asked.

"I knew she was going to do it because she was so calm and intense about it."

Though the talk had gone on for years, it escalated into action around the start of 1986 when Cindy was hired at SeaTac. Her mother said she filled capsules with some poisonous seeds and fed them to Bruce. They only made him sluggish.

"Why would he take them?" Cusack asked.

"My mom always gave my dad capsules," she said, going on to explain that Bruce suffered from bruxism—nighttime teeth-grinding. "My mom gave him stress vitamins to relieve it so she could sleep at night."

Another time, Cindy said, her mother also talked about hiring a professional hitman who could shoot Bruce through his truck window.

"She said how nice it would be if Dad had an accident. A hitman . . . a hit-and-run . . . someone to mess with his brakes on his truck." But her mother didn't have the money, and a lack of cash was the pressure that was pushing all the scenarios.

Over the years there were other aborted plans. Heroin or cocaine in Bruce's iced tea was considered. Cindy claimed her mother brought up the Chicago cyanide case during a ride to the airport one morning.

"She talked about how easy it would be to reenact the case. How people would be looking for someone to take something from a store, not to put it back."

A couple of months before her stepfather's death, Cindy said she noticed a Tupperware container filled with white powder in the airport locker she and her mother shared. There were also some capsule medications.

After Bruce died, the packages and container disappeared.

"I thought it might have been cyanide," she said.

Stella discussed the possibility of driving to her niece Wilma's place in Texas and leaving Bruce, and while she was gone, she'd have a hitman come kill him. Cindy confided that she had seen a diary at her mother's trailer one day. In it, her mother had made entries reflecting a kidnapping plan.

"I saw the diary on the table and read it," she said.

When Dee needed to be at home to greet her teenage daughter, the interview ended. SA Cusack suggested reconvening Saturday at the Seattle field office. It would be quiet on the weekend. The women agreed.

The federal agents knew that if Cindy Hamilton's story could be substantiated enough to hold up in court, Stella Nickell would be behind bars.

"Cindy might be leading us on," Cusack said in the car on the way back. "Here's a woman sitting there at SeaTac having these daily exchanges with her mother, and she says she didn't know for sure her mother was talking about her father?"

Randy Scott agreed as Cusack went on, his mind racing with the outlandish information provided by Stella Nickell's daughter.

"We need to get that girl polygraphed. Maybe she's just trying to save herself."

Two days later, on a characteristically rainy Seattle Saturday, Cindy and Dee arrived at the FBI office. The pair seemed far more relaxed than they had been at the first meeting. Settling into the big black polygraph armchair, Dee even made jokes about it being an electric chair.

Randy Scott took a statement from Dee, which basically echoed what had been said previously.

The agents knew the only way anything could really come of Cindy's allegations would be complete, 100 percent, substantiation. Dee had little firsthand knowledge of anything, so it was all up to Cindy.

SA Scott mentioned the $300,000 reward offered by the drug companies and Cindy blew up at the proposition of collecting any money.

Dee later recalled, "We looked at him, like, 'Get out of our fuckin' face, if you really think we're in this for the fuckin' money, you've got another thing coming.'"

"Cindy," Jack Cusack said at last, "a lot of people who hear your statement will think you're in on it. How is it that you know so much yet are not a part of the crime?"

Cindy fixed her eyes on the FBI agent.

"How many wives have said, 'I'm going to kill him. I'm going to wrap my hands around his throat and I'm going to choke the very life out of him'? They're not going to do anything about it, and if I would have went to my dad and told him, I really honestly don't think he would have believed me."

It was a reason that on the surface seemed easily discounted, but Cusack felt Cindy was, at least partially, telling the truth.

Now that Cusack had Cindy's statement, it seemed that Stella Nickell hadn't just killed for the insurance money. She didn't want to handle divorce proceedings, and wanted to have a business of her own. She also was sick and tired of babysitting her homebody husband, and then there was her affair with Jim.

And while it was true Cindy knew plenty, any lapses in her story would later be attributed by Dee as Cindy holding her cards close to her chest. She didn't trust the FBI just yet. There wasn't any reason to.

Chapter Thirty-Eight

It was a different Stella Nickell who paid a visit to her CB girlfriend Shirley Webbly in early February 1987. Stella was very concerned, very upset, and for the first time seemed even scared.

She was afraid of her daughter.

"Why are you worried about Cindy?" her friend asked.

"Because she'll turn me in for the money." Her tone was resentful and sad at the same time.

"No, she wouldn't," Shirley said. "A daughter wouldn't do that kind of a thing."

The look on Stella's face carried no hint of doubt.

"You don't know my daughter. She'd do it for the money."

But as they talked more, Stella suggested other motives Cindy may have had.

Stella suggested that she thought Cindy had always wanted Bruce ... as a lover. Stella claimed she had seen Cindy in action before with other men, including Jim McCarthy.

"Anytime Cynthia was off work and I was working," Stella said, "she would go keep 'Dad' company. She was usually at the house when I got home from work. Sometimes she would leave before I came home."

Stella admitted to Shirley she hadn't been the best mother in the world when Cindy was growing up. Worry showed on her face. "I think I'm going to be arrested."

"If you haven't done anything, how can you?"

"Cynthia won't stop at anything."

Stella also dropped a bomb. She said she had failed the polygraph.

Shirley was stunned. She couldn't believe it. She allowed herself to buy into the idea that the ordeal of being grilled by a polygrapher could lead to nerves and false results.

Stella insisted she had answered truthfully, but that the way the questions were worded didn't lead to an easy yes or no.

On February 10, neighbor Sandy Scott bumped into Stella and casually asked if she'd heard anything more from the FBI. Stella said things had been quiet on her end, but Mac had been out to the property to tell her the FBI had interviewed him three times recently.

"She seemed mad at him," Sandy wrote in her FBI log.

Cora Lee had a few questions of her own. She wondered out loud to Sandy how Stella was making ends meet with no job.

"She always has money," she said, "and she's always going off without telling anyone!"

Cindy was also flighty during those early weeks following her FBI statement. A trip to the coast, out of the house, and away from Dee's children, became her pattern. She seemed to believe constant movement would keep her mind off the tampering case. When she did sit to talk, however, it was almost always about her mother.

"What's your problem?" Dee asked after a prolonged period of volatile ups and downs.

"What if she didn't do it? What if I'm wrong?"

"Cindy, do you believe she did it?"

"Yeah."

"She did it. She'll never admit it. She'll take it to her grave."

Cindy nodded and bucked up. By now, she knew she was critical to the federal case. She told Dee she felt confident, having passed the polygraph, and she would go before the grand jury.

Dee saw Cindy's taking a stand against her mother as an act of courage, one that would free her from the torments of the past. The wheels had been set in motion for mother and daughter to end up in a courtroom from the very beginning. At least, Georgia Mae Stephenson thought so.

When Stella's oldest sister briefly lived in Orange County during the early sixties, she took care of Cindy Lea while Stella was off running around. Cora Lee was welding circuit boards on an assembly line at Hughes Aircraft and didn't always have the time.

Cora Lee's sister, Lucille, also lived in Southern California, and she too became a convenient, and perilous, caregiver for little Cindy.

Yet Aunt Lucille—who had wanted to adopt Stella when she was first born—had a problem. She beat babies, Georgia later said.

"First time I got her," she remembered, "my mom brought her up. She was bruised ... like a wide belt, a bruise on that baby."

Stella might have ignored her daughter, even neglected her, but Georgia Mae never thought her sister beat Cindy. Georgia thought it had been Cora Lee's sister, Lucille.

"If I ever get my hands on that woman, I'll do to her what she done to that baby," Georgia told her mother one day when they talked about Lucille's beating of Cindy.

Georgia Mae recalled that Stella had lived with Aunt Lucille too. What had she learned from her? Had the cycle of abuse started during those six months the Stephenson children spent in Colorado while their mother was getting a divorce from their father?

Chapter Thirty-Nine

From what Cindy Hamilton and Dee Rogers had confided to Jack Cusack, Jim McCarthy was now a key player in the case.

"He's either a potential witness or an accomplice," Cusack told Ron Nichols on the way out of the first of what would be many meetings.

Community college instructor McCarthy told the FBI agents he had been at the Nickells' home around 7:00 p.m. the night before Bruce collapsed. Such visits were not uncommon, he said, since he lived only a mile or two away. Nothing, he said, was amiss.

"I was over visiting and he was sitting on the couch. He's got his shirt off and he was eating crab salad. They were talking that there was enough left and did I want any and I had already eaten."

He stayed approximately an hour and a half.

"What was Stella up to that night?" SA Cusack asked.

"She was working in the kitchen all the time I was there. Doing her little wifely chores."

"Did you know that she did not go to work that day?"

He didn't.

"I never questioned her work times. When she was home, she was home. I was never privy to a schedule as such."

Jim McCarthy, with his sparkling brown eyes, poured on the sincerity. He was just as shocked as anyone when Stella showed up at his home around noon on June 6. Tears had filled her eyes when she told him Bruce had died the night before.

"She sat on the couch very rigid, on the edge, and said, 'Bruce is dead.'"

Jim McCarthy claimed he was so unprepared that he asked, "Which Bruce? Our Bruce?" Stella was a wreck. But as he would have expected, she held her own.

"She was really stressed out, and stiff. What I would assume somebody that's under a heavy burden of sorrow or whatever would be like. Trying to put up a strong facade, but very sad inside. It wasn't the Stella I knew," he recalled.

"Jim, you're a nice-looking guy. Stella's a good-looking woman," SA Cusack said. "Why don't you make it easy on yourself and tell us what your relationship really was?"

The dancing brown eyes stopped sparkling.

"I was Bruce's best friend. Stella was his wife. End of story."

Jack Cusack asked the man about his photography hobby. "Could we have a look around? Maybe take some lab samples of your processing chemicals?"

"Listen, if you think I had anything to do with this you're wasting your time. But, yeah, I've got nothing to hide. You can take whatever you want."

While the FBI investigated Jim, those closest to Stella were shocked by the recent developments.

When the Churches heard Cindy might have turned in her mother, they could have shrugged it off as a bad joke if it weren't so serious. It simply didn't make sense. None of the family could forget that when Cindy came over to the house after Bruce died, she was steamed at the FBI. She said the FBI seemed to have a vendetta against her mother.

"'My mom would never do this. My mother is innocent.' she said it point-blank to us," Karan Church recalled. "And then, boom! All of a sudden there's talk of reward money and Cindy says, 'My mom did this. My mom talked about doing this!'"

And then Cindy disappeared. No one knew where she was. It all seemed strange to the Churches.

*

Hayley Snow was doing her best to hang on to her mother's memory as her world continued to wither.

Many felt Paul Webking had slapped Sue's daughter in the face when he married the flight attendant Sheri only six months after Sue died.

Paul did nothing to put Sue's daughters at ease. He told them he had lost their mother's jewelry—jewelry the girls had counted on, not for its monetary value, but because it had been their mother's.

Hayley and Exa refused to believe him.

"Lost it? What did it do, hop out of a drawer and walk away?"

Sarah Webb, who was supposed to keep it for the girls, felt it was a lie. Had he forgotten what Sue had meant to the family? To him?

Hayley tossed and turned on Valentine's Day night. Memories haunted her. She and her mother would have exchanged little notes, gifts, and cards.

Paul confronted Hayley about her hostility toward him, but how else was she supposed to ask about the jewelry? It had been under a year since her mother had died and Paul had already moved on.

It was too bad no one thought, or was able, to tell Hayley or Exa, or Paul and Sarah, how the government's case was coming along. There was now a major suspect, and finally, the grand jury was hearing the kind of testimonies that could lead to an indictment.

Chapter Forty

Over the weeks of the drizzly winter, Cindy Hamilton recalled bits and pieces of information which the investigators thought sounded promising, though seldom said so. She had promised Jack Cusack that she'd come up with the names of some people who could back up her claims and then informed Bonnie Anderson that she should expect a call from the FBI any day soon. Cindy also told Jack Cusack that her mother had checked out library books to read up on poisonous plants she could use to kill Bruce Nickell. She said her mother had learned that plants native to the Auburn property had toxic seeds.

"They were very small seeds, and I don't recall from what plant, and she stuffed two or three capsules full of these seeds, some extra capsules that she had had in the house, and she gave them to him," she said. It was interesting information.

SA Cusack wondered how Stella would be able to account for her husband's dying from eating a weed. True to form, Cindy had an answer.

"She mentioned that it would possibly be easy to explain because my dad was always one for reaching down and yanking up a hunk of something, like grass or whatever, and chewing on it. My dad was raised in the country, and he chewed on grass stems and whatever. You know, it was just part of his upbringing, I guess."

Stella told her daughter the seeds made Bruce "lethargic for a couple days" and nothing more. She was disappointed. She had expected him to die.

Cindy said she didn't know exactly where her mother had gone to do the research, but it seemed that she went to the Seattle library quite a bit.

"She also went to University Bookstore quite often and to a little occult bookstore that's just down the road a few blocks from University Bookstore."

It was SA Marshall Stone, young and eager, who was given the assignment to find out where Stella did her research.

Unlike Cindy, Dee Rogers was less informed. But when it was time to see if she could worm some information out of the suspected tamperer under the guise of a tavern get-together, the tough little New Yorker was game. The plan was to have her call Stella and ask her down for a friendly little chat. Easy enough, but was it safe?

The FBI promised an agent undercover in the Virginia Inn.

"That's nice, in case she wants to shoot me. Is your agent going to know when I'm scared? I'll have my own people watch me; you worry about you," she half joked.

When Dee saw the agent dispatched as her protector, she knew her initial instincts had been correct. The agent stuck out like a sore thumb.

"A bearded guy, with a baseball cap and vest on, nobody had ever seen before, in a neighborhood tavern where everybody knows everybody? Here's a stranger drinking a Pepsi!" she said later, laughing.

That night, Dee asked the bartender to keep the corner of the bar vacant so there'd be a clear line of vision—in case

Stella tried something. Dee sat at a back table, drank a beer, and waited for Stella and her boyfriend, Harry Swanson, to arrive. Right on time, they did.

Harry took a seat at the bar, and Stella sat down with Dee.

"Look, I gotta tell you something," Dee said from across the table. "I really don't know what's going on, and at this point I really don't care, but I tell you I can't sleep at night. I feel uneasy about Bruce's death. Stella, did you poison Bruce?"

"No, Dee, I didn't," she said, looking her old bar buddy right in the eye.

"I don't think I can believe that."

Stella remained blasé. "You'll have to believe what you have to believe." Her voice was monotone, deliberate. Dee thought Stella's response was strange. If the tables had been turned and she had been asked the question, she would have slapped Stella and left. But Stella was stone cold.

Though she had received Bruce's pension only a few months before, and had Harry Swanson's wallet to fall back on if need be, Stella was running out of money. She bounced a nineteen-dollar check at 7-Eleven at the end of February 1987.

She needed a job.

She was hired by Burns International, a private security firm on Interurban in Tukwila, an industrial park of a town between Kent and Seattle. The position paid more than $600 a month.

If the new hire was worse for wear because of the stress of the investigation, it wasn't apparent to her boss, Ron Miller, Burns's forty-five-year-old district manager. In fact, within a few short days of her hire date, Stella distinguished herself as an extremely conscientious employee. One of her first assignments had her stationed in a parking lot to provide extra security at a strike site at Southcenter Mall.

"Even the client singled her out as an excellent employee," Ron Miller reported.

Cindy and Dee apparently felt comfortable enough to dream and talk about the reward money. Others connected to the Kent tavern scene also knew of their interest in it.

If they got the $300,000, they'd split it right down the middle.

"Put money in the trust for each of the kids … buy ourselves a house somewhere … and start a new life," Dee Rogers recalled.

Chapter Forty-One

Mary Margaret Stanton, forty-two, had been only a couple of years on the job as the director of the Auburn Public Library when Marshall Stone came calling the first week in March 1987. She'd told him beforehand that the FBI would need a subpoena for a patron's library card. The issue was covered by a patron's right to privacy.

When SA Stone arrived with the paperwork in hand, the librarian readily complied. The subpoena sought only Stella Nickell's library card—Cindy's name was not included; neither were the names of other obvious choices: Cora Lee Rice and Jim McCarthy.

The young agent camped out with the Dewey decimal system and scanned the stacks for books on poisons, chemistry, drugs, poisonous plants, anything that might reference cyanide. He pored over dozens of books and subject catalogs, and nearly two hours into it, he finally found one stamped with Stella Nickell's number.

Deadly Harvest—what a title!

After more searching, the librarian helped him turn up the record of an overdue notice on another book checked out by Stella Nickell but never returned. The title was *Human Poisoning from Native and Cultivated Plants*.

Chapter Forty-Two

Outside the courtroom, friends considered Joanne Maida a bit introverted, even shy. Within the walls of a courtroom, the assistant U.S. attorney was driven to win. When toughness was needed, it was not a problem. She served as a deputy prosecutor, successfully obtaining convictions in a number of notorious cases, including the Wah Mee Massacre, one of the worst killings in Seattle history.

Folks around the King County Courthouse remembered her well. Behind her back they called her "Ice."

On February 19, the Fish Gallery's Tom Noonan was questioned by Joanne Maida as he took his turn before the grand jury. Yes, he told the jurors, Stella Nickell had purchased Algae Destroyer. And yes, he had told her to crush the tablets into a powder and "dissolve it in hot water prior to administering it to the tank."

On Wednesday, March 18, Cindy Hamilton stepped into the grand jury room under the protective wing of Assistant U.S. Attorney Joanne Maida. She stood behind the podium. There would be no turning back. She needed to be believed.

Maida asked for some personal background, and Cindy told of growing up in Santa Ana Heights and her mother's divorce from Bob Strong before moving to the Seattle area.

"After we moved up here, I became rather rebellious. My mother—she was drinking a lot, she was running around a lot, and I didn't get much time to her myself. I didn't like the lifestyle she was leading and I wanted to go back to my stepfather in Southern California, and I was constantly just packing up my bags and going. So I was moved around to a lot of different schools between foster homes and just running away from home and my mother's moving around, also."

She told the jurors about the beating charges that had put her mother in jail and her initial reluctance to tell the school nurses the truth about what had happened for fear of losing her mother. Despite all of it, Cindy said she "adored" her mother.

Cindy told the jurors Bob Strong retained custody of her sister, Leah, "because the courts found my mother was unfit to have her." Eventually Cindy moved in with her grandmother, and she and her mother "didn't talk for several years."

She testified that she didn't care much for Bruce until after he gave up the booze. Then their relationship improved considerably. She liked his sense of humor; he was intelligent.

Maida asked how she felt about his death.

"I think about the closest way I can describe it is as if somebody comes up to you with a bucket of ice water and just slowly pours it over the top of your head."

Cindy proceeded to recount the events of the evening of June 6, 1986. She and Bonnie Anderson were out when Dee Rogers phoned. They returned to the apartment. Cindy was "99.9 percent sure" her stepfather was dead.

"My mother walked in the door. She looked like she'd been crying."

Stella said Bruce was dead and, locking eyes with Cindy, added, "I know what you're thinking, and it's no."

For four years, Cindy testified, her mother had planned a killing, although, she said, she didn't know it was Bruce Nickell that her mother was talking about. It started when Stella was babysitting at White River Estates.

"One day she asked me if I knew where she could acquire some heroin."

"Why did she ask you this? Does she know something about your background?"

"Yes, she does. She knows that when I lived in California, I did a lot of crank, which is speed … and in working two jobs and trying to be a mommy and everything else, you know, it helped a lot. But I told her no, that I had no idea where she could get any heroin. I said, you know, 'I have drug connections as far as crank and cocaine goes, but not heroin. I don't like it.'"

Stella hadn't said why she wanted the drug. Cindy assumed her mother had gotten herself into a financial hole and contemplated being a drug dealer to make some quick money.

The witness also told the jurors that her mother had asked about the dosage needed for overdosing.

"I told her with heroin it doesn't take a whole heck of a lot to OD a person."

Cindy told the jurors she never addressed why her mother was asking nor if anyone was a target. She didn't ask to satisfy her own curiosity, because "you don't ask my mother questions."

Maida asked why that was so.

"Because from the time I was born I was taught that you don't question. There's just a certain attitude that she gets—'I'm going to ask you this and you answer this. Don't question me.' It's very authoritative, it's very intimidating, and that's just the way it is, so—I probably could have questioned her, but my mind wouldn't let me."

Later, she learned the target was Bruce.

"Once it was brought to my knowledge that it was my dad, there was a lot of it that was discussed in depth, and I shouldn't really say 'discussed,' she would do most of the talking, and I in turn would either answer or listen."

Cindy came up short when asked to put the discussions into an exact chronological context. They spread over almost three years. "The next conversation came after I was aware that she was contemplating killing my dad, and she had thought about getting a hitman, but she didn't have the funds to hire one. She still did discuss the possibilities of hiring one and how he could be out on the highway when my dad was coming home from work ..."

"This was your mother suggesting this could happen?" Joanne Maida interrupted.

"Yes, this was what my mother suggested could be done. That he could possibly be shot during rush hour in the middle of traffic, just be shot through the car window or the pickup window; that someone could make him have a very, very severe accident."

The hitmen chat was followed with the cyanide plan.

Cindy said her mother brought up the idea of reenacting the Tylenol murders. It would be easy, her mother said, to put something back on the shelf.

"And that was the start of talking about cyanide. I knew absolutely nothing about it. I told her I believed that cyanide was found in peach pits or something like that. That was probably the extent of what I knew about it, and she had informed me that she knew that you could acquire it through a photography store."

"Why do you remember this?"

"Because it—I didn't know at the time. I gather little bits of information, and I didn't know that cyanide was part of photography processing, but it was just—it was just an interesting piece of information."

She said besides cyanide, her mother researched toxic plants.

Cindy said she remembered her mother talking about hemlock. She also recalled little black seeds that her stepfather could eat in some capsules her mother had. When he died, she could say he ingested them accidentally.

The jurors also learned of Stella's use of the various public libraries.

"Did you ever go with her so that you knew that she went to the Seattle library, or did she tell you that?"

"No, she told me. I don't like to come to Seattle."

Cindy was distancing herself from her mother's research.

In contrast to what she had told the FBI back in June 1986, Cindy then painted a vastly different portrait of the Nickell marriage. When Bruce was an active alcoholic, he and her mother partied from evening to daybreak. "After he was treated and he was no longer active in alcoholism, this tapered off to almost nil," Cindy said. "He was the stereotypical couch potato. He didn't want to go do things anymore. He was no fun."

Joanne Maida, just as SA Cusack had done, made a statement that asked a big question: "Generally people don't talk to other people about such things unless they perceive the other person as being receptive."

"As I stated before, if my mother chooses to talk about something, I didn't argue the fact with her. I'm still intimidated by my mother, basically. It's something you don't just outgrow overnight. If Mom wants to talk, you shut up, you listen ... it gets real nasty if you argue with her or try and tell her that she's wrong ... My mother and I developed a very close relationship when I moved up here four years ago ... even though everything that we had been through when I was younger.

"My mother talked to me about everything, and I talked to her about everything, and when she started talking about killing my dad, I was torn between not really wanting to talk about it and the possibility that should I say, 'No, I don't want to talk about this,' and nothing ever came of it, then there we were back at square one trying to start another relationship again between the two of us."

"That's different from being intimidated, isn't it, where you wouldn't want to squelch whatever your mother was saying? You're making a deliberate decision then to hear her out, to blow off this steam."

"Yes."

"You don't strike me as the kind of person from your demeanor to be easily intimidated by other people."

"No. I guess basically I didn't want to say, 'Look, I don't want to talk about it,' and have my mother cork off and basically destroy a portion of the relationship that we had developed."

Next, Maida moved on to finances. Didn't it make more sense to let Bruce live so her mother would have a decent source of income?

Cindy said her mother wanted to collect on her stepfather's "substantial" life insurance.

"My mother spoke of this around the same time that she was talking about cyanide poisoning, re-enacting the Tylenol incident, and also about the cocaine. She'd asked me about overdosing on cocaine and I said, 'Well, you can't just OD all at once because cocaine stays in tissues in the system,' I said, 'and they're going to know that it was a one-time thing if they do an autopsy,' and I tried to feed her a lot of negative aspects.

"And she says, 'Well, if I were to, like, maybe put it in his iced tea.' They drank iced tea a lot, and they had two separate containers, because my dad drank his with sugar, and my mother, she drinks hers straight. So there were two different containers of iced tea in the refrigerator and she could, like, put some in his iced tea and get it into his system to distribute itself throughout his system, and I told her I had no idea what the difference between ingesting it and inhaling it, whether it diffused through the system differently or not, and she said she couldn't do that before his physical examination in January because he had to pass the physicals to be accepted on a permanent basis for the state and get his life insurance."

It seemed Cindy's so-called discussions with her mother involved more than mere listening. She had told her mother cocaine would be discovered.

"Why would she want his life insurance money?" Joanne Maida asked.

"Why wouldn't she want it?"

The question was repeated.

"Because she indicated that the life insurance policy would pay off the property, the trailer, and she would still have enough left over to live comfortably."

Mother and daughter would share the money.

"She said to the effect of that we could get our dreamed-of fish store. We started talking about that years ago, about going into business together and opening up a pet shop dealing strictly with tropical fish."

She did nothing to dissuade her mother from the idea that she wanted to be in the fish-store plan. She only dissuaded her when she was talking about actually killing somebody.

Why hadn't Cindy warned Bruce Nickell?

Cindy said she agonized over it but she didn't know exactly what to do, whom to tell. No one would believe her. It would ruin her relationship with her mother if the police followed up on it.

She told the grand jury her version of why she had come forward. At first, she didn't believe her mother had murdered Bruce. She tried to convince herself it was a coincidence Bruce had died. She "latched" on to the idea of the emphysema autopsy ruling.

"And when I found out that my dad had died of cyanide poisoning was after I had read about Sue Snow in the paper, and I didn't even connect the two then.

"Then my mother calls me on the telephone one night and told me that my dad had died of cyanide poisoning, and that was another bucket of cold ice water because I knew, but I still kept denying it, and then we had the FBI out to the house. I stayed with my mother for about two or three days after I found out about that. And we had the FBI out there to the house, and internally I panicked when they wanted to talk to me in private. I knew what they were going to question me about because they were out there just tearing the house apart. I mean, they were looking in every little nook and cranny they could find looking for other bottles of Excedrin, looking for anything, you know, that they could find. And I—with the information that I knew, she'd already told me … I was still denying that she could have actually done it. I was still going, 'This is my mother, this is the flesh and blood I was born of,' you know.

"So when they questioned me, I denied knowing anything. I guess you could basically say I lied, because I did … And I was just being protective, and I didn't know for sure. And I thought afterwards when I was done giving my interview and I went back home—I had nightmares. I still do. I'm twenty-seven years old and I've never had a nightmare in my life until this. Never." Cindy said she had hoped the investigation would die down. But the FBI kept on. "… they'll leave me alone, they'll leave my family alone, it will just die down, and I'll figure out a way to live with myself."

It was Sue Snow, her husband, and daughters that really hit her.

"It upset me tremendously, of course, that my mother would kill my dad, but it really, really bothered me that somebody we didn't know, had never seen before in our lives, had no effect on our lifestyle, our family, or anything, was dead because of something that I was almost sure my mother did. And their whole family was basically destroyed because of it."

By the time SAs Cusack and Scott showed up, she still wasn't certain she'd say anything.

"And then it just clicked that I had to say it, I had to get it out. I had to say something to somebody, and I had already discussed it with my roommate, and I had told her—about three months after my dad died, I told her … I told her that I knew that my mom had killed him, and she asked me how I knew, and I told her about the conversations that my mother and I had had, and she was very concerned because I hadn't said anything prior. She knew that it was quite a load to carry around, and Denise [Dee] and I are very, very close, also, and we talked about whether we should say anything or not. And for a few months after that I didn't say anything, because it's going to have a real effect on a lot of people."

A juror asked if Harry Swanson might have been an accomplice. Cindy didn't think so. Harry hadn't been in contact with her mother until after Bruce died. She had someone else in mind. "My mother was intimately and emotionally involved with my dad's best friend, Jim McCarthy, prior to my dad's death."

Characterizing the witness as tough and cool about even the most sensitive subjects, Joanne Maida asked if her assessment of her demeanor was fair.

Cindy, who said she was in "shutdown mode," rambled an answer. "To go through this and not break out into a blubbering emotional mass of Jell-O, it's like—it's like I'm disassociating myself from my mother."

She said she was trying to block out the emotional bond. She still loved her, but her mother needed help. Later, she said, she'd probably break down.

"I just kind of have to shut off all emotion and feeling and just kind of say what I know ... just say what the facts are and just have it done and be over with and don't even associate it emotionally until later. I can't."

She learned all of this from her mother, she said.

"So I just fall back on my rearing of 'you just don't show emotion.' I can't remember my mother ever having an emotional outburst. I guess maybe I'm thankful for part of it, because if I didn't have that I don't know if I could do this … so it's not as hard and crass as it looks."

Chapter Forty-Three

With Cindy singing to the grand jury, Jack Cusack plowed ahead with the investigation. Corroboration remained critical. Cindy had specifically named Bonnie Anderson as someone who could account for her story. It was mid-March when Cusack and another agent interviewed Bonnie at the dimly lit King County offices where she now worked.

The preciseness of her recollections were welcome after the sometimes hit-and-miss information Cindy had offered as she tried to get her story across to the grand jury.

On key points, Bonnie's story was an exact match of Cindy's. She recalled how they'd been out drinking when Dee summoned them.

"On the way back to the apartment, Cindy said, 'It is either Bruce's parents or Bruce...'" Anderson recalled. Stella arrived later.

"She looked horrible. She looked wiped out... that's the impression I got," she said. Most crucially, Bonnie remembered word for word: "I know what you're thinking... and the answer is no."

"Cindy knew nothing about this. She came apart. She didn't even know her dad was in the hospital... She just couldn't believe it. Her reaction was the same reaction I had when my dad died..."

Bonnie summed up her friend's personality and the reason why she turned her mother in: "Cindy's not perfect. She did her things her own way. But she looked on that man as her father. I think it finally got to the point that the more she and her mom talked ... she became convinced that Stella had done it. Regardless of the fact that Stella was her mother, nobody was going to get away with it."

It was raining when Jack Cusack and Marshall Stone checked into rooms on the seventeenth floor of the Showboat in Las Vegas to meet A.J. Rider and her husband, Jim, for a breakfast interview the next day.

The Riders had been open to interviews with the FBI from the start. They had already talked with agents in Yakima, local agents from the Las Vegas field office, and SA Cusack on the phone. By the time they settled down to talk at the Showboat, they were more comfortable with the feds than they could have imagined.

The Riders both wore jeans to the interview. A.J. wore little, if any, makeup. She had light-brown hair she wore in a layered cut. Her husband's hair was darker and longer, but that wasn't the only contrast. Where Vietnam vet Jim Rider was quiet to the point of nearly blending into his surroundings, A.J. made her presence known. She talked nonstop.

The Riders told the FBI men they were still "pissed off" that they had learned of Bruce's death through their foster son's chance meeting with Cora Lee.

"We had only moved out three days before! How hard would it have been for her to tell us?"

SA Cusack asked if either of the Riders ever had any inkling that Stella might leave Bruce. Drawing on a cigarette, A.J.

nodded. "One of the days we were going to pick up Cindy at Dee's, she said she was thinking of taking off to see Wilma."

"With Bruce?"

"Definitely without Bruce," A.J. recalled, adding that Stella dropped the subject.

Did Stella Nickell have a lover? Cindy claimed she did. Dee said she did. Both insisted Big Mac was the man, but Jim McCarthy denied it. If anyone might have had a glimpse of what was going on, it was A.J. She worked with Stella while living at their place.

"Our schedules got switched, and she had Fridays off. She didn't have anything going on those days, but she was never home the whole damn day. And she wouldn't get home until after Bruce on that day."

A.J. wondered if Stella had "gone off to some motel." She doubted she was shopping, as Stella had claimed. She never came home with any packages.

"I also knew she had played around before, so why not now? Maybe she was tired of being the straight-laced little girl who couldn't drink and all this shit because of her husband."

It was Big Mac who seemed the most likely candidate.

"He was there in the daytime when she was home and Bruce was at work. He'd be there and I'd be off on my runs. Most of the time she had someone there, I'd be off on my bike. She'd get pretty hushed when somebody's around. You didn't know whether they were talking business or whatever."

On May 25, 1986, the Sunday before the Riders moved to their foster son's place in Renton, A.J. said she went shopping with Stella. "She bought two bottles of Excedrin."

"Two?"

"She was the typical woman. When you go to the store, do you buy one or two? You buy two. I was with her when she bought the Excedrin. She bought two."

*

If Stella Nickell had worried about losing everything she had fought so hard to get, as her daughter avowed, she was well on her way in the months before Bruce Nickell died. Money was more than tight. It just plain didn't exist.

From the files of North Pacific Bank, the lienholder on the Nickell residence, FBI agents came up with more damaging information on the Nickells' deteriorating finances. Late payments, as records showed, were typical of the Nickells; the file indicated thirty-nine times when payments were received ten or more days late.

It was a problem that wasn't going away. A final notice of delinquency written and sent on April 9, 1986, indicated total payment of $1,892.01 was due by April 25, 1986. By that time, the Nickells hadn't made a payment since September.

A letter from Stella Nickell was sent back on the deadline date.

Dear Sirs,

I know that I am tremendously overdue with my payments. There is a good reason for it. I am having marital problems. They are about solved, and I would like to ask if you will have faith in me, personally. Bruce is no longer involved and I would like a chance for me myself to prove my worth to you…

Sincerely, Stella Nickell.

She closed the letter with a promise to pay $500 a month and enclosed an $800 check. Her marital problems were about to be "solved" ... Her husband was "no longer involved." She never mentioned "we." Stella Nickell sent another letter, this one on stationery showing a smiling girl picnicking atop a checked blanket. *Good feelings make every day sunny.* It was dated June 1, 1986. In it, Stella enclosed a double payment and wrote:

> *My payments will now stay current. Very sincerely, Stella Nickell.*

Bruce Nickell would be dead four days after his wife sent the letter. Cusack wondered where Stella got the money to make the double payment. A friend, a boyfriend? He didn't know Bruce Nickell had been out to see his father in Wenatchee and had returned with $1,000.

SA Cusack felt he knew, however, how Stella was planning to stay current. It certainly wasn't through her job at SeaTac. She was looking for her insurance windfall.

The financial picture supported Cindy's contentions. All of the troubles were coming to a head when Mrs. Nickell started talking about cyanide and the murder of her husband. The clock was ticking and she had to do something, or she'd lose everything.

On March 22, Jack Cusack called Sandy to see if she knew of any toxic plants in the vicinity of the Nickell property. "Nightshade and foxglove are about all I can recall," she said.

He asked her to go down to the Nickells' to see what she could dig up on plants. "Get Cora Lee talking and see what she says."

So Sandy traipsed down the hill, armed with a story for the nice old lady in the trailer behind Stella Nickell's. "I'm worried about my boy eating some of those pretty little berries," she told Cora Lee.

"Oh, I know just what you mean," Cora Lee said, puttering around her trailer, offering coffee or a can of beer. "Before Bruce died we cleaned out that front ditch so [Cindy's daughter] wouldn't get into any of it." She also said Stella had once pointed out some nightshade.

Cora Lee said that years ago she and her children supported themselves gathering cascara bark in the woods of Oregon. Another time, they had harvested flax for its fiber, and even collected foxglove leaves that were needed by drug manufacturers to make digitalis.

Cora Lee gave her neighbor lady a book on Indian herbs. Sandy thanked her and hurried home, eager to see if it held any clues for the FBI.

Jack Cusack and others considered Cora Lee might possibly be involved in the crime. She had a lot to lose. It was her property and trailer home that teetered on a wire as the Nickells' considerable financial troubles escalated in 1986. When fingerprint analysis was done, hers were on the list for comparison. Might mother and daughter have schemed together? Cora and Stella? Or Stella and Cindy?

Some sources suggested Cora Lee was mad at Bruce Nickell. Cora Lee had put up the $20,000 for the land, with promises no doubt from Bruce and Stella. But Bruce was a couch potato and didn't get the chores done as fast as the old lady had wanted.

The fact remained that if Cora Lee was involved, Cindy wasn't implicating her. Stella Nickell told friends her mother stood by her. She said it was more than a mother hoping her daughter was not involved. "I know for a fact that you did not do this," Cora Lee said time and time again. "If she gets you convicted," she said, "I'll kill her."

"Mother," Stella said, "you're angry; it's something you're saying."

"No, I'm serious. If Cynthia puts you in prison, I'll kill her."

Years later, A.J. Rider's most vivid memories of testifying before the grand jury were the questions they asked her.

She was asked point-blank if she thought Stella had killed Bruce. "Yes," she answered.

"Why?"

"It's not one specific thing. It's all the comments, actions, innuendos … that didn't mean anything, but you put them all together and the big picture says she's guilty."

Jim McCarthy, laughing eyes no more, also stood before the grand jury. But whatever his testimony was would remain secret. Jim later said he stated firmly that he and the suspect had not been lovers.

*

Cindy Hamilton needed irrefutable backup. It was possible Stella's daughter conceived the story to get back at her mother or to collect the reward money. Maybe even to save herself. Whatever the case, it was almost certain that if Cindy's charges against her mother were devoid of substantiation, it would end up as a spitting match between mother and daughter. Neither could expect to hold up under even the poorest cross-examination—if the case even got to court.

Case Agent Jack Cusack and Asst. U.S. Attorney Joanne Maida both knew that. Early one morning, SA Mike Byrne called Cusack into his office and handed him a "greenie," or teletype, from the FBI lab. "Look at this," he said, a big smile on his face. "The bureau has made Stella's latent prints on the library book."

The library books gathered by SA Stone, the Excedrin, and the Anacin had been forwarded to SA Carl Collins Jr.'s Washington, D.C., laboratory for processing. It was there, under the eerie glow of lasers and meticulous examination, that the FBI truly made a breakthrough.

The bottles, surprisingly, were a bust.

None of the bottles recovered from Stella Nickell's home had any fingerprints of evidentiary value. Not even Stella Nickell's. Nor Sandy Scott's, who claimed she touched the mysterious third bottle.

Likewise, SA Collins was unable to record any prints on the capsules themselves. Perhaps the tamperer had used gloves; perhaps his or her hands were devoid of oil or perspiration.

The books from Auburn Public Library, however, were another story.

SA Collins saturated book pages with ninhydrin, a chemical agent sensitive to amino acids found in perspiration. The resulting chemical reaction leaves a blue-violet-colored indicator disclosing latent prints.

The copy of *Deadly Harvest* became so mottled with prints, it looked as if it had been pelted with overripe blueberries. In time, SA Collins found more than eighty finger and palm-prints matching the ink-print cards of the suspect.

Though some forty-six book pages, and the checkout-card holder page, had fingerprints belonging to Nickell, some pages had more than others. Pages 88–89, with passages on cyanide, showed the greatest number of prints found on any two facing pages. It also featured an exceptionally clear print with forty-seven characteristics matching Stella Nickell's.

That was an astounding forty more points for comparison than SA Collins required before testifying in court with utter conviction.

One print was severed in half, indicating the reader had held a piece of paper or a tool with a straight edge to the page to aid reading or note-taking.

Facing pages 66 and 67 showed the second highest number of prints: seven. Those pages dealt with hemlock and toxic seeds.

A fingerprint belonging to the suspect was also recovered from the membership enrollment card for Bruce Nickell's All American Life Insurance policy.

The FBI expert also found two latent prints on Bruce Nickell's January 8, 1986, long-term disability enrollment change form from the SEIB. Again, the fingerprints were not Bruce Nickell's, but those of his wife, Stella.

Finally, the Stella Nickell product-tampering case was moving along after a drought of information. Holed up in his office after dinner, SA Jack Cusack could only imagine Stella Nickell's surprise—and likely outrage—when the Harborview pathologists hadn't detected a telltale smell. Through the library books—books with her fingerprints all over them—it was clear

Stella Nickell had read that a gassy derivative of potassium cyanide gave off the odor of bitter almonds.

The bottle of Anacin-3 was interesting. When had she mixed that one? Mike Dunbar of the Auburn Police told the FBI he thought she had put it on the shelf after Sue's death had been in the news and after the FBI had been out to see her.

"It was getting a little hot for her. She knew she made a mistake with the two bottles of Excedrin, and needed a diversion," Detective Dunbar had said.

SA Jack Cusack wasn't so sure. After all, the green crystals were present, pointing to the same mixing as the Excedrin.

He also disagreed with Joanne Maida's theory that the additional bottles were placed on shelves after Bruce Nickell's funeral. Jack Cusack believed it was all done at once.

Chapter Forty-Four

It was time for hapless Harry Swanson to leave Auburn. Stella Nickell had her reasons. Perhaps it had been boredom. Or she had used him for all he could do around her place. It was even possible she had Harry leave for the reason she gave: she loved him.

"I'm going to be the scapegoat," she told him one morning. "They don't have anybody else; it's going to be me." She said it would be best for him to leave town.

"Honey, you better get your motor home off the property. They'll confiscate it. I don't want that."

When Harry didn't move fast enough, Stella became derisive and more direct. She told him to get the hell off her property; she even cleaned out his motor home to send him off in a hurry.

"It hurt like hell for her to tell me those dirty things," Harry Swanson recalled years later. "She wanted to come out and say, 'Get the fuck out of here! They're gonna eventually pin this on me, and it will give you some time.'"

Weeks before he pulled his Winnebago off the property for the last time, Harry also discovered another reason his time with Stella was coming to an end—Stella had met someone else, a man named Fred Phelps.

"I knew that's who she was working with out in Renton," Harry said of Phelps. "This was when she'd start treating me real bad."

Harry never believed Stella was in love with Fred. She was only getting rid of Harry to save him hurt later. "When she turned her head, she'd cry. Every dirty word she said to me, she cried."

Jack Cusack advised Sandy Scott that the FBI was concerned that Stella might flee. Since the grand jury had talked to just about everyone who had anything to do with her, word was likely getting back.

Sandy went undercover—under the cover of brambles and bushes—to keep a watch on the Nickell place. Of particular interest was Harry Swanson's RV. If Stella was going off somewhere in that rusty little Winnebago, Sandy Scott was instructed to notify Cusack immediately.

Cloaked by alder seedlings, sword ferns, and other waist-high spring foliage, Sandy crouched across the road and watched as Stella said goodbye to Harry.

If Stella only knew, Sandy thought as she crept back through the thicket to make her report for Cusack.

The second week in April, Wilma Stewart had a baby girl, a beautiful little blue-eyed blonde. A month later, mother and her new baby visited Stella at her Auburn trailer. Aunt Stella was clearly not herself; she was preoccupied with the investigation and the insurance money. Her niece could certainly understand that. It had been getting rougher.

SA Jack Cusack set about interviewing Dick Nickell, Bruce's cousin. Dick, the retired Chelan County Sheriff, had sputtered on for months about Stella's killing Bruce. He offered SA Hill a litany of anecdotes about her, mostly having to do with character.

Stella had stolen from Walter and Ruth; Stella had a boyfriend just after Bruce died; Stella had acted inappropriately at the funeral.

As Cusack sat in the comfort of Dick Nickell's western-decorated home, he could tell that all of it had weighed heavily on the man's mind. Yet he couldn't be sure if it was because he cared for Bruce or that he just wanted to solve a case as a law enforcement man himself.

Cusack was receiving more information than he knew what to do with. He received regular calls from many close to Stella. Dee Rogers put in a call with something of her own to contribute to the investigation. And it was just bizarre enough to be true. She told Jack that she and Stella shared an interest in the supernatural. Dee, raised Catholic, said she had had some frightening experiences associated with the occult when she lived in New York. Both women had their own Ouija boards and decks of tarot cards while living at White River Estates.

Dee now remembered how Stella Nickell, shaken and distraught, had come to her Kent apartment the fall before her husband died. Though Cindy was living with Dee at the time, she was not home.

"She had a steno book with a spiral binding. In this book, she had all these different things and says she wants me to do Ouija."

Dee refused. She was afraid. Yet Stella was frantic. She said she was reading the tarot cards and they indicated Bruce was going to die. She said she tried to pinpoint it but couldn't.

"Dee, it's real important to me. I've got to know what's going on; what is going to happen."

Dee told SA Cusack she looked at the steno pad and saw notes Stella had written indicating Bruce was going to die in a car or truck accident. She was looking for a date.

"Stella, you cannot change this. It is destiny. You cannot change it, and if you do you'll pay. If this is how Bruce chose to die, you have no right to change his destiny."

"She begged me to do it." Dee added that she finally gave in. "If it is really that important to you, I'll do it. But I don't own a Ouija."

"I'll get you one," Stella said quickly.

She never heard from Stella again on the subject of the Ouija.

SA Cusack told Marshall Stone about this latest update from the Rogers/Hamilton camp.

"It would give us some traction if we could get that damn notebook out of Stella's house."

"Yeah, if it exists," Stone answered.

The steno book was interesting because it clearly was different from the diary Cindy had seen in the trailer setting up the kidnapping plot.

Cusack didn't doubt the story. Others might have thought Dee was painting in the colors to fill in the gaps because she wanted the reward. He didn't think so. He believed her.

Cora Lee and Sandy both liked to air their latest woes to one another. Cora Lee stopped by the Scotts' place and chatted for a while the morning of April 13, 1987. They talked about insurance. Sandy was still bothered by a recollection of three policies Stella had fanned out at the kitchen table in front of SA Ike Nakamoto. Cora Lee said that as far as she knew, her daughter had only a single policy—for $20,000—on top of the one from Bruce's job.

Stella's mother then complained to Sandy that Dee hadn't been out to the property to see the Nickells since Cora Lee moved there in June of 1985. But the minute Bruce died, the pushy New Yorker was there.

"She came out here and took over," Cora Lee said, still bitter over the camping trip she and Stella had taken after Bruce died. "She said she was 'going to take Stella away from all of this.'"

Cora Lee said she knew why: Dee Rogers smelled money, and that was the reason she re-entered their lives.

Cora Lee also admitted to having her own concerns about money. She was afraid Stella would lose their mobile homes and the five acres.

"Stella is so far behind on her bills!" she told Sandy Scott.

That same week, Cora Lee phoned daughter Berta in Michigan. "I might say the wrong thing," a frightened and tense Cora Lee told her daughter about her upcoming appearance before the grand jury. "They might take anything the wrong way!"

In mid-April, another pack of Stella Nickell's friends and others gathered to testify before the grand jury. As they sat in the hallway, waiting to go into the jury room, the SEIB's Sandy Sorby and Pam Stegenga listened to an old woman who identified herself as the suspect's mother.

Though they had been instructed not to talk with one another, Cora Lee was not one to follow orders. She asked Sandy Sorby if she was a friend of her daughter's, and the Olympia woman explained that she had met her only once.

"I know they are thinking Stella did it," Cora Lee said, "but there is no way she would have done it. I don't know why they are doing this."

Cora Lee talked quite a bit about cyanide, saying that her daughter did, in fact, have some of the deadly poison. "She uses it in her aquarium ... we also used it to kill coyotes."

Sandy and Pam could see the pain Stella's mother was enduring. All the old woman wanted to do was protect her daughter.

Harry Swanson also appeared before the grand jury in April. Despite their recent break-up, he had spent the previous night at Stella's place.

Stella had been trying to convince her closest friends that she and Jim McCarthy had never been intimate. Harry, for one, believed her. Fred Phelps, however, refused to buy it.

Early in his affair with his co-worker, he came into her mobile home and saw her engaged in a "passionate embrace" with the man she introduced as Jim McCarthy, or "Mac."

Stella maintained that nothing had happened, and Fred said he didn't care either way.

Chapter Forty-Five

Living with Paul Webking and his son, Damon, was like living with roommates, unencumbered by the limitations typically set by parents. Hayley Snow's nighttime curfew utterly disappeared. She could do whatever she wanted. Some teenagers would jump for joy at such freedom. At sixteen, Hayley felt abandoned, with no reason to come home.

Money pulled them even further apart.

"He told us when he got the insurance money he was going to pay off the house bills and put the rest into CDs for us. We trusted him," she said later.

But in the spring the year after Sue died, money became inexplicably tight. Paul told Hayley she'd have to dip into her Social Security to help keep things going on N Street.

Hayley felt lost.

*

Stella hoisted herself out of bed one morning and told Fred Phelps she had to meet with her lawyer. It was an excuse she often used. In fact, she had heard the indictment could come at any time, and she needed an attorney. The Nickells' lawyer, Bill Donais, was in way over his head, and he and Stella both knew it.

On May 14, 1987, Stella did what she had to do. She filed a financial affidavit for a government attorney. She listed her salary as $621, and monthly payments of her property, two Visa cards, and a MasterCard totaling more than $650.

The next day, a thirty-nine-year-old federal public defender with a faint country twang named Tom Hillier was appointed to represent her.

Tom Hillier's most famous case was one he lost. It involved his defense of a Puget Sound man named Steve Titus who was wrongly convicted of a rape "because of police shenanigans and a polygraph that made him out to be a liar." Hillier knew firsthand that polygraphs were not an exact science.

Stella found great comfort in that. At least that was one area she wouldn't have to argue. Defense Investigator Sal Ramos considered Tom Hillier "pathetically committed" to his client.

When Stella walked into the Federal Public Defender's office in Seattle, she walked with confidence and her head held high. She wore her fringed buckskin jacket, western shirt, even a scarf. She also carried a briefcase, a kind of 1970s vinyl relic, that contained the start of her war chest.

She was cool. Guilty or innocent, she carried off the whole matter as if it were some kind of major inconvenience. When she spoke, she often seemed remote. She used a short laugh to punctuate her conversation. She posed for fake mug shots, and then, with a click of her cowboy boots, she was on her way.

*

Katy Hurt's life had improved substantially since she and Cindy had been roommates at the low-income housing of Auburn's River Terrace in 1985. She was married and had a second baby, another beautiful daughter. She had given up drugs and alcohol and had happily settled into a calm new life. Katy and her new baby and Cindy were driving through Kent one afternoon when Cindy told her that the FBI might be contacting her.

"I gave them your name," Cindy said at the time, "and I told them about that incident that I told you about where I came back from my mom's."

Katy didn't hesitate.

"I'll go for you. I don't have a problem with that."

Cindy told her friend that there was a $300,000 reward being offered and some were saying she was after the money.

"I wasn't even supposed to know about it, but some FBI agent told me," she said, adding that he was taken off the case for telling her. "I really don't care if I get it," she told Katy.

"If anyone deserves reward money, you do. Nobody else does. You're the one stepping forward, and it is your mother. You're the one who should be compensated. It's never gonna make everything all right."

And while Cindy Hamilton was shoring up her story, Sue Snow's survivors finally learned that someone else, in fact, was being investigated for Sue's murder—and it wasn't Paul Webking.

Sarah Webb got the news about Stella Nickell from an attorney working on the suit against Bristol-Myers. It was hard to swallow. She told a friend visiting in Artesia:

"I still think Paul's the killer … we just can't prove it …"

Hayley and Exa Snow just wanted to know who had done it.

*

Jack Cusack made enough appearances down at Olympic Security to give Stella's old boss Gerry McIntyre cause to believe his former employee was the tamperer.

The FBI agent had searched in vain for traces of cyanide in the locker Stella had used. He dug up employment records and timecards showing Stella had been off the days before Bruce's death.

But so had Cindy.

The fact that Cindy had waited before coming forward with her story didn't surprise Gerry. She was biding her time for a reason: the reward.

"Knowing what I know of Cynthia Hamilton, the majority of people on the face of the earth, if there's a way to make a buck, they're gonna do it. Somebody saw some money. Cindy was no fool," he said.

*

Stella Nickell came into Ron Miller's office at Burns International one June morning with an offer to resign. A front-page article in the *Seattle Times* was the impetus. Though it did not mention her name, the headline read:

TAMPERING PROBE CENTERS ON 1 SUSPECT NO CHARGES YET IN YEAR-OLD CASE

She said it was she who was under suspicion for the tampering murders. She was concerned the media would find her at her job.

"I know that adverse publicity can affect you."

Once over the shock of his employee's confession, Ron Miller felt he owed her some measure of loyalty. She hadn't been charged with the crime, and she was a good worker. Ron listened with great sympathy—and mentally scratched her name off the promotion list.

"Ron, I didn't do it. I want you to know that I didn't do any of the things they are saying." Then she talked about Cindy. Stella said her daughter and another person had cooked up the story to try to get the reward.

"She was not real complimentary," Miller recalled later. "She said she was a 'money-grubber' and she was strictly after the money—a large amount of cash."

Ron couldn't bring himself to believe Stella was shrewd enough, conniving enough, even smart enough to have done the crime.

"I just didn't think that it was possible that she could concoct the whole thing and carry it out," he said later.

*

In mid-July, newspapers across the state carried an AP story about the cyanide case. The *Wenatchee World* headlined it:

PILL VICTIM WIDOW NOW CHIEF SUSPECT

That same day, Marshall Stone arrived at Stan and Laurie Church's place, now an apartment in Pacific, a tiny town south of Auburn. It was the first time an FBI agent had contacted the Nickells' closest friends.

SA Stone set his briefcase on the kitchen table and they all sat down on the yellow dinette chairs. Stan explained that he was on the way out the door for the shipyard, but he wanted the young FBI agent to know that while their friend might have been smart enough to carry out such a crime, she flat out didn't do it. He told the agent his wife would tell him the same thing.

Laurie appreciated the vote of confidence. She needed it. She was so anguished about the whole thing, she could barely look the agent in the eye. She wanted to help her best friend.

SA Stone worked from a prepared list of questions pulled from his briefcase, marking them off as he asked. He wanted to know how Stella had acted when she came over to tell them Bruce had died.

"She cried. Any woman who lost her husband would," Laurie said.

"Did you know the Nickells were filing for divorce?"

"No, they weren't. If she was, she would have told me about it." Karan Church did not like this FBI man.

"Did you know Bruce donated his eyes to the Lion's Eye Bank, and that's how we were able to test for cyanide?" Stone asked.

"Bullshit!" Karan Church sputtered.

"What do you mean, 'bullshit'?"

"Stella turned in the lot numbers from the Excedrin bottles . . . that's how they found out he died of cyanide."

Can't you see? How could she be guilty if she had been the one to call about the poisoning in the first place? Karan thought.

Later when the Churches met with federal public defender Tom Hillier and investigator Sal Ramos, however, they felt they were with allies. These men were going to do something to help their friend.

Tom Hillier asked if Laurie thought Stella could have done the crime. "No. Poisoning someone is a sneaky way of doing things, and Stella is not a sneak. If she wanted to get rid of Bruce, she'd have blown his brains out. That's the way she is."

They talked about Stella's daughter. Cindy's name came up so frequently that later the Churches would insist Hillier must have considered the young woman the more viable suspect. In that light, they told Hillier about Cindy's strange appearance at Kim Church's wedding.

"She acted as if there was no problem," Laurie said. "You could not tell that her family member had passed away two days before."

Cindy had no credibility: the drugs, the neglect of her little girl, and the list could go on. Tom Hillier seemed to take it all in.

By the time Stella's defense lawyer left, Stan and Laurie had agreed to testify if needed.

Because of the rules of discovery, the defense, of course, didn't have anything in the way of real information on the government's case. All they had was Stella.

When the defense learned that A.J. Rider was considered a key government witness, Sal Ramos asked Stella why. She didn't know.

"What could she tell them?"

Again, a blank.

"Well, where is she?" he persisted. "Think, Stella, think."

It wasn't much of a lead, but after a couple of days meandering around in a place he considered "ugly" and "desperate," Sal Ramos knocked on A.J. Rider's door. It was midmorning.

While her son and daughter played in the pool, A.J. jumpstarted her lungs with a cigarette and drank some microwave-heated coffee. She did not mince words. A.J. told Ramos the story of going with Stella to buy several bottles of Excedrin just days before Bruce collapsed.

Stella's former friend was adamant and foulmouthed, another of the hardcore, hard-living persons who ran in Stella's throng of friends.

He asked if she thought Stella killed Bruce.

"You're goddamn right the bitch killed him."

That was all he needed to know.

*

SA Jack Cusack built a timeline that appeared to back up the bizarre story given by Cindy Hamilton.

Work records showed several instances when Bruce had complained of stomach troubles that might have resulted from little black seeds his wife slipped into his iced tea.

In late April 1986, Stella had written to the lienholder of the Nickell property saying that her problems were about to be solved and her husband was no longer involved.

On May 27, a foreclosure notice was sent to the Nickells. That very same day, Stella shopped at Johnny's and Pay 'N Save North.

A.J. Rider said she saw Stella buy more than one bottle of Excedrin.

On June 1, Stella wrote to North Pacific Bank and said her payments would stay current.

She still didn't have any money, so how could she have told them that?

Two days later, she shopped at Albertson's and Johnny's—two places where tainted capsules were later recovered. On June 5, Bruce Nickell was dead.

Chapter Forty-Six

Cigarette smoke braided the heavy air of her aunt's trailer as Wilma Stewart sucked on a menthol-eucalyptus cough drop and suffered the push-me pull-you battle the FBI and her aunt had waged for her allegiance. SA Ron Nichols approached her to talk about her aunt and her life. Not the crime. Wilma enjoyed their conversations. It had been a while since someone had listened to her.

She said little as she listened to her aunt drone on.

"Those goddamn FBI! Every time I turn around they're here, poking their noses in someone else's business. Killed Bruce for insurance money! Give me a break! They're trying to hang that on me as some kind of a motive ... I didn't even know about the Visa policies! No money could replace your uncle Bruce!"

It went on and on ...

Wilma was sick of hearing about the money. She heard it from Aunt Stella and Ron Nichols every time she sat down with either one of them.

Her aunt had no reason to kill Bruce, not when the man was worth more alive than dead. He had a good job. He was back on his feet. No cause at all. She said so herself.

"Now, if the man had beat me into the floor every day and beaten me to a pulp, I might have possibly had a reason. But Bruce was not that type of person."

After hours of listening, with barely an instance when she could offer anything beyond an occasional nod, Wilma grew weary of the tirade.

She wanted to talk about what was going on in her own life. Since Aunt Stella had so many problems, they never got around to discussing any of Wilma's.

The night before she was to testify before the grand jury, the government put Wilma Stewart and her baby in a Seattle hotel overlooking I-5. She adamantly maintained that her aunt was innocent, and that was the way she was going to approach the jurors.

Aunt Stella did not kill anyone. She just wouldn't.

Her aunt was both a much wished for mother figure and a trusted friend. Stella was a woman who had overcome great hardship, and though she did not always make the best choices in life, she had survived. She'd found the American dream on that acreage in Auburn.

"I did not agree with the way she lived her life. But I also did not condemn her for it, because mine was very similar," Wilma said later, holding back tears.

Stella was not the mothering type, and Wilma, at least before she had her daughter, had considered herself of a similar mold.

When she looked at her aunt, she saw the single family member she could love and trust. Her own mother, Georgia, had never showed her any kindness.

Aunt Stella was innocent, and the FBI and all their arguments about money could go straight to hell.

Wilma testified about her aunt's phone call to Houston. She had asked her not to say anything to Bruce about her plans to leave him.

See? Why kill him? She was going to leave him!

Joanne Maida asked if insurance money as a subject of conversation ever came up, and the witness said it had "all the time."

"I mean, my uncle had died and he was a really neat person, and I was getting sick and tired of hearing about what she was going to get."

After the grand jury, Wilma returned to Auburn and stayed the night at the property with Stella and Fred. Stella entertained her great niece with a musical teddy bear, and the sight of it filled Wilma with hope that things would work out, after all. Something would save her aunt.

Maybe Cindy would come to her senses.

Wilma also wondered whether her aunt might consider changing her story. From what she was hearing from the FBI, it didn't look like there was any way that her aunt would walk away from this without going to prison.

"Has it ever dawned on you to confess and throw yourself at the mercy of the court?"

"I'm not doing that," Stella said, her face frozen in that look of iron-strong determination she wore like a mask.

*

One evening in early September 1987, while Bob and Pat Strong were eating take-out pizza in their Ranchero Way home in Garden Grove. When Pat went to answer a knock on their door, they were met with a surprise. A shock, really. It was Cindy. Not only that, she acted as though she'd never been away, though it had been at least seven years since they'd seen her. She just showed up. She and her trucker boyfriend needed a place to stay. It was the two of them. Her little girl was living with her father's ex-wife since Cindy had sent her there shortly before Bruce died.

"I guess you heard about Mom," she said.

They had.

"Well, I'm going to be testifying against her."

The information stunned them. The Strongs knew Stella was in big trouble, but they hadn't known Cindy was going to testify. Yet both Pat and Bob felt it was somewhat believable that Stella might discuss Bruce's murder with Cindy. The two were extremely close.

"I can't discuss any of it until after the trial," she went on. Cindy said she was there to hide out and wait for her mother's trial. Only Jack Cusack of the FBI knew her whereabouts.

Bob was certain he wasn't getting the whole story.

"It seemed like she was always trying to hide something," he said years later.

Cindy said she had nothing to hide. She said she had even been polygraphed by the FBI and passed with flying colors.

Bob didn't say it, but didn't give a hoot about any polygraph.

*

As if the whole story at once was too painful, or too difficult to recall, Cindy Hamilton dropped information in erratic snatches. At one point, she told SA Cusack she recalled something about her mother's using library encyclopedias to research cyanide. Although, she seemed a bit unsure.

She did not know where, but a good bet was the Auburn library.

SA Marshall Stone returned to Auburn and added another win to his successful library search for evidence.

The young agent packed up several "C" volumes from the Auburn Public Library, and again, more pay dirt from Carl Collins and the FBI lab.

Sections on cyanide in the various encyclopedias also turned up prints. McGraw-Hill's *Encyclopedia of Science and Technology* revealed nine of Stella Nickell's latent fingerprints and one latent palm print. Two more of her fingerprints appeared in the *New Caxton Encyclopedia*.

Finally, five additional fingerprints and another palm were detected in the cyanide section of the *Merit Student's Encyclopedia*.

Chapter Forty-Seven

Contact became infrequent between neighbors Stella Nickell and Sandy Scott as the weeks of the investigation piled up. When defense investigator Sal Ramos contacted Sandy for an interview, she called Jack Cusack. He told her she could decline if she wished, which she did. Sandy wondered if that had been some of the reason for Stella's distance.

In October 1987, they finally crossed paths on the gravel road between their properties.

"Any news on the case?" Sandy asked.

Stella shook her head. There wasn't much to report. "If the grand jury can't or won't reach a decision, then the case will be allowed to just fade away," she said.

"Heard from Cindy at all?"

"No, I haven't," Stella replied. "But I have an idea where she is."

Two days later, Cora Lee walked up the hill to get some tomatoes Sandy had promised. The visit was pleasant, but it was the last the two would share.

A week and a half later, another neighbor returned some books Cora Lee had borrowed.

"Stella's mother doesn't want to talk with you anymore."

Defense lawyer Tom Hillier dispatched Sal Ramos to interview after interview with friends, as well as those considered adversaries by his client. The one they could never pin down, and who flat out refused to talk with them, was the government's leading witness, Cindy Hamilton.

*

Stella Nickell's days of freedom were slipping by. She knew it. The FBI told her so. Finally, on November 4, US prosecutor Joanne Maida filled out an indictment status sheet. Arrest was imminent, albeit with a few loose ends needing to be tied up.

It was the prosecutor's nearly obsessive need to mitigate loose ends that caused some frustration down the hill at the FBI office. No one doubted the prosecutor's capability but for some, the grand jury process had dragged on too long. Jack Cusack, for one, wanted Stella Nickell picked up right away. Cindy had told the Seamurs case agent that her mother might commit suicide if faced with a prison sentence, and the FBI didn't want Stella to avoid incarceration.

It was now obvious the government's case was going to hinge on the insurance money and the proceeds from a civil lawsuit she filed against Bristol-Myers the month after Bruce died as the motives. The alleged affair with Jim McCarthy, although it might have been the impetus for the need to get rid of Bruce, would not be stressed because it would only serve to cloud the issue and confuse the jury. SA Cusack ate lunch with documents expert Lee Waggoner at the Metropolitan Grill across the street from the Federal Building.

All were frustrated with Joanne Maida. In her zealousness to tie up the case, she had pressed Lee Waggoner on the subject of the Nickell signatures he was still unsure about.

"You can't tell me that Stella Nickell signed for this insurance?"

"No," he'd said. "She may have, but I can't say with certainty."

While Stella waited for the FBI to come with an arrest warrant, she passed her free time and days off drinking Wild Turkey and reading the Bible.

Stella Nickell had made a fine scheduler for Burns, but it wasn't to be a career.

"I've got the word they are going to arrest me at work," she said with a matter-of-fact calmness that continued to amaze manager Ron Miller.

He put Stella on a leave of absence and told her they'd play things by ear. If she wasn't arrested soon, she'd be reinstated as an active employee.

"Fred was a lot more nervous about the whole thing than Stella appeared to be. Fred can be very jittery, visibly nervous. She didn't show anything," Ron Miller later said.

Stuck at home and unemployed, Stella drank and waited to be arrested. Fred joined her and her bottle when he got home from Burns. Since she didn't want to go out anymore, she usually planted herself on the davenport, cuddled up with an afghan, drinking Wild Turkey and coffee.

One night in early December while the couple was watching a video, some old Conan-type flick, Stella reportedly let her guard down.

For the first, and only, time.

She rested her head on Fred's shoulder and started to cry.

"I'd looked at her and she had tears coming down her face," he said later.

"I did it," she said.

"What are you talking about?"

"I did it," she repeated.

"I know," he said.

Stella cried some more, and Fred held her.

"We never talked about it again. I didn't give a shit one way or another. It didn't bother me," he said later. Fred never told anyone about what Stella had said.

Nobody ever asked him.

Tom Hillier arranged to have his client surrender when the inevitable indictment was finally handed down. She was no danger to society, he said, and she'd had ample time to run over the past year and a half.

SA Cusack thought the very idea was not only ridiculous but insulting.

"Send a goddamn letter! Here's a woman who killed two people, one she didn't even know, and the government was going to send her a note or make a phone call so she could waltz into jail?"

December 9, 1987, eighteen months after the case began with Hayley Snow's call to 911, SA Cusack took the stand before the grand jury and provided his testimony about the fingerprints on library books.

He told Ron Nichols to get a car from the garage ready to go before he went to testify. If a True Bill indictment was sent down, both wanted to be able to make the trip to Auburn in time to be the ones to make the arrest. Auburn police detective Mike Dunbar and SA Marshall Stone were already there, watching the Nickell place from the road.

After the assistant U.S. attorney asked her last question, the silver-haired special agent asked if he'd be recalled. She said no, he was finished, and Cusack and Nichols set out for Auburn.

At around 11:00 a.m., they arrived at the dirt road separating the Nickells' and Scotts' properties when the call came in that the five-count indictment had been handed down. Five counts; one for each bottle.

Fred Phelps answered the knock at the door.

"We're here for Stella," SA Cusack said. "You must be Fred." An agent frisked Stella's boyfriend.

"Stel doesn't feel good," Fred said, letting them in, "she's laying down. We knew you were coming... just didn't think it'd be so soon."

SA Cusack asked, "Are there any guns in the house?"

Fred nodded toward the bedroom.

"Yeah, a .357 pistol in the bedroom, a .22 automatic in the other bedroom," he said. "There's a rifle out here, a shotgun out here; they're all loaded."

While the agents gathered the weapons, Stella emerged, still in her bathrobe. She looked pale. She didn't even have her signature red lipstick on.

"Stella, you are under arrest," SA Cusack said. "Consider yourself in our custody. Don't move."

An agent held out the warrant and she was advised of her rights.

"I understand," Stella said. She was resigned, nearly emotionless. Or maybe it was stoic? Or bravado. No screams she was innocent. Just flat. Agents checked out the bedroom one more time before allowing the prisoner to dress for the ride downtown to the King County Jail.

Stella put on a pair of dark slacks, cowboy boots, a plain shirt, and pulled her thick, black hair back in a barrette. She allowed herself a ring, a watch, and a lion's-head pin as her only adornment. She chose a jacket that would provoke the most comment later—a blue windbreaker embroidered with her late husband's name.

With her daughter swept away by the FBI, Cora Lee told a lone reporter seeking a comment that her daughter was innocent. "If she is not found innocent, I tell you I will take it to a higher court!"

Down in Garden Grove Cindy found out her mother had been arrested when it came on the TV news. She called SA Cusack and railed at the agency's incompetence.

"Goddamn it!" she said. "Doesn't anybody do their job and keep me informed?"

Over the next few days, Stella Nickell made two court appearances. First a detention hearing in which a U.S. magistrate denied bail, citing that the government's evidence—which was sealed—indicated their case was a strong one. In a five-minute appearance at the end of the week, Stella pleaded not guilty to each of the five counts before a federal judge. She managed a faint smile for Fred Phelps—like the Churches, still in her corner.

Trial date was set for February 16, 1988.

Chapter Forty-Eight

Fred Phelps saw a different woman when he went to visit Stella at the jail. It was as if a switch had been flipped and she now had the unmistakable air of confidence. She even looked younger, somehow. Refreshed. The waiting and Wild Turkey could no longer drag her down.

"I know one of the reasons Cynthia Lea is doing this," she finally said, seated in the visiting room: "She owed us money."

Stella said she and Bruce had bailed Cindy out financially more than a time or two. They were glad to do it, but they had always expected they'd be reimbursed. Cindy had found a way to get out of her commitment: by killing Bruce and setting up Stella to take the fall.

"I have it all written down somewhere," she said, but she needed Fred's help. In her briefcase, which was in her car, he'd find three ledgers. In the back of one were some entries outlining her daughter's debts.

"Get them and go through them and look for the entries," she said. "She owes me twenty-three, twenty-four hundred dollars." He'd also find a board in the back of the truck.

"I want you to burn it. Will you do that for me?"

Fred wanted to know what kind of board.

"You'll know it when you see it," she said. "It's in a thin box."

That afternoon, Fred Phelps poured himself a drink and sat at her kitchen table. The stack before him included the ledgers and a Ouija board he pulled from the truck.

He figured he had the board Stella had told him to destroy. *Why burn this?* he thought. *Who believes in this shit anyway? What's the big deal?*

The first two ledgers showed no entries for anything concerning Cindy and any money she owed her mother. The third volume, a red-cornered and green-colored leather-like bookkeeper's ledger, gave him pause. Three quarters into it, Fred found some questions and statements, relating, he believed, to the Ouija board.

"I remember reading it," Fred said several years later. "They were up in the woods and stuff like that. She wanted to know basically when Bruce was going to die. If he would die by Christmas ... Fourth of July. And would her boyfriend—the Indian guy—if he would leave his wife by then and when Bruce would die and come to her and shit like that."

There were about a dozen such handwritten pages; every third or fourth question related to Mac. And from what Fred read, he believed Stella's friend Dee Rogers was involved in some way. It was possible, he thought, that she had been camping with Stella when the questions and answers were written.

When Stella called Fred the next day, he told her he couldn't find anything about Cindy's owing money.

Stella was impatient. "Well. I know damn well it's there."

"I looked at every page ... but what is this shit I found in the back?"

"I don't know what you're talking about."

He read a line from the ledger.

"I want you to burn that book for me," she said.

Long after, Stella and Fred parted company because of what he had found in the truck—and what she had asked him to find. Stella's attorney, Tom Hillier, had told her to find proof that Cindy owed the Nickells money.

"Tom wanted a page where I wrote down that Cynthia had owed me money. I asked Fred to look for that page. It was in a red notebook … and it had two rings and something like a ledger. And I described it to Fred and told him to look for it and look to see if that page was in the back of it, because Bruce wanted me to keep track of everything Cynthia owed us so when she got on her feet she could pay it back…"

Stella emphatically dismissed the very idea that she had kept a ledger or used a Ouija board to predict her husband's death.

"For one thing, if my husband's ever going to die, even if he had had emphysema and I knew for a fact that he was gonna die, I wouldn't wanna know when. So why would I question cards or whatever on this and then write it down? I believe in living the days right up to the last and letting come as a surprise wherever may be in store."

Fred later claimed he broke the Ouija board into pieces, doused it with gasoline along with the ledger, and burned both in the barrel behind the Nickells' mobile home.

"Right after I did it, I was sorry I did it. As I was watching it burn, I thought I should have kept this. I don't know why." Later, when Fred told Wilma about the journal and the Ouija board, she didn't believe him.

It sounded like some kind of a joke.

*

Even with Stella arrested and awaiting trial, Jim McCarthy, the man who Cindy swore up and down was her mother's lover, wasn't going to budge.

Jack Cusack met with him again.

"What would it take to convince you?" he asked over coffee.

"The source of the cyanide. Where she got it. The motive. Things like that that are concrete, not circumstantial."

The FBI agents didn't know the source of the cyanide but were still working on it. The motive, SA Cusack said, was insurance money.

McCarthy refuted the idea.

"I don't think the paltry insurance was reason enough for murder. He had just gotten on permanent with the state. He got $30,000 a year and the place would have been paid off."

SA Cusack asked if Stella had access to Mac's photographic supplies and darkroom equipment. "No, I don't think so, but even if she did, I don't think I have anything in there that qualifies as cyanide. So it's a moot point." They knew that. He had given them chemical samples from his darkroom, and none had contained cyanide.

"Did you know she has an interest in herbs and plants?"

"Yeah, she liked plants. Like every woman does."

"Did she buy fertilizer that had cyanide in it?"

"How the hell should I know? I don't have a green thumb in the first place. And how many people read the ingredients on a package of fertilizer?" *You're not convincing me, Jack*, he thought.

"How do you explain all of the bottles in this area, and Stella having two of the five found?"

Jim ranted on about manufacturing line processes and how Stella would be an unlikely candidate to have had access to all five bottles, of different brands, and even different-sized capsules.

Cusack just listened.

Jim McCarthy told Cusack he thought the government would do just about anything to solve one of these cases. Even fabricate evidence.

"No, we wouldn't."

"There are just too many things in this case that don't smell right. Been out in the sun too long."

*

Why wasn't anybody helping her aunt Stella? Why would the feds believe someone like Cindy? If only Wilma had a way to come up with money to hire an attorney who could see that her favorite aunt was being railroaded by a band of federal agents.

In the way that only she could, Stella Nickell asked her niece to change her story. "You made an awful mistake, babe, telling the FBI that I was coming to Houston to live."

"But you were."

Stella took her "let's clear up this little matter" posture. It was very familiar. Wilma had seen it since she was a child.

"Say I was coming to Houston to visit. Not to live. You made a mistake, you didn't hear me right." Her tone was insistent.

Wilma didn't say anything. How could she? Her aunt was in jail, and she didn't want to lie to the federal government and end up joining her. She couldn't alter her testimony. Besides, her words had been offered to protect, not indict.

"Aunt Stella wasn't going to kill Uncle Bruce ... she was going to leave him!"

"I didn't realize they were using it against me," Wilma said later, embarrassed by her naiveté.

Chapter Forty-Nine

The United States courthouse for the Western District of Washington sits solidly on Fifth and Madison in Seattle. In the right light, it is a seemingly rose-hued ten-story box punctured with vertical slits of tiny windows. The imposing architecture underscores its "federal" purpose. For the defendant, it would be home for the weeks of her trial.

Judge Bill Dwyer's courtroom was adjacent to his chambers on the fifth floor. Gold letters proclaimed the number: 506.

It took only two days to empanel the Nickell jury; surprisingly fast, given the extensive publicity of the case. The defendant sat quietly, even smiling faintly as Tom Hillier and Joanne Maida narrowed the jurors from a field of ninety-seven to thirty-six and finally to twelve—five men and seven women, plus two alternates.

Among those on the jury were a dental technician, a secretary, a real estate agent, and an automotive painter. All would be considered average, hardworking, but none had lived a life like Stella Nickell's.

*

The Stephenson girls gathered around little sister Stella to show support and to see what was going to happen. Cora Lee had brought them all together: Mary from Redmond, Berta from Michigan, Wilma from Pasco. Even Georgia said she'd be coming, though no one knew when.

Cora Lee, now seventy-one but looking a decade older, still wanted to find Cindy to "tell her a thing or two," but the feds kept her whereabouts secret. No one knew if Cora Lee would hug the girl or wring her neck. Her true feelings were mixed. Inside her purse was a wallet photo of a curly-topped baby, Cindy.

"She looks just like Shirley Temple," Cora Lee would say proudly, before her words trailed off to questions of why and how Stella's daughter could do this to the family.

During noon recess on Tuesday, April 19, 1988, the Stephenson women made their way to the 6th Avenue exit of the courthouse to dodge the reporters and get a cup of coffee. No one was hungry. Cora Lee ranted about Fred Phelps, whom she considered to be taking advantage of her daughter's incarceration. She was also angry that Georgia Mae hadn't shown up for the trial.

The women left the courthouse and walked across the steep grade near the corner of 6th and Madison—one of those Seattle streets that plummet from hilltop to the Sound. As she started to step, Cora Lee fell backward on the pavement, hitting her head. Her glasses flew off; her hearing aid popped out from her ear. A bystander rushed over and put his sweater over her trembling body.

The Stephenson girls looked on in horror as Cora Lee lay on the steps, passed out.

Their mother was rushed to Harborview, where she was listed in critical condition.

While Cora Lee lay in the hospital, Berta returned to her mother's trailer to look for medical and insurance documents. Among the considerable stash of papers, she found a letter

Cindy had written to Stella during the time the girl lived with
Cora Lee in Ukiah. It had never been mailed.

"She was sorry, please take her back, she couldn't stand
it with her grandma anymore. Her grandma was all sorts of
things, words I cannot even speak. She wrote she couldn't go
anywhere, she couldn't do nothing, how she hated Mother,"
Berta said later, recalling the contents of the letter that made
her sick to her stomach.

Cora Lee had saved the letter for a reason. Berta thought it
was her mother's intention to show it to Stella.

Later, going through more of her mother's papers, Berta found
a copy of a "will" Stella had written in her own handwriting:

*Cora Lee Rice has invested $23,000 into 5 acres I have
purchased. Her portion is one-half… to leave in her will
to my 3 sisters and 1 brother…*

Stella reserved the right to buy out her siblings.

*If anything happens to me the property goes to my daughter,
Cynthia Lea Slawson Hamilton. But all will be held in
trust for her by Cora Lee Rice, my mother, until such time
as Cora Lee Rice dies.*

Signed, Stella Nickell.

Oddly, the will made no mention of two people: Bruce and
Leah. Leah and Stella had not been estranged, except for the
brief time after she made her daughter leave White River
Estates when she found the photo of the marijuana. Why leave

her youngest out? And why omit Bruce? Was it simply Stella's take-charge way of writing, as she had to North Pacific Bank? Or was Bruce already dead? The paper was not dated, but since Stella used the name Hamilton, it clearly was written after her daughter's 1984 marriage to the trucker, Pepper.

Was the document an agreement, a promise, or an inducement?

Over the days of the trial, an unconscious Cora Lee would be scanned for a blood clot. When she woke, she called her daughters by her sisters' names.

"I'm not Lucille. Mother, I'm Bert."

Her daughters knew the tough old bird would never be the same.

For friends who hadn't seen Stella Nickell since prior to her arrest, their first glimpse in the courtroom on the morning of April 20 must have been a shock. Stella, who had once had a lovely figure and thick black tresses, now looked puffy and dull. Twenty pounds heavier, she wore her old skinny clothes.

As she moved to her seat, she still managed a kind of confidence and swivel in her walk. It wasn't quite "The Walk," but it was as close as the circumstances would allow. She wasn't going to let anyone get the best of her.

Projecting her buttoned-up, cool version of confidence, the defendant sat rod-straight in a black leather, brass-riveted chair. Before her, a pencil on a legal pad. Throughout the morning and the days to follow, she wrote note after note for Tom Hillier. At times when the attorneys discussed matters among themselves, she gazed out the window on her left and looked at the city beyond.

Of Stella Nickell's boys and men, only Fred Phelps took a spot on one of the walnut benches provided for spectators. Harry Swanson claimed he had been told by the feds to stay away. Jim McCarthy also made himself scarce. He had wanted to be a witness on Stella's behalf, but had been told by the defense lawyer that that wasn't a good idea.

Ron Nichols and Jack Cusack sat on chairs next to the double doors leading to the courtroom. Their job was to make sure the witnesses were ready.

Judge Bill Dwyer directed his instructions to the jury, imploring each to listen to the evidence, and solely the evidence presented in the courtroom. He reminded each not to discuss the case with anyone, even another juror.

With that, the trial began.

Assistant U.S. Attorney Joanne Maida spoke with an impressive deliberateness, a preciseness that jurors would grow to accept as her trademark delivery. Her salt-and-pepper hair was pulled back from her forehead tightly, then released down into a short mane in back. She opened with a detailed recounting of the case against Stella Nickell, a woman who wanted more from life than her marriage could provide. She described a chilling scenario involving tampering with consumer products and an insurance payoff that depended on someone discovering the tampering. When Stella's husband died, Maida suggested, the defendant had expected the pathologists to rule death by acute cyanide poisoning. But that didn't happen. Instead, pathologists ruled emphysema—a natural cause.

Sue Snow had died to give Stella Nickell a reason to call attention to the circumstances of her husband's death.

There was plenty of evidence to incriminate the defendant, the prosecutor said. Insurance policies, inconsistent statements, and out-and-out lies. And the defendant's own daughter had come forward with information against her mother.

"You will hear a lot of talk about money in this trial. You will hear about money to be collected from insurance proceeds, about monetary damages requested by the defendant, who had sued Bristol-Myers, the manufacturer of Excedrin, one month after her husband's death. You will also hear about a $300,000 reward that was put up by a pharmaceutical association for the arrest and conviction of any person brought to justice for this cyanide poison case, this one among several in the nation.

"You will be asked to make decisions about people you will hear testify during the course of this trial. Some of these people may be questioned about that financial motivation, what financial motivation, if any, exists for their cooperation with the United States.

"I represent the United States. They have been promised nothing by the United States in return for their testimony in court. The reward is offered through a private organization, which will make an independent determination regarding any payout terms."

The jury was told that Cindy revealed to the FBI that for several years preceding her stepfather's death, her mother had talked of killing her husband and that six months before Bruce Nickell died, the talk had become more concrete.

"You will learn the specifics of these discussions between mother and daughter at this trial. You will also learn that mother and daughter have certainly had their share of disagreements, but they are still mother and daughter and they relate as mother would to daughter. You will see that Cindy Hamilton and Stella Nickell resemble each other physically, so much so that in the past they have been mistaken as sisters."

Joanne Maida warned the jury that Cindy might appear to be flat and unemotional. "Lessons learned from childhood die hard, and her mother taught her that a display of emotion was a sign of weakness."

*

Tom Hillier stood next to Stella Nickell as he began his opening argument. His style was warmer. He was the kind of guy jurors immediately liked. Folksy and friendly, that was Tom Hillier.

If spectators, friends, family members, the media, had thought the trial might be a daughter up against a mother, Stella's lawyer gave the notion greater foundation.

"We invite you now and encourage you now to give your closest attention to the testimony of Cindy Hamilton. As outlined by the prosecutor, her testimony and its credibility is central to the prosecution's case. Ms. Hamilton's testimony will be contradicted in all essential details by Mrs. Nickell, who will testify on her own behalf and tell you about the events that led to and after Mr. Nickell's death."

Yes, Stella Nickell and her husband had life insurance.

Yes, she was the one who filled out the paperwork. An FBI handwriting expert was not needed to verify that. She was not forging his name for nefarious reasons, just signing it as she had done on all such papers during their marriage.

"The evidence will show that when Bruce died, that question of his taking a physical to obtain the coverage he had applied for was unresolved. He hadn't taken a physical yet, and Mrs. Nickell was unaware when Bruce Nickell died just how much insurance he really had coming, if any, from the state of Washington."

Yes, there had been books. Tom Hillier boasted that his client was a voracious reader. But the subject of poison plants was a concern related to her babysitting responsibilities, first at White River Estates, and later on the Nickells' rural property. Stella was concerned about her granddaughter.

The jurors were told to pay careful attention to when the books were handled by his client.

"Significant will be the dates concerning the checkout time of these books, the dates of the checkouts in mid-1984—May of 1984 and September of 1984. Dates absolutely consistent with the time frame that the Nickells moved onto their property in Auburn, Washington. That was in May of 1984."

Yes, she read encyclopedias.

"Again, there is no controversy concerning the fact that Mrs. Nickell read in the encyclopedias about cyanide. Mrs. Nickell will testify and tell you why, and I invite you and encourage you to listen closely to her and her explanation. She will say that she did do some general reading about cyanide after she found out about the tragic circumstances concerning her husband's death.

"Who wouldn't?"

It was also true … Bruce and Stella Nickell had struggled financially. At the time of Bruce's death, both were working full-time and still unable to make ends meet.

That was not in dispute, he said. Why had Cindy changed her story? Tom Hillier implored the jury to pay close attention to the defendant's daughter.

He repeated the word "anticipate" in reference to what testimony Cindy would give.

"We anticipate that she will say she decided to let it play its course, even though she knew in her heart, as people say, that she thought this was going to actually happen. We anticipate this because we don't know what Cindy will say, because the evidence will show since January of '87 when she went to the FBI, she has fastidiously avoided contact with her mother and cleverly avoided each and every contact attempt by Sal Ramos and myself to interview her, in stark contrast to the cooperation and availability of Stella Nickell."

Maida objected. Hillier's statement was an "improper characterization of Ms. Nickell's availability to the government and of Cindy Hamilton's nonavailability to the defense."

Judge Dwyer agreed that the claim the defense had made was arguable, but let counsel proceed.

Finally, Hillier mentioned the reward.

"The prosecution disavows any governmental interest in that $300,000. That doesn't matter. What matters is, it was out there, in the public domain.

"Your considerable task will be to weigh against the testimony of Mrs. Nickell the story of Cindy Hamilton, because resolution of that conflict will necessarily control your verdict."

The case against his client was circumstantial, but he could easily reconcile all of it with her plea of innocence.

Chapter Fifty

After morning recess on April 20, King County volunteer firefighter Bob Jewett sat in the freshly polished witness box between the judge's bench and the jury box.

He told the court the squad had arrived at 5:13, June 5, 1986, just eleven minutes after the defendant's 911 call, uncertain about whether they were at the correct address. Stella Nickell stared from the doorway.

Joanne Maida asked if the fireman knew if it was the right place.

He did not, but after thirty seconds or so, Mrs. Nickell finally started to wave him over. " ... It looked like someone was just watching us."

The firefighter testified that Bruce Nickell was inside, lying on his back as they set out to stabilize him. He showed signs of agonal breathing. His eyes were fixed, his blood pressure rapidly falling. Stella told the witness that her husband had taken a physical for state employment and had passed with no problems. She also emphasized that Bruce had been having problems with headaches.

Though her hands shook, she "seemed pretty calm."

Tom Hillier stepped to the microphone with great assurance for a brief cross-examination. "Do you see a full range of physical responses from people who have made the call?"

"As far as their reaction to the situation?"

"Right."

"Yeah."

"So you see people who seem calm outwardly and you see people, as you say, so hysterical that they can hardly talk?"

"Oh, well, I'm not saying that all people I see are that way, no."

*

Sue Snow's widower was the government's second witness. Paul Webking looked lost in the witness box, his pain obvious. He testified about their life together, the phone calls from the road. He described his wife's morning ritual of taking two Excedrin capsules for caffeine, instead of coffee.

He recounted his story of his June 8 comment to Sue to buy more Excedrin as he left on a long haul to Chico, California. In fact, Sue had already written Excedrin on her shopping list.

Phone records indicating their conversations the days before Sue died were received into evidence. They were followed by more documents identified and admitted without objection—Sue's Albertson's and Safeway checks from June 8.

"Mr. Webking, what was Sue Snow doing the last time you saw her alive?"

"She was sleeping."

The last question was a nice touch, the kind prosecutors often use to elicit sympathy for a victim. Sleeping. Unaware of impending doom.

*

More testimony that first morning came from King County medical examiner Corrine Fligner, who explained autopsy procedures and how her assistant had picked up the smell of bitter almonds, the first clue that Sue had died of cyanide poisoning. She told the court that the ability to smell cyanide is genetic, and that anywhere from twenty to ninety percent of the population is unable to smell it.

Dr. Fligner said that the toxicity report indicating cyanide was received on the morning of June 16, 1986. Two days later, Bruce Nickell was suspected to be a possible victim; testing later that day also showed cyanide.

Tom Hillier's cross-examination went nowhere in particular. He restated some of Dr. Fligner's testimony regarding under whose jurisdiction Bruce Nickell's death came. Suspicious deaths were autopsied by the M.E., and the physicians at Harborview hadn't felt Nickell's death fell under such guidelines.

It still didn't change his cause of death.

The medical examiner testified that the hospital doctors had requested the autopsy, and then sought permission from the widow.

"And the reason for that normally would be to try to confirm the cause of death if there was some question?"

"Yes, I think the physician's desire to know the cause of death."

"Did you have any personal contact with my client, Mrs. Nickell, during the course of your investigation of this case?"

"Yes, I did."

"When was that?"

"I spoke to Mrs. Nickell twice, to my recollection. One time was to inform her that her husband had died of acute cyanide poisoning, and that was, I believe, on Wednesday, the eighteenth of June, after the testing had been performed and the cyanide tests were positive."

*

Ed Sexton, still with the King County Sheriff's Office, though now based in the Federal Way precinct, was sworn in. He told the court that on June 17, 1986, he answered a radio request for help at the Nickell home. When he arrived, the defendant gave him two bottles of Excedrin—both with lot numbers matching Sue Snow's.

"Did you see how many were left in this particular bottle of capsules?"

"Yes, I believe there were seven."

The witness went on to tell the court that Stella said Bruce had been taking the capsules from the bottle because he "had been having severe headaches and the only pills that he likes to take were the Excedrin . . . he would take three to four pills a day."

Stella had told him her husband had been suffering from headaches for around eight days.

When the prosecutor tried to determine the number of times Stella contacted medical authorities concerning her husband's autopsy, she was again met with a vague response.

The best he could offer was "more than once."

"Did she tell you what had been reported to her about the cause of her husband's death?"

"Yes. She said they determined natural causes."

"Did she use the words 'natural causes'?"

"Yes."

When asked about the second of the two bottles given to him by the defendant, the police officer said Stella had retrieved it from the upper kitchen cabinet. Unlike the first, it was in a box. He noticed it didn't have a safety neck band.

Sexton said the defendant told him she had purchased one bottle at Johnny's in Kent, the other bottle from either Johnny's or the North Auburn Albertson's store.

When Joanne Maida sought details, the witness reviewed his report. The one she bought at Johnny's was the one in the box. She had purchased it two weeks after the first one, he said.

Tom Hillier had a good chance with the diminutive King County officer, and he knew it. He started with the suggestion that the old recollection was not as fresh today as it had been two years before.

The witness agreed.

"All right. You testified on direct that Stella Nickell said that her husband had been taking Excedrin for eight days prior to his death. Is that what you testified to?"

Sexton said that was correct.

"Could you find in your report where it says that Stella Nickell indicated her husband had been taking Excedrin for eight days before?"

Sexton futilely searched the document. His face reddened.

"Doesn't say that she said it. I asked Mrs. Nickell how many pills Bruce was taking. Mrs. Nickell mentioned he took four at a time. Being that there was only seven capsules in a forty-capsule bottle; that meant Bruce had been taking the Excedrin eight days."

"So that's arithmetic that you accomplished, isn't it?" Tom Hillier prodded.

"Yes, but she also mentioned that he had been taking them eight days."

"Look at your report again."

Sexton admitted it wasn't there, and the defense lawyer had him read a line from his report: "Mrs. Nickell told me that Bruce had been feeling ill several days before his death and that he had been taking the Excedrin for his headaches."

"So that's what Mrs. Nickell told you, isn't it?"

"I remember her saying seven to eight days."

"So at first, it was eight days, now seven to eight days."

Hillier did the same with the officer's recollection of the number of calls Stella Nickell had made to Harborview.

That hadn't been in his report either.

*

After the afternoon recess, FBI Special Agent Ike Nakamoto took the stand. Nakamoto was there to testify about the interview he and the FDA's Kim Rice conducted with the defendant on June 19, 1986. After establishing the basics surrounding the interview, Joanne Maida launched into her direct examination.

Ike Nakamoto's retelling of Stella Nickell's story of her husband's death, matched, without exception, the defendant's account. Bruce came home a little after 4:09 p.m., took a shower, watched television, had a headache, took four Excedrin capsules ... collapsed ... was airlifted to Harborview.

Agent Nakamoto reviewed his notes concerning the number of calls the defendant made to medical authorities regarding her husband's autopsy. He reported three calls: June 7, 13, and one after she heard of Sue Snow's death on television.

On the subject of where she shopped for the two bottles she turned over to Officer Sexton, SA Nakamoto said that the defendant said she shopped at Albertson's North, Pay 'N Save South, and at the Johnny's Market in Kent.

"What did she tell you about where she purchased, she thought, each bottle?"

"The open bottle was purchased probably two weeks prior to Bruce's death, probably at either the Albertson's North End or the Johnny's Market."

"And the new bottle, the one that was in the box?"

"The unopened bottle was purchased probably two days prior to Bruce's death at Johnny's Market."

SA Nakamoto also referred to his notes when he testified that the defendant had told him her husband had taken a physical as a requirement to gain full-time employment with the Department of Transportation.

The prosecution continued on the subject of the deceased's "depressed mood," just before his death. Stella Nickell had told the FBI agent her husband was unhappy about missing a physical necessary for an additional $100,000 in life insurance.

"Do you have any question in your mind that she was talking about an amount of $100,000 being contingent on the taking of a physical examination, as opposed to any greater or lesser amount?"

"No doubt."

Next, the prosecution produced the June 16, 1986, letter—written three days before the interview with the defendant.

The letter carried the initials of Wally Strong, Senior Special Underwriter, Group Division. It was read into the record.

Dear Mr. Nickell,

We have received your letter in which you are requesting additional information as to why we incompleted your

application for the requested $25,000 of life coverage offered
through the State of Washington.

According to the underwriting guidelines which we
must follow for this group, anyone age 51 and applying
for over $20,000 of life coverage must complete a medical
examination. Our first request for you to take a medical
exam was sent out on March 11, 1986. We closed out your
file as incomplete on June 2, 1986.

We would be happy to reopen your file if the completed
medical examination would be sent in to us...

"Mr. Nakamoto, the letter references requested $25,000 of life coverage. At any time did Stella Nickell in this interview that you had with her ever revise the $100,000 figure she gave you, that according to her was contingent on taking the medical exam, and say she was mistaken; that it was $25,000?"

"No."

Maida pulled the statement of insurance again, and with the FBI agent's help, deciphered the state's coverages for Bruce Nickell. They totaled $135,000.

Further, according to SA Nakamoto, Stella Nickell stated that she and her husband each had applied for an additional $20,000 through Bank Cardholders of America, but a clerical error had left her husband without insurance. Only she was covered.

The membership enrollment form from October 14, 1985, was identified by the agent. The cardholder was Stella Nickell; spouse, Bruce Nickell. The document showed the defendant had checked off that she and her husband were both beneficiaries and insured.

Maida asked how the defendant explained the clerical error that left her, and not her husband, insured. SA Nakamoto recalled Stella Nickell showing him a small card indicating she was the insured. She said she had called the insurance company's 800 number and discovered "a clerical error had been made and that her policy was issued but Bruce's was never issued."

Under further direct, the FBI agent said that the third Excedrin bottle had been recovered from the cabinet under the bathroom sink and was turned over to FDA investigator Kim Rice.

On cross-examination, Tom Hillier prevailed with his prepared questions, promising to wade through them and get on to some new ones based on the Assistant U.S. Attorney's direct examination. Hillier recalled that the unopened bottle had been said to have been purchased at Johnny's "a couple of days before" her husband's death ... around June 3.

When the defense lawyer asked about the Albertson's receipt from June 3, the agent didn't recall seeing it.

Hillier had the witness confirm that Stella retrieved some papers to provide information on insurance, that it had not been something she said off the top of her head.

"She told you that—she expressed some question about what insurance coverage they actually had in view of some correspondence concerning a physical, didn't she?"

"Yes."

And yes, the witness also agreed, Stella didn't think her husband had $100,000 coverage. And yes, there had been a delay in receiving notice from the insurance company regarding the insurance. No, she didn't know the exact amount from the state policy.

Tom Hillier recalled the June 16 letter Nakamoto had read into evidence.

Bruce Nickell had not been alive when the letter was written.

"And this letter, was it given to you on that day?"

"This is the first time I've seen it."

"All right. So you don't know if Stella Nickell had seen it on June 19 when you were interviewing her, do you?"

"No."

Hillier had the witness take a look at the document addressed to Bruce by Northwestern National. "And are there two dates on there, one of which is scratched out and one of which is stamped on?"

"The scratched-out one looks like March 11, 1986, and the stamped one is April 17, 1986." Hillier asked the witness to read the message into the record.

We are pleased to receive the request for insurance coverage which was recently submitted…

Next, Hillier had SA Nakamoto read the letter to North-western from Bruce Nickell, dated May 27, 1986. It had been stamp-dated June 2, 1986.

I received a letter from your company today informing me I have to take a physical. This letter is dated in final notice and my application had been delayed… I was not aware I had to take a physical. I would appreciate more information… as I am in the dark on this matter.

Under further questioning, Nakamoto conceded that the defendant had said her husband was depressed that she was the one covered and not he. It was also true that Stella Nickell had given the FBI agent information on the All American policy, stating that a clerical error left her insured and Bruce uncovered.

FDA investigator Kim Rice followed Nakamoto with testimony about the third bottle, the one from under Stella's bathroom sink. He testified that the defendant told him she didn't know of its existence.

Maida had the clerk hand the sixty-count Excedrin bottle, still in an evidence bag, to the FDA investigator. He identified it and the bottle was received into evidence.

The Albertson's receipt from June 3, 1986, was next.

Maida asked if he had asked Stella where she purchased the tainted bottles. He had. When searching for the source of the bottles, the defendant produced some receipts. The one from Albertson's was among them.

"There was really not much that she did say about this receipt," he said. "She had no recollection concerning what the items might have been on here that were purchased."

Hillier took the podium and drew from Kim Rice support for his opening statement that his client had been cooperative: She had recovered the Albertson's receipt, along with others, at the request of the FDA and FBI. Rice told the court that, in fact, the Albertson's receipt had a price—$3.39—that matched a price sticker on the intact forty-count bottle of cyanide-laced Excedrin.

Rice agreed that Stella had told him that, to the best of her recollection, Johnny's was where she bought the unopened bottle.

"And she indicated that she thought she bought that a couple of days before Bruce's death?"

She had.

"Which, of course, would be June 3 or thereabouts?"

"Yes."

"Did you ask Mrs. Nickell why that conflict? Albertson's or Johnny's?"

"I did not."

Equifax insurance investigator Lynn Force was called to fill in the last bit of the day. His voice was so soft that Judge Dwyer asked him to speak up. Force told the court he was in the process of investigating on behalf of Northwestern National, both its $100,000 accidental death and $36,000 life insurance policy when he met Stella at the airport to have her sign a release so he could obtain the autopsy report to complete his investigation. She accommodated his request. He had asked her if there were any other policies, and she said no.

Under further direct and subsequent cross-examination, the insurance investigator told the court that although he hadn't written the $136,000 total on any paperwork, he recalled telling the defendant the amount.

*

After Cora Lee's fall, her condition was of prime concern to her daughters. Berta visited Stella to tell her she had to get to the hospital. Mother needed her.

Though concerned about her mother, Stella had other things to worry about. She told her favorite sister she had braced herself for her daughter's testimony.

"You watch and you're going to see one of the greatest performances you've ever seen. Cynthia is a good actress. She could make you believe anything."

Stella told Berta that she knew her daughter would never back down.

"She sticks to what she says even if it is all lies. Because she will never admit when she is wrong, and never has in all her life, unless it is to her advantage."

Chapter Fifty-One

Jack Cusack went to SeaTac to pick up the government's star witness for her day in court. Cusack's goal was to make sure the defendant's daughter didn't completely back out of testifying. If she did freeze up, Jack Cusack would need to take the stand to testify about what she had told him. That, of course, would be an extremely weak presentation compared with a firsthand account from the suspect's daughter, no less.

Words of assurance did little good, however. Cindy kept saying she was worried that if her mother were acquitted, she would seek revenge.

"She'll come after me … she'll kill me."

"Cindy, it won't happen. Stella's going down."

"You don't know my mother!"

She told the FBI agent that she didn't want to check in to a Seattle hotel, which would have certainly been more convenient for the trial. "I don't want the media to find me and hassle me," she said. "I can't handle it."

Cusack drove Cindy to the Bellevue Holiday Inn, just ten minutes east of Seattle. Cindy, professing great concern lest the media locate her, told the front-desk clerk, "I'm a witness in a very important federal trial. I don't want anyone to know I'm here."

It was Cindy goes to Hollywood, Cusack thought. She was lapping up the attention.

Back at the Seattle offices of the FBI and U.S. Attorney, clocks were watched in anxious anticipation of Hamilton's testimony.

SA Cusack had told Cindy that she couldn't see or talk to Dee Rogers before the trial, but she called her from the Holiday Inn anyway.

"She didn't give a shit what they said," Dee Rogers said later.

Paul also understood that the defendant's daughter was the key witness. He wondered how it was that she could know so much and yet not be involved in the crime.

"At the very least," he said later, "she could have come forward after Bruce died . . . she could have saved Sue."

*

The defense finally got its hands on Cindy Hamilton's grand jury testimony, only hours before she was to take the stand.

Tom Hillier asked Stella to go through the sixty-nine pages of testimony page by page. He told her to make note of anything that could help her case.

And so she did. When Cindy whined about moving around from school to school, Stella bristled and wrote: "*She went to one school 'til 6th grade. I changed her school because of behavior problems.*"

Cindy said she was rebellious when they moved to Washington because she "didn't like the lifestyle" her mother was leading.

Stella wrote: "*She was all of 14 and she didn't want me to marry Bruce.*"

When Maida inquired about the beating and other corporal punishment, Stella scrawled: "*The only other corporal punishments she had was Room Restriction or no T.V.*"

Cindy testified to her fear about being a child abuser herself, and how she read up on the subject.

> *"She had no worry about that except in her own mind. So she would know what to say to convince people she was an abused child … she also told everybody at one time she was adopted."*

Maida asked if the relationship with her mother had remained constant. Stella wrote: *"Yes it has remained constant—she doesn't like me."*

On the beating: *"She never got hit. She got a spanking when called for and that wasn't often. From the way she turned out, not often enough."*

Every time Cindy mentioned her first husband in California, Stella scratched it out and wrote "man." She amended marriage to "living with."

When Cindy told the grand jurors her mother was intimidating, Stella scribbled: *"Where she got that, I don't know."*

On the page showing Cindy's statement that "she was 99.9 percent sure" it was her stepfather her mother was going to say had died, Stella wrote: *"Why was she so sure it was Bruce? Why wouldn't it have been her own grandmother?? She knew Mother was not in the best of health."*

Stella also noted that she, not Cindy, was at Dee's apartment first. She made numerous notes refuting the whole story. She claimed the "I know what you're thinking" statement came later.

> *"I was trying to relieve her guilt feelings about sending [her daughter] to Cal. away from her Grandpa. Bruce was very*

*upset about that. I was trying to tell her that Bruce didn't
die still being mad at her..."*

Stella wrote more: "*We were in financial problems to where I was
supposedly 'thinking of dealing drugs'? Now we are talking 'Hit
man'? As far as I had ever heard that is Big Money on the spot.
Where did I have the money??"*

With respect to conversations at the airport when her mother
could talk in half sentences and Cindy said she'd know what
she meant, Stella wrote:

> "*If I was talking half sentences, then she filled in the rest
> from her own imagination, thoughts, wishes, desires, etc. Is
> that the way it went???"*

When Maida got to the subject of Stella asking her daughter
about cyanide, Stella wrote: "*Why would I ask her about something I was sure she had no knowledge about??"*
Stella corrected her daughter's testimony concerning the
idea of the cyanide tampering coming from a discussion of the
Chicago Tylenol killings.

> "*If she is referring to the only time we talked about anything
> of the sort, it was about the news article about the guy
> in Texas that put Rat Poison in Caps. The Tylenol was
> mentioned in that article."*

The defendant also wanted to know "where did I get the extra
caps to do this with?" when Cindy informed the grand jurors
that her mother had filled some extra capsules with toxic seeds.

On why Cindy said she didn't tell Bruce about the murder plots, Stella wrote: "*She knew he wouldn't have believed her. Bruce knew beyond a shadow that I loved him and still do.*"

Cindy "panicked" when the FBI first questioned her at the trailer. "*Why would she panic?? (a guilty conscience? Maybe).*"

"And I thought more and more about Sue Snow and her family, and it bothered me ..." Stella wrote: "*It should have!!*"

Cindy used half a page of testimony to tell why she hadn't told her daughter Bruce had died. She didn't know how to. "*Tell her the truth, that you set grandma up and sent her to prison.*"

Cindy said she sent her daughter to California because she was "moving around a lot," and Stella wrote: "*from one bed to another and [the child] was in the way.*"

When Cindy's testimony indicated that her mother was "intimately and emotionally" involved with Jim McCarthy before Bruce's death, Stella wrote: "*She believes that because she couldn't get into Jim's bed, from what she told me. All he talked about was how great her mom and Bruce were.*"

Cindy ended her grand jury testimony stating that although she might project a hard exterior, inside she was still having problems, nightmares even, as a result of the ordeal.

Stella wrote: "*As well she should have.*"

Tom Hillier made a number of notes of his own, mostly pointing out how rife the testimony was with time conflicts and mismatched stories.

In the margin next to Cindy's testimony about her mother's plan to mix Bruce's iced tea with drugs, he wrote the words: "Accomplice to plots."

Chapter Fifty-Two

Ron Nichols took the stand on the second day of testimony. The blue in his suit brought out the red of his hair, though now it showed more gray than it had when the case began. After establishing his role in the Nickell investigation, Joanne Maida turned the court's attention to the interview he and SA Cusack conducted with the defendant in November 1986.

The witness identified the stores the defendant had said were places she shopped, and probably where she purchased the tainted bottles. SA Nichols named the same stores as SA Nakamoto had the day before.

Concerning life insurance, SA Nichols testified the defendant "stated that she had a life insurance policy that paid approximately $25,000, and that she was supposed to have a life insurance policy that paid $100,000, but Bruce did not take a physical."

"Did Mrs. Nickell at any time during this interview correct any of her statements to you by calling to your attention the existence of such a letter?"

"No, she did not."

And though she had many months in which to do so, the witness said the defendant never contacted the FBI to correct her statement about the $100,000 coverage. Further, the defendant said she did not have any other insurance policies.

"Did Mrs. Nickell indicate whether she had any interest in any money benefiting from her husband's death?"

"Yes, she did indicate."

"What did she say?"

"She said that she was not interested in benefiting from her husband's death in any way."

Asst. U.S. Attorney Maida asked the clerk to give the witness the next exhibit, Stella Nickell's lawsuit against Bristol-Myers.

SA Nichols read the date it had been signed: "July 30, 1986."

Throughout all of Nichols's testimony, Stella continued to write on her legal pad, occasionally looking up to brush a loose strand of hair from her face. She never once betrayed her feelings.

"Moving on, Mr. Nichols. At the conclusion of this interview with the defendant, did you tell her anything to indicate that your investigation of her was over?"

"No, I did not."

Hillier began his cross-examination by asking if it would be fair to say that when Stella said she didn't want to benefit from her husband's death, what she really meant was she'd prefer he was alive.

SA Nichols said he didn't take it that way.

"So what you've testified to today is your impression?"

"Yes, sir."

It was true, the witness also said, he didn't know whose idea it was to file a lawsuit against Bristol-Myers. Hillier turned his attention to the June 16 letter. "Is there anything in that letter which suggests or states that a $100,000 policy is intact?"

"No."

"Does it even mention the number 100,000?"

"No, it doesn't."

"Does it give specifics concerning what insurance is covered or isn't covered?"

"No, it doesn't."

Yes, SA Nichols said, the November interview repeated questions from June's. Yes, her responses concerning where she shopped, purchased the Excedrin, were consistent with what she had said back that spring.

*

It was time to talk insurance, the motive of the government's case against Stella Nickell. Up first was Sandy Sorby, of the State Employees Insurance Board. Wishing she was anywhere but the federal courthouse, she testified that Bruce Nickell's death benefits through Northwestern National totaled $136,000.

The attorney asked her to step down to review the chart of insurance policies. She asked the witness to explain the numbers on the right-hand side of the chart, under the label: "Northwestern, January 6, 1986 Application."

The witness said that $100,000 was accidental death and dismemberment, and another $5,000 AD&D was provided by the State. A figure of $26,000 was optional life, taken by the employees at their own expense. That figure increases as salaries rise. Another $5,000 basic life is provided by the state to all employees.

Joanne Maida asked about a bracketed figure of $25,000.

"The employee had applied for an additional $25,000 that was incomplete. That means that he did not get that amount of insurance because he was requested to take a physical exam by the insurance company and that was never done."

Next, Sandy Sorby identified a life insurance enrollment form used by state employees and reviewed by her office.

It had been signed by Bruce on January 8, 1986, and indicated the following amounts purportedly requested by Bruce: optional life for $25,000; supplemental life for $25,000 (the one that had been incomplete); optional life or optional accidental death and dismemberment for $100,000.

"The sum that you have originally testified to of total coverage on the insured Bruce Nickell came to $136,000. What is the $1,000 amount that appears on its surface to be a discrepancy, the extra $1,000?"

The witness said optional life automatically increases with the employee's salary. Records showed Bruce had received a raise.

The insurance enrollment form was admitted in evidence.

Sorby also told the court about her meeting on July 7, 1986, with Stella when she came to file the claim. Stella told her she had waited for an amended death certificate, since her husband's cause of death had been changed. She also testified about the hundred-plus news clippings she saw in the widow's briefcase.

Tom Hillier stepped forward to drill the nice lady from Olympia on the news clippings. She told the court she had not counted them. And yes, they were originals, not photocopies. "So you're saying that there were a hundred original newspaper clippings in there?"

"I'm not saying a hundred. It was a full briefcase and—"

"You saw—"

"—a hundred is the largest amount I could imagine in a briefcase."

"So you're imagining that's a possibility?"

"Yes."

Under more cross, she told the court the clippings were brought appropriately, necessary for the processing of an accidental death claim.

She said Bruce Nickell's supervisor, Dick Johnson, contacted SEIB on behalf of the defendant on July 2. When the defendant showed up five days later, it had been a month since her husband's death. The time frame was not unusual.

It was fitting that Sandy Sorby's friend and work colleague, Pam Stegenga, was next. She stepped up into the witness box and said her contacts with the defendant had only been over the phone.

Stella Nickell called three times in late 1986, each time wanting to know when the insurance claim would be paid. During the call on November 20, Stella Nickell said the FBI agents had met with her two days before. "And what, if anything, did she say about the status of the investigation?" Joanne Maida asked.

"She said that she thought the investigation was completed."

Under cross, Tom Hillier tried to pin down who had made the late-September call—the witness or the defendant. There was much give and take over who had called whom. Finally, after cross and re-direct, the jury learned that Stella Nickell had placed the last call and the witness returned it.

Joanne Maida commenced direct examination of Auburn Public Library director Mary Margaret Stanton by asking about checkout procedures for library patrons. At the time in question, it was a simple system of stamp-dated book cards, imprinted with due dates and patron numbers.

Stanton identified Stella's registration card and a checkout card for *Deadly Harvest*. It had been stamped with Stella Nickell's number, with due dates of June 16, 1983, and May 22, 1984.

The librarian also identified a book card for *Human Poisoning by Native and Cultivated Plants*. It had been due on September 19, 1984.

But the book, Mary Margaret Stanton testified, had never been returned. An overdue notice was sent to Stella on September 26, 1984.

After the lunch break, librarian Stanton identified books belonging to the Auburn Public Library: *Deadly Harvest*, volumes of McGraw-Hill *Encyclopedia of Science and Technology*, *New Caxton Encyclopedia*, and *Merit Student's Encyclopedia*.

All were admitted into evidence.

Tom Hillier, of course, had no cause to pick on a librarian. He asked if she had looked at *Deadly Harvest* before it went to the FBI labs.

She said she hadn't.

*

Valerie Williams, a compliance officer, whose responsibilities also included managing bank records for North Pacific Bank, took the stand. North Pacific was the lienholder on the Nickells' mobile home. The witness identified various documents, including the Final Notice of Delinquency dated April 9, 1986. The letter indicated that total payment of $1,892.01 was due by April 25, 1986.

Next, she identified the letter written by the defendant on April 25, 1986.

I know that I am tremendously overdue ... I am having marital problems. They are about solved, and I would like to ask if you will have faith in me, personally. Bruce is no longer involved ...

Williams identified a second letter, dated June 1, 1986, in which the defendant promised to stay current, after making another double payment.

Dear Sirs, I am trying to figure out where I can get my payment in by the 12th of the month and not be behind ...

The next letter, also from Stella Nickell, was undated. Joanne Maida had the witness read the letter for the record. *If you just have patience, I will eventually catch up—just don't push ...*

Maida had the witness point out that in none of her letters concerning payments due did the defendant use the words "we" or "our."

After discussing payoff of the loan, the Asst. U.S. Attorney had nothing further.

Hillier pointed out that the letters' chronology was suspect—the March 5 letter from the bank to the Nickells did not reference a $100-per-month insurance increase.

Further, Hillier had the witness consider that the letter in question might be only a portion of a larger one. Somewhat reluctantly, the witness agreed it was a possibility. The defense had no further questions.

A pivotal moment in the morning's proceedings occurred when Tom Noonan of Fish Gallery and Pets took to the stand. If there was a chance for trouble in the government's case, Tom

Noonan was it. Not that he wasn't truthful, but sometimes his story changed slightly, and that left room for the defense to discredit him.

He identified Stella as a regular customer and told the court that although he recommended the liquid Algae-Gon, Stella preferred Algae Destroyer. At her request, he said, he even ordered her a supply.

He told the court that the blister-packed product sometimes admits moisture, causing the tablets to become insoluble. "I told people when they bought a product like this that to make them easier to use they could crush them up and dissolve them in warm water before administering them to the tank."

"Do you have any specific recollection of having discussed that with Mrs. Nickell?"

"I can't really say if I did, but my general—"

Tom Hillier bolted up. "Your Honor, I think he's answered the question."

Judge Dwyer agreed. "The question has been answered."

Unflappable Joanne Maida went into damage control. In order to make the record "understandable," she asked if Tom Noonan made a general practice of advising purchasers of the algaecide how best to use the product.

He said he told them to crush and dissolve it in warm water. Maida asked the question again: had he given Stella Nickell the same advice as his other customers?

He said he had. In fact, he remembered "to try to get her to purchase a product we already had, I told her the drawbacks of the product she wanted to purchase, that you had to crush it up to make it effective."

Tom Hillier stood to ask Tom Noonan how he was doing.

"I've been better," the young man deadpanned.

The response drew laughter. After a brief testimony concerning the defendant's interest in opening a fish store—with her husband as partner—the defense hit back upon Noonan's recollection of events.

Hillier pointed out that at first, Noonan couldn't remember talking to Stella specifically and then, suddenly, he was able to recall an exact conversation.

The defense wanted to know when this exact conversation had occurred. Hillier had the witness tell the jury he started working at the Kent store in December 1984 and left for the Renton store in January 1986.

"One year, through 1985," Hillier stated. "Did the conversation take place in '85?" The witness said it did, in the wintertime.

"What month?"

"Probably October, to the best of my recollection."

"So this would have been the first time she would have talked to you about algaecides?"

"That particular product, yes."

"So she didn't buy that particular product before October of '85?"

"Not from me, no."

"Let me ask you this: Is it possible that you didn't tell Mrs. Nickell that you should crush and dissolve in warm water these tablets?"

"No."

Maida stood for re-direct. The Asst. U.S. Attorney had the court clerk hand the witness his grand jury testimony. Yes, he said, his memory had been better in February 1987 than it was at that moment.

She directed him to the passage just before the question Hillier had read during cross. Yes, he said, reading it, he did suggest she dissolve the tablets by "pounding them into a powder" and adding warm water.

"And this is something that it is quite conceivable that you would have told her because she purchased this product all the time?"

"Right."

*

Having worked out some problems with the defense, Joanne Maida made a run at having Stella Nickell's checks and bank records admitted into evidence. Marshall Stone was recalled to go over his summary chart, which itemized the defendant's checks from Albertson's North and South, Johnny's Market, Pay 'N Save North, Fish Gallery and Pets, Auburn Market & Garden, and Carousel Pets in Auburn.

The SA testified that six checks had been written at Pay 'N Save North between February 23, 1986, and May 27, 1986.

The witness also testified about the defendant's work schedule on the days before Bruce Nickell died. Stella Nickell had not worked May 27, or June 3 through 5.

Next, Bonnie Anderson took the stand, telling the court she had met Stella in November 1985 when she started working at Wells Fargo at SeaTac. She said she met the defendant's daughter four months later.

She told the court Stella could be intimidating.

"She had a way of staring you right in the eye, and you got the impression that either you did it her way or you didn't do it."

"During the course of this professional relationship with her, did you ever have occasion to challenge her or to question her judgment?"

"You didn't do that with Stella."

Hillier asked that the answer be stricken as not responsive, and Judge Dwyer told the jury to disregard it.

The witness said the defendant would occasionally talk about her marriage while on the concourse. Stella said when she got home she'd read a book while her husband watched TV or talked on his CB.

"Did she tell you whether she was happy or unhappy with this state of affairs between herself and Bruce Nickell?"

"I can't say that I remember that she actually said, 'I am unhappy with this situation.'"

"Then how did she describe it to you?"

"She said that she liked being on the late shift because that way she didn't have to see so much of Bruce."

"Did Mrs. Nickell ever discuss with you leaving Bruce?"

"Yes."

"Would you tell us what she said about that?"

"Well, we were talking about this plan that some of the employees there had of opening a security system in Mexico, and evidently Stella had been asked to go, and I asked her what Bruce thought about it and she says, 'Well, I haven't told him.' I asked her if she was going to, and she said, 'No. I don't care. I'm just leaving.'"

To the best of Bonnie's recollection, the conversation occurred "sometime between January and March."

Maida directed the witness to the day Stella made her announcement that Bruce had died. Bonnie told the court that she and Cindy left a bar when Dee Rogers called. At the apartment, Stella arrived and told Cindy, "'Your dad is gone.'"

"Did she say anything else?"

"She looked Cindy straight in the eye and she said, 'I know what you're thinking and the answer is no.'"

The witness said mother and daughter stared at each other for "maybe ten seconds" before pouring drinks in the kitchen. At that point, Cindy "got very upset and almost hysterical."

"And how did her mother, Stella Nickell, respond?"

"Stella was pale, but quite composed."

The assistant U.S. attorney had nothing further, and because of the lateness of the hour, Hillier deferred his cross-examination until Monday.

Chapter Fifty-Three

Wilma Mae Stewart brought her baby to Seattle for her day in court, Monday, April 25. She knew she wouldn't be able to take her daughter into court with her, but she had been assured that a woman from the FBI office would look after her.

Wilma Mae had struggled for months with the conflict of speaking to the FBI when they were after Aunt Stella. Wilma didn't doubt that SA Nichols felt Stella was guilty, but that didn't mean she had to think so.

Fifteen minutes before she was due in court, Wilma put her one-year-old on the hotel bed to diaper her. The baby rolled over and onto the floor and hit her head. In a frenzy, she called the hotel's emergency number. She needed help! Her baby was hurt!

A moment later, someone was at the door.

"About the same time I got a knock on the door, I got my [daughter] in my arms and obviously I'm shook up, went to the door, and it was Ron Nichols. I told him that I couldn't testify, I had to make sure [she] was okay. But he was adamant: 'You are going to go testify,'" she later recalled.

It was a turning point. Nichols didn't care about her life. All he cared about was the conviction. Wilma felt she had been used.

Wilma kept thinking she should have listened to Aunt Stella and never spoken to the FBI. She should have seen it coming.

A Seattle reporter approached Wilma, her aunts Berta and Mary, and other relatives outside the courthouse. "Any comment on the trial from the family?"

Stella's sisters looked at the ground and said nothing.

Where's all the power, the strength you had while I was growing up? Wilma thought as the women shifted from side to side. "We have no comment!" Wilma finally said to end the discomfort of the moment.

"We'd like to know …" The reporter pushed forward.

"You don't understand," Stella's niece said, her words growing harsher with each syllable. "We have NO comment."

The Stephenson sisters sighed with relief as the reporter backed off.

At that moment, Wilma Stewart's world had turned.

"I could no longer look up to anyone in my family," she said later.

*

After a weekend of rest—if rest was possible in jail—friends had hoped Stella would put on a better appearance than she had the week before. Her clothing had seemed frayed and strained at the seams. Fred Phelps, for one, thought his girlfriend should have dressed up. She was a good-looking woman, but you couldn't tell by what he saw in the courtroom.

Stella Nickell later said Tom Hillier and Sal Ramos were trying to make her dress up, but she didn't want to go along with any of it. They even suggested she wear glasses instead of her usual contact lenses to make herself look more demure.

At half past nine, Bonnie Anderson resumed the stand for Tom Hillier's cross-examination. The witness testified that when Jeanne and Jim Rice left the airport that spring, the bodyguard business left with them. Stella Nickell's plan for going to Mexico had been dashed.

Shaking from the ordeal with her baby daughter back in the hotel room, and now being forced to testify, Wilma, dressed in a striking dark blue suit and looking every bit the beauty of the Stephenson clan, took the stand.

She testified that she and her aunt were so close she considered her "my mother." Her aunt and uncle's marriage was normal; occasionally Stella got a little irritated at Bruce.

"He would come home from work sometimes and sit in front of the TV and she might need to have something done, so she'd get a little irritated with him."

The two women kept in contact at least once a month, up until just before Bruce died. Wilma was in Houston preparing for a trip when her aunt made a phone call out of the blue.

"She just wanted to know if she could come to Texas and stay with me."

"Was that a matter of surprise to you, or had you expected that?" Joanne Maida asked.

"It was a surprise because, you know, why would she not want to stay there."

"What did she tell you had happened between her and her husband Bruce?"

"She didn't say anything had happened."

Even though she was a prosecution witness, her tone made it clear whose side she was on.

"How did she characterize, then, her relationship as the reason why she was coming down?"

"I don't understand what you're getting at."

"Was she happy with Bruce or was she unhappy with Bruce?"

"Well, I don't know how she was with Uncle Bruce, but you know, she wasn't happy when she called."

"What did she say about that?"

"She was just upset."

And so it went. Wilma Stewart trying to defend her aunt, but her words falling short. Yes, she thought her aunt was serious, but she wanted her to move to Houston. Stella Nickell didn't fly off the handle. She didn't get mad often.

"Did she make the statement to you that she was sick and tired of fighting with Bruce all the time?"

"She may have made that comment."

"Did she tell you whether this would be kept from Bruce if she decided to come down to stay with you at Houston?"

"Well, I don't recall that part of the conversation." Wilma sank in her chair as Maida had the clerk give the witness her grand jury testimony. She hadn't counted on that at all. After looking at it, she finally answered. "Well, I don't know that she wouldn't tell him. It was more me keeping my mouth shut and me not to say anything to him."

"She asked you not to say anything to him?"

"Yeah."

Wilma testified she returned to Washington around Labor Day 1986 and contact with her aunt increased. Often the two talked about the case.

"And how did your aunt, if she did, make it clear to you she wanted to talk about the investigation?"

"Well, it wasn't a matter of being clear. It was a matter of we'd sit down and she would talk awhile about what went on in her life, and then as soon as I could pleasantly do so, I would interrupt and tell her what was going on in my life."

Maida asked if insurance money came up and the witness said it had. "All the time."

After Wilma's cross-examination, she was escorted out of the courtroom by Ron Nichols. As they turned toward the elevators, a woman stepped out with FBI Special Agent Jack Cusack. Wilma didn't recognize her cousin at first. She was made up—perfect hair, perfect eyebrows. It was her, but it wasn't.

Wilma felt herself lunge forward. She wanted to smack the girl. Hard. Decisively. She had taken Aunt Stella away. But they were in a Federal Courthouse. There was nothing she could do.

It was the last time she would see Cindy.

Robert Lesniewski, vice president of underwriting of Amex Life Insurance Company, formerly Firemen's Fund, took the stand to identify Bruce Nickell's application for $50,000 life insurance, dated January 20, 1984. The beneficiary was the defendant. The policy was canceled as a result of a letter written by the defendant on May 14, 1985, protesting an increase in premium payment rate from $27 to $45.65.

The premium had been raised in March of 1985 because of Bruce's age following the first anniversary of the policy. The witness identified a form letter sent by customer service.

"Apparently we got a telephone call from Stella Nickell and we couldn't locate that in our alpha index, so we sent this inquiry out to try and find out what policy they were referring to." The letter, entitled "Insufficient Information," was sent to Stella Nickell on June 3, 1985.

The form was returned, completed by Stella Nickell. It indicated that the insured was Bruce Nickell; the policy in question was Life and Accidental Death, $50,000.

It was admitted into evidence.

Next was a letter from Stella Nickell canceling the policy, though only the applicant-owner, Bruce Nickell, could make such a request. Another letter was sent out by the insurance company, and it was returned signed by Bruce Nickell on June 10, 1985.

This was also admitted into evidence.

Morning recess was longer than usual. Tom Hillier had concerns about the next witness, and what she might say. The government's trial brief had referred to the polygraph, and he wanted firm directions given regarding the subject. He cited three pages of Cindy's grand jury testimony. None of it indicated the polygraph as the reason she came forward.

Maida said the witness had been instructed not to mention the polygraph. Maida said she had, in fact, told Cindy not to mention the polygraph to the grand jury because she did not want to have the grand jurors "tainted" by the information. But trial was a different animal. Maida said she didn't seek to offer the polygraph for its worth, but for its relevance to Cindy's decision to come forward, "especially if Mr. Hillier gets up on cross-examination and says her motivation was the reward money."

Tom Hillier said he did not intend to cross-examine Cindy on the reward; that he wanted to probe the witness's prior inconsistent statement—six months before she came forward.

"I don't intend to open any doors and I have been careful with the way I've prepared my cross-examination. I don't want this polygraph stuff to come in because it's so confusing, so prejudicial, and so unreliable, as my past cases can testify," he said, referring to the Steve Titus case.

Both parties had agreed to stipulate that the reward money was available. As far as Tom Hillier could see, it was as relevant as the insurance money the government said had been Stella's motive.

Judge Dwyer needed more time for his ruling. If the cross-examination attacked the witness's motivation, he tended to lean toward admitting the phone call Stella purportedly made to her daughter with a limiting instruction to the jury.

That phone conversation wouldn't go away. Both mother and daughter were adamant in their positions about the call. Cindy said it was the reason she went to the FBI. Stella said the call never took place, that it was one more of her daughter's lies.

Chapter Fifty-Four

Cindy Hamilton, looking every inch her mother's daughter, took the stand the afternoon of April 25. She wore a yellow skirt and jacket. Her hair was a bright orange-red.

Everyone hushed as Jack Cusack handed her off to Ron Nichols to be sworn in. Spectators stared at mother and daughter again and again, tracing the lines of resemblance in their faces. The witness seemed nervous. Even frightened.

Stella stared a hole through her daughter's chest. She thought Cindy looked terrible. The government had tried to make her look weak and distraught. Stella knew better.

In what was clearly an attempt to show the difficulties the daughter had had to endure during her childhood, Joanne Maida established family relationships, including a mention of Leah.

"What did you strive to be, based on your mother's upbringing of you?"

"I tried very hard to be everything that I thought my mother wanted me to be, to always have control of myself, to present myself in a fashion that would please my mother at all times."

When not looking at the witness with a hard stare, Stella scribbled notes on a legal pad. If her movement was any indication, everything the witness said could be refuted. The defendant's arms and hands worked overtime as Cindy told the jury that she and her mother did not have a close relationship prior to her move up to Washington in late 1982.

Whatever problems they had were gone. They became more like best friends than mother and daughter.

"What prompted the move out of the house in April of 1983 after living there for four months?" Joanne Maida asked.

"My mother and I were having some disagreements as to my lifestyle and the upbringing of my daughter."

Stella wrote angrily: "*Because she would be gone for 2 & 3 days at a time and no phone calls to let me know how she was nor to ask about her daughter.*"

The witness said she didn't like Bruce when she first met him, because he was an alcoholic. By the time she moved back to Washington in 1982, however, he had stopped drinking.

"He was a lot less obnoxious. He was a very intelligent man, very funny and witty when he wanted to be."

She testified that after Bruce dried out, he became a homebody. The days of running around and partying were gone. And her mother wasn't happy about it.

"Well, she was very pleased and very grateful that he had stopped drinking, and she made sure that he knew that, but she was discontented with the fact that they didn't do anything anymore. Oh, they would go camping or they would go and visit Grandma and Grandpa east of the mountains, his mother and father."

"Based on what your mother told you, how did their social life change after Bruce became a reformed alcoholic?"

"Their social life changed in the effect that most of their friends and acquaintances he chose not to associate with anymore because almost everyone that he knew—and they knew together—drank."

"How did your mother feel about that in the relationship that she had with Bruce?"

"She made friends of her own, but she was discontented with not being able to go out partying anymore."

Next, Maida focused on the shift hours of Cindy's time at SeaTac; the fact that mother and daughter often rode to the airport together. They were alone for much of the time and passed the time talking.

"Most of the time we were able to talk was in the morning on the way to work, on the shuttle bus, on the concourse."

"Were you able to talk about a lot of personal things during these times?"

She said they were.

Maida asked the witness to tell the court how she learned of Bruce Nickell's death.

Cindy said she and Bonnie Anderson were out drinking when Dee Rogers called from their apartment and told her to come home. Within a few minutes, Stella arrived.

"She came in. She sat down at the kitchen table and she told me that my dad had died."

"Did she say anything else?"

"Yes."

"What else did she say?"

The witness started to cry. "Just a minute …"

Judge Dwyer called for a recess so the witness could calm herself.

Ron Nichols noticed that one of the women jurors was crying too. That was a good sign, he thought.

When the questioning resumed, Maida asked, "Did she say anything else?"

"She looked at me and she said, 'I know what you're thinking, and the answer is no.'"

"Based on your past relationship with your mother, your past conversations with her, did you feel you knew what she was talking about?"

"Yes, I knew exactly what she was talking about."

"In the days following this announcement made by your mother about your dad's death, did you ever confront her about his death?"

"Not after that, no."

"Did you ever ask her point-blank, did she cause his death?"

"No."

Even with a microphone, Cindy's voice was so soft that Hillier strained to hear.

She said she stayed with her mother for a short time after Bruce's death. She even went with her mother to the family doctor to find out why Bruce died.

"Based on what your mother told you, what did you think to be the reason he died?"

"Based on what my mother had told me prior to my dad's death, I believed that she did it. I basically knew that she did it, and—"

Hillier objected to the witness's rambling, but the question had been answered.

Maida asked for Stella Nickell's reason concerning her husband's death. On the verge of tears, Cindy further stated that she didn't press her mother for information, in light of the emphysema ruling.

"Why not?"

"I didn't want to ask her."

"Why not?"

"Because I didn't want her to tell me the truth and I didn't want her to lie to me."

Under further direct, Cindy told the court that her mother called her and told her the FBI would be coming out to the property for an interview. Cindy made arrangements to be there too.

"Why did you plan to be there?"

"I was scared for her, and I guess to protect her. I've always been very protective of my mother. I was afraid they were going to find something there that was going to be proof of what I basically knew she had done."

She testified that FBI agents asked her the "obvious" questions about the Nickell marriage, if her "dad" had any enemies, if her mother could have done it. She told them their marriage was relatively happy, and no, she didn't think her mother did it.

"Was that the truth?"

"No."

"Why did you lie?"

"To protect my mother."

While her mother looked on, shaking her head slightly, Cindy proceeded to tell the jury that the truth was her mother's marriage had soured by the time Bruce died.

"There was a lot of dissatisfaction on my mother's side."

"And how did you know that?"

"She told me."

The discussions occurred over a period of several years.

Joanne Maida had the witness discuss her version of the Nickell finances. The young woman was aware of the bankruptcy petition and the layoff from McDonald Industries.

"What, if anything, did your mother tell you about this period of time, the six months or so that your dad had been laid off?"

"She—at first everything was fine. He was making out applications and sending out résumés, and then towards the end of that time period he wasn't really making a great effort at finding another job. He had already sent out his résumés and he wasn't really following up on them, and she was very upset about it."

"According to your mother, what was the relationship between her and her husband?"

"Their relationship progressively worsened."

Cindy told the court her mother had even discussed divorce in the year before Bruce Nickell's death.

"According to your mother how, if at all, did this option of divorce remain?"

Cindy said her mother considered divorce for a "short time," but decided against it because "she was not going to lose half of everything that she had fought so hard to get."

"What options other than divorce, then, did she discuss with you, if she did?" the prosecutor asked.

"She discussed killing him."

"Did she, over a period of time, discuss how she would accomplish this?"

Her mother had, but Cindy did not know it was Bruce when her mother started talking about it. The first conversations were about "two years prior, at least."

Maida tried to get Stella's daughter to nail down the time frame.

"At least two years prior to Bruce's death, and a maximum of four to five."

"And why do you put it at four to five?"

"Because I can remember certain questions that were asked of me shortly after my moving here on a permanent basis."

"What kinds of questions did she ask you in and around December of 1982?"

"The first question that I can definitely recall had to do with heroin, and she asked me if I knew where I could acquire any." But the witness said she had no idea where to get any. Her mother also asked her about cocaine and speed.

"What did she ask you about cocaine, particularly?"

"What it would take to overdose a person."

Cindy's recollection of the date was interesting. Katy Hurt Parker had told the FBI that Cindy talked with her about Stella's interest in cocaine overdoses in the fall of 1985. How could that have been one of the first conversations?

The witness said the questions about speed and cocaine were general, with no names attached.

Cindy explained that, yes, she had used drugs, primarily speed. It was a habit that her mother had known about, hence the questions about it.

"What about cocaine? Did you ever use that?"

"I have indulged in cocaine, but very few times. It's—it wasn't of use to me for the same reasons that I was using speed."

She went on to testify that she was a single mother at the time, holding down two jobs, coupled with an active social life. "… There just wasn't enough time in the day to do all that and sleep too."

"Did you have a reaction to your mother when she asked you questions about heroin and speed and cocaine, where she could get them?"

Cindy stammered, "I was—I didn't have any real severe reaction, no. I was curious as to why she was curious, but it didn't strike me as odd, no." She said she had no information on heroin.

"I do know that it doesn't take a lot to overdose a person, through what I've heard and seen on documentaries."

Concerning cocaine, Cindy claimed that she told her mother she was unsure what quantity would cause an overdose. She also told her mother that the drug stays in the system even after the user ceases taking it.

"What did you say to her about speed?"

"About speed? It depended. It's a lot harder to overdose a person on speed. It also stays in your system, and I don't know how the body treats it in distributing it, whether you ingest it or whether you inhale it, the different methods of using it, and I really didn't know how much it would take to overdose a person."

"With respect to which drugs was she asking about overdosing?" Joanne Maida asked.

"Over different periods of time, at different times she was asking about overdosing on all of them."

As direct continued, Cindy said her mother also did some research on drugs.

The next question was important. Maida asked if Cindy knew which books her mother had read when she told the FBI about library research. It was important because of the possible charge that daughter and mother had been co-conspirators. Cindy could know too much, and that would be damaging.

The witness said she did not.

"Did there come a point in time that your mother began specifying names of people in these conversations about death?"

"Eventually, yes. Names were brought into it."

"Whose name?"

"My dad, Bruce Nickell."

Court adjourned until the next morning.

Chapter Fifty-Five

Before eager spectators and the jury were seated for Cindy's second day of testimony, the intention of the government to bring up the polygraph and phone call were argued again before Judge Bill Dwyer.

Judge Dwyer addressed the dilemma. He acknowledged that the government had not sought to probe the content of the phone call, only to establish that a call had been the catalyst in Cindy's coming forward. Since such testimony would lead to much speculation as to what had been said, Dwyer had suggested the question be: Did you hear something about the case you had not heard before and then decide to go talk to the FBI?

But considering the preceding day's testimony, that wouldn't work either. Cindy told the jury she knew all along her mother was the killer. The phone call would invite speculation about a confession, or the reward being discussed. A curative instruction admonishing jurors not to speculate on the conversation wasn't worth the risk.

After considerable discussion it was agreed that whether the phone call would be mentioned would depend on the defense's case and rebuttal later. Dwyer told the attorneys that if the reward came into play, and if Cindy's testimony reflected no motivation related to that, then she should be allowed to testify to the call.

*

Cindy Hamilton returned to the witness box as Joanne Maida renewed the testimony that the young woman had heard her father's name connected with her mother's interest in drug overdoses sometime after the discussions began.

Cindy said her mother told her that her stepfather had been treated for alcoholism at Schick Shadel, and through subsequent experience with counselors and tapes, Stella had learned that "it was not uncommon for an alcoholic to turn to other substance abuse."

"What did your mother say when she became more specific to the point where she mentioned your dad's name in conversations about drugs?"

"I can't remember exactly the first time, but in some references of bringing up his name and in overdosing him, specifically with cocaine, that it could be placed in his iced tea."

"And according to your mother, why would she put cocaine in your dad's iced tea?"

"It basically couldn't be tasted in the iced tea, therefore being able to be distributed throughout his system, and then eventually to just overdose him on it."

Cindy said her mother told her that when Bruce was autopsied, the cocaine could be explained as an accidental overdose. She said the conversations occurred in late 1985 and early 1986.

Asst. U.S. Attorney Maida asked how Cindy could pinpoint the date.

"Because my dad had to pass a physical in January to become a permanent employee of the state, and the idea was shoved around that she could not do that prior to the physical because there would be—it would be found in the physical."

She said her mother was concerned that if doctors found cocaine in his system, Bruce would lose his job, and she'd lose his life insurance. The plan was dropped.

Describing how she felt when she learned of her mother's intent to kill Bruce, Cindy said she "was hoping she was just talking out of frustration and dissatisfaction, and then on the other hand, the actual thought and fright that she was going to do it."

Her words trailed off and she started to break down.

"Actually, it was somewhere around the time of April of '85 that the discussion and the questioning of hitmen came into being, and more intensely to the end of the year, after I knew for sure when it was my dad. By late '85 I knew for sure."

When the hitman idea was discussed, Cindy said again, she passed it off as more information-gathering on the part of her mother.

Her mother wanted to know if she had any connections or knew the cost. Cindy said she didn't have any answers.

"When you heard these questions from your mother, did you take them seriously or did you just dismiss them as being outlandish?"

"No, I didn't dismiss them … Once getting to the subject of hitmen, I knew someone was in some trouble."

Maida returned her questions to SeaTac, to establish when the discussions occurred. Cindy said they started February 1986, and as she said the day before, she and her mother talked during the drive to the concourse.

"It was towards the time after I started, because she had plans to become a bodyguard. And when the position with the bodyguard operation fell through, then she couldn't just up and disappear."

Cindy said co-worker Jeanne Rice had been behind the Mexican bodyguard-company idea. "She told me she was just going to leave the airport one day and not come back.

"She told me the way she was going to arrange that was she was going to keep a diary, and in that diary she was going to make entries of a strange person watching her at the airport, just a slight mention in her diary, because she found it strange that this person was there every day watching her. And these entries in some way were going to be made into this diary so that when she just disappeared, it would look as if she was kidnapped or abducted and she would never be heard from again. There was talk of the possibility that while she was away, that a hitman could be employed to kill my dad and she would not be anywhere around to be found responsible for that. She also entertained the same thought in going to Texas, to go to Texas to visit my cousin Wilma Mae, and that while she was on her way down for vacation or a visit, that a hitman could kill my dad in some way and then she would be all the way in Texas and pretend not to know anything about it."

Joanne Maida asked if Stella Nickell was to fake an abduction and disappear, how she would collect life insurance. "There was never any discussion of her coming back from being a bodyguard."

Was the Texas plan the same as the Mexican plan—a complete disappearance?

Cindy said it was not. Her mother was going to Texas to live. She had even invited her daughter to come too. The hitman idea frightened her.

"I just had a—I was scared. I was afraid she was going to do that."

"Did you see the idea as being realistic?"

"Oh, yes. Very much so."

"How so?"

"Because of the modes of death that she talked about—things that the hitman could do."

Cindy explained: "He could be shot in traffic going to or from work; he could be run head-on into by a truck, or just plainly run off the road with a truck. Different other methods in just a very violent way and seeming more as a random killing."

To the witness, it all seemed plausible. But her mother didn't have the money to hire anyone.

The diary had been mentioned so often, and so many had claimed to have seen it or something like it, one might have thought it would be entered into evidence. But it wasn't among Joanne Maida's vast arsenal of paperwork.

SA Cusack had heard Cindy talk about the diary. Girlfriends heard her say she had actually read it, and that was how she knew of the kidnapping plot.

"I was over at my mom's trailer and I saw it on the table and read it . . ."

But in court she didn't say that. She distanced herself from the book by saying that her mother had told her about it. Reading it would have been a bit too close to home.

Fred Phelps and Cora Lee Rice later joined Dee Rogers on the list of people with claims to having read the Ouija ledger with questions pinpointing the date of Bruce Nickell's demise. Had Fred burned it?

No one could say. Stella Nickell said none of the documents existed. "Another of Cindy's lies," she explained.

*

Berta and her sister Mary left for the hallway outside the courtroom aghast and disgusted by Cindy's testimony; in the hallway they overheard one woman say with a sigh, "Oh, that poor girl. She lost her daddy."

Berta couldn't hold her tongue. "That was not her daddy; that was her stepfather. She never called him that until court."

"Oh, really?" The woman looked puzzled. "Why would she do that?"

Stella's sister went on. "What would you do for a lot of money?"

Berta considered the encounter "a little of our own input" to help Stella. The things that needed to come out in court hadn't come out yet. "Of course," she said later, "we couldn't get to the jury."

After recess, Joanne Maida asked her star witness if the disappearance of her mother to Texas or Mexico would mean she would lose all of her property.

"My mother told me that in going to Mexico to be a bodyguard that she would acquire a substantial amount of money in salary for doing this and would basically have no need for the property or anything having to do with my dad or the property or the trailer or anything."

The Texas plan differed.

Stella's daughter said her mother's plan was to come back for "the property, the trailer, because of course with my dad dead, it would all be hers."

Cindy said she was "very relieved" that her mother had considered just disappearing.

"Because if she just packed up and left and went to Texas to be employed as a bodyguard, then she would drop the whole idea of trying to kill my dad."

Maida moved on to testimony about discussions mother and daughter might have had concerning toxic plants. Cindy's mother had said she could put a toxic plant into her husband's food, and the resulting poisoning "could be explained as an accidental ingestion due to the fact that my dad was one for picking something, a piece of grass or a twig, something, and sticking it in his mouth and chewing on it."

"Did your mother tell you about any opportunity she had to feed him a toxic plant?"

"Yes."

"What did she say?"

"She told me specifically on one occasion that she had indeed fed him . . . it was either two or three capsules full of small black seeds. I cannot tell you for sure exactly what plant but I'm sure she told me at the time. I know that the plant was lethal, or supposed to be . . . The name 'hemlock' stays in my mind, and foxglove, and foxglove seems to stick out more."

"Why?"

"Foxglove, to the best of my knowledge, is a very common plant, and she also had in turn discussed foxglove at one time."

Maida had pointed out with other witnesses that memory deteriorates and grand jury testimony is a great aid to recall. Yet Cynthia Hamilton could recall things now that she never could before. Foxglove had not been mentioned in her grand jury appearance.

Cindy said her mother told her she was doing some research on toxic seeds, though she couldn't recall any besides hemlock and foxglove.

"What did she say about the capsules containing the seeds?"

"She just said that she had given them to him and that they had had no real adverse effect."

Cindy said her mother told her of the seeds in the capsule six months before her stepfather died. Her mother indicated she had done it within two weeks of telling her daughter.

Under direct, the government's star witness said her mother told her she had researched cyanide at the library within three months of Bruce Nickell's death.

"The discussions came up having to do with the Tylenol tamperings back east; that it would be very easy to re-enact those tamperings."

"Why?"

"The actual act itself of putting something tainted or tampered with back on the shelf, in her own words, would have been easy because they were looking for people to be shoplifting and taking things from the store, not looking for somebody to put something back."

Cindy also claimed her mother told her cyanide could be purchased at photography stores and Stella planned to call on different stores to see if identification was required.

"Was any of this discussion, according to your mother, related to your dad?"

"Yes. She—these plans per se were being made. The foundation was being laid to kill my dad in a way that she would not get caught in doing so."

"Was there any discussion in particular among all these different methods that concerned you the most?"

"The hitman and the cyanide were the two that actually panicked me the most." The witness said her mother abandoned the hit as too costly, and she focused on the cyanide.

While her mother discussed the insurance money during the time of the cyanide discussions, the witness said, she did not mention specific amounts, though it would be enough to pay off the property, the trailer, "and the possibility that she would have enough to live on comfortably, and the possibility that we could entertain the idea of starting a fish store."

The question was: Could this intimidating young woman with the tear-streaked eyes really have thought her mother would carry out her murder plans?

"I knew she was capable of it, but when it's your own mother, you don't want to believe." The witness said she didn't warn Bruce because she didn't think he'd believe her.

"What proof did I have?" she asked, tears falling again. "I had nothing that I could take to him and present him with the truth. How do you make your stepfather who you've only been close with for four years, believe that his wife of almost twelve years who is supposed to love him is going to kill him? How do you approach somebody with that?"

"Did there come a point in time, after that, that you came forward with information to the FBI, basically what you've testified to in court today, that information?"

"Yes."

"The second time that you talked with the FBI, was that in January of 1987?"

"Yes, it was."

"That's about a six-month lapse between interviews. Is that correct?"

"Yes."

"Did you do a lot of serious thinking in those six months?"

"Yes, I did."

"And by January 1987, had you decided to tell the FBI what you knew?"

"Yes, I did."

"Ms. Hamilton, you came forward to the FBI, as you've indicated, in January of 1987 and then to the grand jury in March of 1987, and now to this jury. As a general principle, why have you been willing three times to come forward with your knowledge about your mother's involvement with your father's death?"

"It was the right thing for me to do. It was a decision that I made and I knew it was the right thing to do."

Maida asked when the witness had last talked with her mother.

"The last contact that I had with her was when I went to go get my dog from her property, where I was keeping her, and that was the last time I seen or spoke with my mother."

"Was this in the same year that your dad died?"

"It was—no, it was after my first two statements to the FBI."

Cindy's testimony suggested going to the FBI before January 1987.

Only mother and daughter know for certain when it took place and what their last meeting truly was all about, but both agree that it was out in Auburn at the Nickell mobile home.

"She asked me if I had been spoken to by the FBI. I told her no, that they hadn't contacted me. She said, well, they had contacted so and so, and so on, some friends of hers, and went on to tell me about the plans with her lawyers and etcetera, and I really didn't have much to say. I just listened a little bit, and said, 'Well, we got to go,' took my dog, and left."

Chapter Fifty-Six

In the afternoon session, Tom Hillier prepared to cross-examine. Since he planned to clear up some of the confusing time frames, he requested that Stella's daughter have her grand jury testimony available to her for reference. Cindy had said the discussions had occurred sporadically over several years.

"So, you have no real firm time frame to offer us with respect to, for example, the first discussion you talked about, which related to heroin, the date that took place, that sort of thing?"

"No, I don't."

Referring to her grand jury testimony, Tom Hillier asked if she recalled a specific event that occurred in April 1985 that she was able to pinpoint relative to the time the hitman was discussed.

"In April of '85 I received a DWI."

"Okay. So you're able to put that conversation within a context because of something specific that occurred to you?"

"Yes."

"Now, I'm a little uncertain as to when you began working at the airport. Was that in February of '86?"

"To the best of my recall right now, yes."

"And Bruce, of course, died as we all know on June 5, so most of these discussions you've related took place during that four-month period of time, would that be true?"

"Yes."

The federal public defender asked a series of questions relating to conversations the witness had with the FBI, as well as her appearance before the grand jury in March of 1987.

"Before that you had, I thought I heard you say, two major conversations with FBI agents?"

"Yes."

"And those would have occurred in January of 1987?"

"Yes."

The defense then established Cindy's movements over the previous five years.

"When you moved in with your mother in December 1982, indeed you discovered a different Bruce Nickell than the man you had met some years previous?"

"Yes."

"In fact, years ago when you first met Bruce, you resented the fact that he and your mother had gotten married?"

"No."

"No?" Tom Hillier feigned a surprised look. "Do you recall testifying to that effect to the grand jury?"

"No, because I didn't resent their marriage." She said she was upset because her mother hadn't contacted her to let her know of the marriage.

Yes, Bruce was boorish when he was drinking. And yes, he was good-natured, loving, intelligent when she moved in in December 1982 because he had stopped drinking.

"And it's true, isn't it, Ms. Hamilton, that your mother was instrumental in bringing that change about?"

"Yes, she was."

"She helped him, supported him, and encouraged him to stop drinking?"

"Yes, she did."

"And she stood by him through that ordeal?"

"Yes, she did."

Through his cross-examination, Tom Hillier established Stella "doted" on her husband and stayed home with him because he had stopped drinking. She didn't even drink around the house as a show of support. Stella also paid all the bills and ran the household.

Cindy admitted she didn't socialize much with the Nickells after Bruce stopped drinking. Yet, she said, she did visit now and then after moving out in April 1983.

"Now, as I understood your testimony today and yesterday, your first conversation regarding drugs with your mother occurred some four years before Bruce died?"

"Yes."

"A very generalized discussion about heroin?"

"Yes."

"She asked you where it could be acquired?"

"Yes."

"In fact, you had shared with your mother the fact of your prior problems with drugs?"

"My prior usage of drugs, yes."

"Yes. Would it be accurate to say that you moved from California in part not only to escape your marital difficulties but to disassociate yourself from that drug past?"

Cindy bristled at the question. "No, that wasn't necessarily a major portion of it."

"You and your mom talked about that, though, didn't you?"

She said they had.

Hillier prodded on. As he understood the witness's testimony, later there were additional "generalized conversations" about overdosages and drugs such as heroin, and later more discussions concerning cocaine and speed. Bruce Nickell's name was not a part of the discussions. The same was true of the hitman idea.

Cindy agreed.

"And did there come a time during those general conversations that Bruce's name was mentioned?"

"Not that I recall."

Hillier asked the witness to turn to page twenty-six of her grand jury testimony.

"Did there come a time that Bruce's name was mentioned specifically with regard to these numerous hitmen-type plots you talked about today? The answer is yes or no to that question."

"During the general conversations—"

"No, later on. I'm not trying to trap you or anything. Did his name ever come up in relation to any of those conversations?"

"Yes, in later conversations it did."

He referred her to Joanne Maida's question: How did your stepfather's name first get introduced into this whole business about eliminating people?

Cindy read:

"*I honestly can't remember exactly when it came as far as me knowing definitely that it was my dad, and I honest to God cannot even recall if she brought up his name or if it was just that I knew, because you have to understand my mother, you know, you know it sounds strange, but my mother and I are like on the same wavelength. It's like I know what she's thinking before she says it, and vice versa. I recall . . . can't recall if it was just there and then from that point forward. I can't remember when she first brought up his name, but…"*

The defense lawyer waited for the young woman to look up.

"In view of that testimony, do you remember your father's name, your stepfather's name, being mentioned at all in relation to this hitman testimony?"

"I cannot with actual positive recall on exactly when saying the name of Bruce."

Under further cross, the witness agreed her testimony had indicated that at some point she knew her mother had been talking about Bruce Nickell. And, yes, most of the conversations had taken place during the four months she worked with her mother at SeaTac.

And as convinced as she was, she didn't warn Bruce or the police. No one would believe her. "Perhaps more importantly, you didn't angrily confront your mom and ask her to knock it off, did you?"

"No, I did not."

"You testified that this plot concerning stuffing tablets with black seeds seemed feasible to you because your father was always chewing on grass or whatever. What else did he chew on besides toothpicks?"

"He would chew on matches, he would chew on anything out on the property. Sometimes he would chew on pieces of grass."

"Did you ever see him chewing on any foxglove or anything that appeared to be foxglove?"

"No. I probably couldn't point out foxglove if I saw it."

Tom Hillier described the plant in detail, but she still couldn't recall if she had ever seen it.

Cindy told the jury that she had told her mother to divorce Bruce Nickell but Stella didn't want to lose her community property.

Again, as she testified, it was conversations that reportedly took place while at SeaTac, before and after her employment. She was certain of the time frame.

Tom Hillier referred the witness to her grand jury testimony indicating that the bodyguard venture fell through in April or May of 1986. "She definitely knew by May."

"So your testimony in March of 1987 was that specifically Bruce Nickell's name never came up in relation to drug overdosing until after the Mexican affair fell through?"

"Yes."

"That would have been in April or May of 1986?"

"Yes."

"And indeed, as I read your testimony here, instead of dissuading your mother, you offer her some information concerning overdosing?"

"I offered her negative information, yes."

Stella's daughter agreed that it was after those particular discussions that the subject of cyanide first came up.

"Did you ever see your mom with any cyanide?"

"I don't know what cyanide looks like."

"You have no idea that she ever had any cyanide. Is that true?"

"I have no idea."

Further, the witness said she never saw her mother crushing Algae Destroyer. Never saw her mother go to the library to research cyanide, either. Never saw her mother buy Anacin-3, or Excedrin capsules. Never saw her put them back on the shelves.

"She never told you she had done that, either, did she?"

"Not that she positively had done it, no."

And, as she testified, she never asked.

Tom Hillier had nothing further, and Cindy Hamilton finally stepped down.

SAs Cusack and Nichols speculated on what they had perceived to be weak cross-examination from the defense lawyer. A lot of what Cindy had said might have been the first time Hillier had heard any of it.

"I don't think Stella told him the truth," SA Nichols offered later. Even the defendant was surprised.

"At first he said he was really going to nail Cynthia when she got on the stand and I was making notes to help him, like he told me to. And then when it came time for him to question her, he told me he was going to go kinda easy on her because he wanted to prove to the jury that we were on friendly terms."

Next, Katy Parker was called to the stand. But after Joanne Maida called her, Tom Hillier requested a sidebar, and Katy Hurt Parker sat on the stand wondering what in the world was going on.

Hillier apologized, but within the last day or two he had received the young woman's grand jury testimony and was concerned about her trial testimony's being hearsay.

Joanne Maida disagreed. The testimony would be offered as corroboration of a conversation between Cindy and the witness regarding overdosages of cocaine.

"As Mr. Hillier knows and as the Court is aware, the government's case rests on the reliability of Cindy Hamilton in the jury's eyes," she said.

The assistant U.S. attorney wanted to offer it as a prior consistent statement to corroborate Hamilton. The government felt it would show that its star witness had made the statement long before there would be any reason to fabricate it.

The attorneys argued whether the cross-examination had challenged Cindy with a recent fabrication, which would allow it, but Judge Dwyer ruled on the side of caution: the witness would not testify.

Jeanne Rice was called to the stand.

On direct examination, Jeanne Rice told the court how in February 1986 she became a victim of "burnout" at her job as a screener at SeaTac. Before she left SeaTac, she had worked with the defendant. It was at the airport that she told Stella Nickell about a business venture she was developing.

"I wanted to start a service in Monterrey, Mexico, to bodyguard wealthy people there ... And she was very interested, and after a time she was interested for her daughter Cindy, also. I talked to her about what I was doing and what the ambitions and the hopes were for this service, and at that time she broached with me the subject of possibly working for me there."

There was money to be made, she testified, from guarding the rich of Monterrey.

"Did you discuss with the defendant how she was going to accomplish going down to Mexico with you, since she was married?"

"Well, at the time that Stella and I had talked about this, this occurred over several conversations, she said to me she would just be willing to leave with no suitcase or whatever."

"According to her, what would happen to Bruce, her husband?"

"She never stated that to me."

Chapter Fifty-Seven

Tom Hillier and Joanne Maida met before court the morning of April 27. Hillier had been thinking about the case the night before, and wanted to inform Maida of his intention to offer the stipulation about the reward so the defense would not need to call in someone from the Proprietary Association to testify it existed.

In that case, Joanne Maida argued that the polygraph/phone call testimony be admitted as that was the reason Cindy came forward—not the reward.

Tom Hillier naturally opposed the idea. Testimony about the reward should not automatically allow the prosecution to bring up the phone call. How the court would rule on the matter was critical.

Judge Dwyer had several things to consider. The testimony of Katy Hurt Parker, offered as a prior consistent statement of Cindy in 1985, was not allowed since the government hadn't shown there had been an attack on the young woman's credibility or improper motive.

Judge Dwyer did not believe the admission of the reward stipulation would justify the admission of the polygraph or the phone call. It would be prejudicial and outweigh any value it might have in explaining why Cindy came forward. Joanne Maida planned to ask the Court again later.

Later that morning, Carl Collins was on the witness stand and testified to what would not be disputed by the defense.

Stella Nickell's fingerprint was on the All American Life enrollment card from September 5, 1985. He also found two prints belonging to the defendant on Bruce Nickell's Long-Term Disability Enrollment Change form dated January 8, 1986.

The United States finally rested. It was the defense's turn to present his case.

Chapter Fifty-Eight

Tom Hillier's list of defense witnesses was small. With the exception of the defendant, none were insiders who could refute what Stella's daughter had told the jury.

Dr. Dennis Reichenbach, Harborview's chief of pathology, was called first. He testified that after performing a routine hospital autopsy on Bruce Nickell, which determined pulmonary emphysema as the cause of death, he spoke with Stella Nickell. He couldn't recall specifics of the conversation.

"Is it unusual that next of kin contact the hospital to discuss what the results of an autopsy were?"

"No, it is not."

Two weeks later, he said, there was another call from the defendant.

"In fact, it was at the time of the examination of the brain when she had contacted the pathology department and wanted to talk with me—this was right after Sue Snow had died and there was some publicity about the capsules, and she wanted to know whether there was any possibility that her husband could have died of cyanide poisoning."

At that point, the doctor testified, the medical examiner was involved. The cause of death was amended to acute cyanide poisoning.

"During your discussions with Mrs. Nickell, did you find anything out of the ordinary or odd about those contacts?" Hillier asked.

"No."

Soft-spoken Bruce Stone, a social worker who was on duty at Harborview when the defendant died, took the stand next. Hillier needed someone to tell the jury his client wasn't the cold-hearted, dying-husband abandoner that the prosecution had suggested.

Bruce Stone's testimony was very brief. He told how he had met with Stella Nickell in a "quiet room" at the hospital for about five minutes. She and her mother were not permitted to be in the emergency room with Bruce Nickell.

"She was very quiet, withdrawn," he said. Such a response was consistent with others he had seen in similar circumstances.

The witness was turned over for cross-examination.

The assistant U.S. attorney reminded Bruce Stone of his interview with SA Jack Cusack at the beginning of the investigation. "Do you recall what your response was at that time?"

"I believe I told him that she did not go in to see him."

"Didn't you tell Mr. Cusack, when your memory was fresher in 1986, that someone extended the opportunity to the defendant, Mrs. Nickell, to be by her husband's bedside when he died?"

"I may have, because that again is, you know, standard procedure for the hospital."

"You talked again with Mr. Cusack this morning, did you not?"

"I did."

"And in discussing that, did you agree with him that Mrs. Nickell declined the opportunity to be by her husband when he died?"

"I don't think it was worded quite that way this morning. If, in my documentation in the chart, you know, if I could see that, I think I could clarify this."

Joanne Maida asked if he had the chart, but he didn't.

"In any event, do you have any factual basis today to dispute any statements that you made to Mr. Cusack back in 1986?"

"No, I do not."

Bill Donais, thirty years a lawyer, twenty of them spent in Auburn, took the stand. He told the court how he had met the Nickells in the early 1980s when they waged the battle over cable TV service at White River Estates. Later, in 1983, he represented them in their request for bankruptcy declaration. He testified, a day or two after Bruce's death, that the defendant called and asked if she should meet with him in the event something needed to be done immediately. He told her to wait until things calmed down and get in touch with him then.

Later, she made an appointment for June 17.

"What was the substance of that meeting?" Hillier asked.

"We went over the assets of the estate—the real estate was about all there was, a little personal property—and discussed the insurance that was involved, at least the two credit card policies."

"What did you see in that respect?"

"I was a little bit concerned when I first read it. The documents she gave me indicated that there was only one policy and that she was the insured."

"Did you express that concern to her?"

"Yes. I told her we might have a problem because I thought there should be another policy, or at least a rider indicating that Bruce was insured. However, the application had been returned by the company and the application was very clear that both were insured ... So I told her she didn't have to worry and to go ahead and make the application for the insurance."

"Did she ever bring to your attention a state insurance policy?"

"Yes. She brought in a number of papers. One of them was sort of an outline that the state had probably given Bruce when he got the insurance information, but one page of that was a breakdown saying you have a basic $5,000 life insurance coverage, and I think it was $5,000 accidental coverage, and you also may apply for $100,000 additional accident policy and $25,000 life."

Yes, the witness said, Stella was concerned about what coverage Bruce truly had. A missed appointment for a physical left her believing she was entitled only to $5,000 basic life.

Further, Bill Donais said, it had been his suggestion to file the lawsuit in connection with Bruce Nickell's death. The discussion occurred two or three days after Bruce's cause of death had been formally amended to cyanide poisoning.

Hillier asked why.

"The legislature in the prior session had passed what they referred to as the Tort Reform Act, which very seriously affected the possibility of damages, the amount of damages that a plaintiff could receive in an action of this sort. I consulted with Sue Snow's estate's lawyer, who was also concerned about the cyanide, and we had to file the action prior to August 1."

Joanne Maida reiterated information gleaned from Bill Donais's direct.

"With respect to your testimony about the coverage of the insurance policies, you indicated that she brought to your attention that there were two other credit card policies?"

"No. She brought those to my attention first."

"And the point of my question being, the policies were group term life insurance policies, were they not?"

"That's correct."

"Taken out on their credit cards?"

Again, correct.

"Were you aware at the time, Mr. Donais, that your client had denied the existence of those policies to the FBI?"

Tom Hillier jumped up. "Your Honor, I would object. That is not accurate; it's argumentative."

"The objection is sustained."

"Did you know whether your client had made any previous inconsistent statements to the existence of those policies?"

Another objection, and Judge Dwyer sustained it.

Maida continued her line of questioning.

He was aware that his former client had been interviewed by the FBI in June, and had had some contact with an insurance investigator in July, and again with the FBI in November.

Each time Bill Donais answered, his testimony was marred by uncertainty and inexact recall.

Yes, he said, he and Stella discussed the two All American policies, but he didn't know if she provided information on them to the FBI or Equifax.

The clerk was asked to produce the June 16, 1986, letter from Northwestern noting the $25,000 coverage was contingent on a physical.

"At any time during this association with your client up until Mr. Hillier stepped in to represent her, did she ever bring this letter to your attention or tell you that she stood corrected about the amount—it was actually $25,000 and not $100,000 that was contingent on the medical exam?"

"No. At the time she came in to see me on the seventeenth, she was not clear on what the amount of insurance was."

Next, Maida had the court clerk hand the witness the copy of the lawsuit against Bristol-Myers. Over the defense's objections, she ferreted out the status of the damages contingent on Stella's criminal case.

Bill Donais said that in the event they won damages, he'd receive one third, plus costs.

Dick Johnson was the third witness for the defense. No longer with the Department of Transportation, Dick had retired a few months before trial. He told the court that he hired Bruce as a temporary welder in November 1984 and that Nickell became permanent in January 1986. At that point, he received full state benefits.

Dick met Stella only after her husband died.

"As I recall, on June 6, 1986, I received a phone call in my office, approximately seven o'clock in the morning, from Mrs. Nickell stating that Bruce would no longer be coming to work, that he had passed away the night before."

He talked to the defendant again several days later. They arranged a meeting at Johnson's office in Seattle approximately a week and a half after Mr. Nickell's death.

"I had informed Mrs. Nickell that there was certain paperwork that she had to take care of in order to collect the wages
and sick benefits that were coming to Bruce Nickell."

Johnson explained he had directed her to the accountant
who handled that type of work, and consequently she was
directed to the insurance board in Olympia.

After Hillier's cross-examination of Cindy, the defendant's
best chance for "reasonable doubt" lay in the testimony of
the next witness, Dr. David Honigs, an assistant professor of
chemistry from the University of Washington.

Dr. Honigs was a young and imposing man. His PhD was
in analytical chemistry, and, in fact, he had written a number of
articles on the analysis of cyanide as related to product tampering. He had received $70,000 in grants to explore preventive
techniques developed in his lab.

For the record, the witness defined the "elemental fingerprints of cyanides," as related by the experts at the FDA. He
told the court how potassium cyanide contained some trace
metals that when analyzed could determine which of the three
manufacturers produced it.

"They [FDA] found they could take the cyanide from the
different companies and match up different lots and different
batches." With that in mind, Dr. Honigs said he had set out to
determine where the Seamurs cyanide had come from.

"The analysis was performed by the FDA and submitted
to the FBI at their request. The analysis in this particular case
was less than the ideal case—that is, the cyanide was not pure.
Rather, it was mixed substantially with the Excedrin or with
the Anacin-3. This meant that you couldn't simply take the
powder and do the analysis in a straightforward fashion. You

have to allow for the dilution and also perhaps for any other trace metals that might have been in the aspirin."

Yet, according to the chemistry professor, the FDA did its analysis in two ways. First, they analyzed the bulk powder, which did not reveal the elemental fingerprint. Second, it analyzed individual cyanide crystals.

"The numbers," Dr. Honigs said, "matched the fingerprint of the manufacturer DeGasa, a West German manufacturer of cyanide."

"Did the FBI and the FDA reach conclusions similar to yours?" Hillier asked.

"No, they did not. They had a little bit of difficulty in interpreting the results, both in their written report and then verbally when I contacted Mr. Martz with the FBI."

Dr. Honigs said he talked to SA Martz a couple of weeks before the trial, and at that time he asked his opinion of the source of the cyanide. The FBI chemist told him that the analysis was "too garbled" because of the presence of sodium.

But the witness insisted barium was also a fingerprint. It was his analysis of the barium concentration that led him to believe the cyanide was manufactured by DeGasa.

"The other manufacturers of cyanide, Du Pont and ICI, which is in England, do not have any measurable levels of barium at all in their cyanide. So both the amount and the identity confirmed my analysis."

"Did you explain that to Mr. Martz?" Hillier asked.

"Mr. Martz said that I could say whatever I felt was important and that he would stand up in court and say that he was the expert; he had been doing this longer than anybody else, and that in his opinion it could not be done."

The defense moved on to the green specks.

Dr. Honigs said the FDA's analysis of green particles had in fact made up approximately 190 of the 200 pages of chemical documentation he reviewed.

He also said he went to the FBI office and analyzed the powder that had been dumped out of the capsules.

"Any conclusions?" Hillier asked.

"The conclusion I reached was that the particles were in there not by accident, that they were put in there on purpose. The reasons I concluded this were, first of all, particles were found in almost all of the capsules. They were found in the vast majority, and in most of the cases, most of the tampered bottles, particles were found in every single one of the capsules, so it was not, therefore, in my opinion, there by chance. It was too common.

"The second thing is that the capsules had to be mixed up, the poison with the material put in the capsules had to be mixed up more than once."

He had two reasons for his conclusion.

First, the tampered Excedrin capsules contained Excedrin, cyanide, and the green particles. The tampered Anacin capsules were filled with cyanide, Anacin, and the green particles.

"... So they had to be mixed up at separate times in separate containers."

Of additional concern, he noted how the number of contaminated capsules and the total number in the bottles was very consistent.

"In the cases that I looked at in all the evidence, the tamperer took out between eight and nine capsules, dumped out the contents of those, mixed them, and then put them back into the capsules. Since every bottle had some capsules missing, it's very likely, then, that they were all done individually, that they were taken apart, dumped out, mixed up, and placed back together," he told the jury.

The final reason he believed the Algae Destroyer was added intentionally was that it was so visible against the whitish cyanide.

"If a person is mixing these up, they can see the green particles in there. It was evident to the analyst as soon as the analyst dumped the contents of the capsules out, you could see the green particles, and so it seems to me that the person who was mixing this up had to be able to see that as well as the analyst could later on."

Hillier wondered if the witness noticed a difference between the powders found in the Anacin capsules and those found in the Excedrin capsules.

"I took a look at the cyanide because of the particle size. While you can't tell chemically from the fingerprint what the material is, sometimes you can tell how it's been treated. The particle size ranged—the particle size was different in the different bottles. In some bottles the particles of cyanide were very large. Crystalline-like, larger than crystals of salt or sugar that you would see. In others they were very mossy and very amorphous, kind of a blob sort of shape, and so from that evidence as well it would appear that they were not mixed up from one batch."

Maida stepped from her chair with a quick deliberateness to question his conclusions that the cyanide was mixed in different batches, deliberately and not accidentally.

"Now, you have to make a number of assumptions about the facts in order to get to that conclusion," she said.

"I have to make assumptions if I assume it was mixed up more than two times. The chemical evidence directly supports two times. There is additional evidence that supports more than two times."

"So you're telling us you did have to make some factual assumptions?"

"That's correct, to support more than two times."

"You made an assumption that the green specks had to have been noticed by the tamperer, and that is a factual assumption that you have no factual basis upon which to make. Isn't that correct?"

The young professor responded: "There is an assumption that the person can see. I could see the green particles. The FBI analysis, the FDA analysis, they all saw the particles in that same situation, and I assumed that the person doing the tampering could have the same faculties of observation that I and these other people did."

"And that is an assumption that has no basis in fact, isn't it?"

"I don't know the tamperer; therefore, I am suggesting, then, that the tamperer should have the same facilities that I or these other people do."

"And, Dr. Honigs, you have no idea whether the tamperer would have noticed or could have noticed the green specks in the cyanide, do you?"

"I know that they were obvious—"

"Do you, sir?" Joanne Maida snapped, cutting him off.

Judge Dwyer stepped in, letting the witness complete his answer.

"I know that to the average person, they would be visible. I don't know if the tamperer looked at it."

"And, sir, you don't know whether the tamperer performed the tampering under as good lighting conditions as you would have in your laboratory, do you?"

He did not.

Maida inquired about the witness's statement, from a preliminary report, that there was no reason why the defendant would have a container of the green particles sitting around the house.

"That's speculation, sir, isn't it?"

"It is speculation, based upon the fact that she had a fifty-gallon aquarium, that the instructions, if she followed them, would require that she use and would drop in several of these tablets at once. She wouldn't be using fractions of tablets, and so it's based on the size of the tank and the manufacturer's instructions."

"And you speculated as to whether she kept a container with these particles lying around the house. You don't know that, sir, do you?"

"The speculation was based on the facts that I stated."

"Correct. And you don't know that was a fact, do you, sir?"

"It is speculation."

"And you used these two factual speculations to arrive at your conclusion that the cyanide was mixed in different batches, sir?"

"These are some of the speculations and some of the facts that were used. There are additional ones, which I stated."

"Sir, you are a scientist and not a detective, is that correct?"

"This is correct. My training is as a scientist."

The prosecutor questioned the witness's purported analysis of the evidence in the case during his visit to the FBI office.

"Dr. Honigs, it's fair to say that you never obtained a sample of the cyanide that's in this case, in evidence, and chemically analyzed it as Mr. Martz did at the FBI?"

"Mr. Martz, as I understand it, did not analyze the samples. He sent them to the FDA."

"Can you just answer the question, sir?"

"You compared me to Mr. Martz, and I don't think that was phrased so that the answer could be either yes or no."

Judge Dwyer again stepped in. "The question did include 'as Mr. Martz did.' The best procedure is to let the answer come forth and then go on to the next question."

Joanne Maida went after him again.

"You're aware that Mr. Martz did handle the capsules in this case, the contents of those capsules, and chemically analyzed them, aren't you?"

"The reports that I have document the analysts as other than Mr. Martz."

"Aren't you aware that Mr. Martz analyzed the substances in question and concluded it was potassium cyanide with traces of Algae Destroyer?"

"The conclusions that I have say that the person drawing the conclusion is Mr. Martz. The documentation on who run the chromatograms, who run the flame ionization and the like, some of these analyses was done at the Food and Drug Administration. In every case, Mr. Martz's name did not appear as the analyst."

Yet it was true, he said under further cross, that he did not chemically analyze the contents of the capsules.

"From your gross observation of the way in which these capsules were mixed, it doesn't take any level of special expertise for a layperson just to sit down and mix them in the same way, does it?"

"The capsule showed no special expertise in terms of mixing."

*

Sal Ramos helped a trembling Laurie Church, dressed in her best suit, a gray-and-maroon pinstripe, to the stand to give some rudimentary testimony on her background and the fact that she and the defendant had a very close friendship.

Laurie told of a good friendship, one of dinners out, CB radios, visits at one another's homes. She and her husband saw Bruce every weekend up until he died. Laurie saw Stella at least once during the week.

Hillier asked how the witness learned of Bruce Nickell's death. "My daughter was married June seventh and that evening, later that evening, Stella came over and told me that Bruce had died on the fifth."

Hillier asked why Stella had waited.

"She didn't want to let us know beforehand because my daughter had made these great plans for her wedding and Stella didn't want to ruin her day. She wanted that to be her day and so she told us later."

Maida went after one of Church's last answers, which was that Stella and Bruce "had a very good marriage."

"To you it appeared on the surface that they had a happy marriage?"

"I thought all the way around they had a happy marriage."

Yet under cross, Church admitted she was unaware of any financial or personal problems the Nickells might have had. Stella never told her she was unhappy in her marriage. Never said she was going to leave Bruce and run off to Mexico or Texas. "Oh, no. No."

"Did your friend Stella Nickell tell you at any time about plans that she had to open a fish store?"

"She said she wanted to open it and have Cindy work it with her, yes."

No doubt Cindy had been the star witness for the prosecution, but it was now her mother's turn to push back. Hard. Stephenson girl style.

Chapter Fifty-Nine

"Call Stella Nickell!"

The defendant flanked by Ramos and Hillier, her bearing stoic, took the stand. The tone and cadence of her voice matched her appearance—stiff and earnest.

Stella Maudine Nickell gave her version of her life story: born in Colton, Oregon, moved to Washington in the late forties, Seattle, then California, back to the Northwest in the early seventies where she met Bruce Nickell. She sketched a simple life of CBs, bowling, working on the property.

She told the court how she had helped her husband to stop drinking in 1979.

"Did you find a change in the lifestyle you and Bruce had as a result of his decision and yours not to drink?"

"Yes. Our life together improved considerably because he did not have the aftereffects of the alcohol. He was easier to get along with. His temper was not quite as quick as it used to be."

When Hillier asked if she had found the new life boring, Stella offered an emphatic "No."

At no time, Stella testified, did she tell Cindy she was bored with her marriage and resented that she could no longer go out and drink. In fact, her love for her husband grew.

"Well, we got along a lot better. We were at home more often. It wasn't a constant running uptown or going here or going there. We were able to settle down, catch our breath, and get to know one another more easily."

Next, the defense focused on the Nickell finances. According to Stella, they had their ups and downs. She, of course, did not deny the bankruptcy filing, but reported that they had been fortunate enough to be able to pay off the creditors.

Yes, they had "discussions" or arguments over finances— Stella pointed out that any couple did. Yes, there was stress over money.

No, there had been no physical altercations.

Under direct, the defendant said her husband had been "climbing the walls" during the summer and fall of 1984 when he was unemployed. He had things to do on the property, but he wanted a real job. He finally started working for the state in October.

Hillier asked if Stella's employment at SeaTac was a source of contention for the couple.

Stella said it wasn't. Her husband "realized what I had been trying to tell him about my inactivity around the house, being he went through it for six months."

Steady employment for both of them eased the financial problems, she said. But in early 1986, there was another "slump" in their finances.

"We had gotten behind, and the banks and our other companies that we owed were sending us letters, wanting us to make our payments."

Stella referred to the April 25, 1986, letter to the bank.

"The purpose of that letter was in answer to the letter that I had received letting our creditors know that we were having financial difficulties. We were having a little bit of family difficulties because of arguments in discussion over finances, and that I was trying the best that I could to pick up the payments and keep them current."

"You mentioned in the letter that 'your marital problems are about to be solved.' What marital problems were you talking about?"

"Our marital problems as far as finances go."

"What did you mean by 'about to be solved'?"

"Bruce had taken over the finances for a short time. He was—dictating is not the right word—but he was telling me what bills that we were to pay, what ones he wanted paid. That was the ones that I paid and we were falling behind. I had contacted these people and told them that this problem was about to be solved because I was taking the finances back over again."

"When you say 'Bruce is no longer involved and I would like a chance for me myself to prove my word to you,' what did you mean?"

"That meant that I was not at that particular time listening to Bruce. We had had a discussion about it, which was part of our marital problems, and I told him that I was taking the finances back over and trying to catch us back up to date where we should be."

"Were you meaning to suggest anything sinister by that letter?"

"No, I was not."

Tom Hillier asked if finances were improving immediately prior to Bruce Nickell's death.

They were, she said, "because we had finally gotten on permanently with the State of Washington."

Prior to her husband's full-time insurance benefits with the state, Stella Nickell told the court she and her husband satisfied their insurance needs with policies purchased through credit cards.

Stella said she had filled out applications, even to the point of signing her husband's name. Anyone who knew Bruce knew he "despised paperwork."

She identified the insurance enrollment forms from Bank Cardholders of America and admitted filling them out.

When Hillier asked about the defendant's meeting with SA Nakamoto, she said it was after her meeting with Bill Donais. She was uncertain about who was covered on the credit card policy. In addition, her attorney thought it was a single policy "because both policies that were in the envelope looked exactly the same."

Stella told the court that since she didn't have the certificates of insurance, that Bill Donais had them, she turned over a wallet card to SA Nakamoto.

Yes, he asked if there were any other policies and the witness told him no. No, Bill Donais did not process the claims, but he might have made some phone calls on the witness's behalf.

"I did try to contact him to find out if he had found out, and he told me that it looked like it was a clerical error and for me to go ahead and process them and see what the company sent back to me."

Next up were the letters to All American on October 20, 1986. Stella did not deny writing them, nor sending them to the same place on the same date. The defendant said she filled out the claimant's statement. She identified her original and the photocopy, but she could not recall submitting two claimant statements. Concerning the All American letter from October 29, 1986, Stella Nickell said she had written "both policies are the same."

"What do you mean that they were the same?" Hillier asked.

"There were the same contents in them. They were the same all around. They were identical."

"Did you think there was one policy?"

"Yes, I did," she said.

Stella said that it was her husband who filled out the state policy while the two of them sat at their kitchen table. At that time, they discussed the kinds of coverage they should have. Bruce had wanted $25,000 optional life and $100,000 supplemental.

Just before Bruce's death, there "was a foul-up with the insurance company's communication and us. They had sent out a packet for Bruce to have a medical examination, and we did not receive that package in the mail in time because there was a dated letter in it saying he had fifteen days to take a physical."

The letter, she said, was received about a month after they were supposed to get it.

When Tom Hillier turned to the amount of insurance Stella Nickell said she believed her husband was covered for, she stuck with the $25,000 figure from the state.

Prior to the All American policies, Stella Nickell said, she and her husband had applied for Firemen's Fund insurance through their American Express card, but premiums got out of hand and they canceled.

Hillier switched the defendant's direct to tropical fish. The witness said she had been interested in fish for some twenty years. Her husband enjoyed the fish too, she said. At the time of his death they had one tank. Her daughter was also interested in fish.

"Her knowledge is more technical than your own?"

"Yes. She had quite an advanced knowledge. To me it was advanced. It wasn't professional or anything, but she had quite a knowledge of fish tanks."

Tom Hillier asked how she handled her algae problem. The defendant said she preferred scavenger fish over chemical remedies.

Stella Nickell said she shopped for fish ninety-nine percent of the time at Kent East Hill Fish Gallery & Pets, so yes, she recognized Tom Noonan. But she did not recall any particular conversation about algae control in October of 1985. She could not recall a particular conversation about Algae Destroyer, but conceded it "could have entered into our conversation."

She said she did not buy the product from Noonan. "Do you recall ever crushing Algae Destroyer and using it in your aquarium?"

"No."

"Do you recall receiving advice from Cindy concerning a different kind of algae control, a liquid product, through Aquatronics?"

"Not to the best of my recollection. She could have mentioned about me controlling the algae in my tank, because it's very unsightly. We discussed several fish products."

Stella did not refute her daughter's claim that she had read up on poisonous plants. It was her concern for the children she babysat at White River Estates that prompted the reading. A girlfriend told her dieffenbachia, a houseplant she had, was poisonous.

Concern for her granddaughter led her to do more reading after they moved to the wooded property east of Auburn. She identified poisonous plants there—foxglove and nightshade.

"Did you ever mention foxglove or any of those observations to Cindy?"

"Yes, I did. I told her that I thought these plants were out there and that I had to check to find out if there was any other type of plants out there, for fear of my granddaughter getting into them, because when she came out, we told her she had the run of the property and she was only six years old."

"Did you ever research cyanide?"

"No, I haven't."

The response surprised Hillier. He asked again. "You've never researched it?"

"Before Bruce died when we moved on the property, no. After Bruce died, yes."

The defendant said she had done some reading about it in late June, once she knew that her husband's death had been caused by cyanide poisoning. She did not dispute that she touched any of the books in evidence.

Stella's next answers were a succession of "No." No, she never discussed poisoning Bruce with her daughter. No, she never wondered where she could get cyanide. No, she didn't talk about photography stores. No, she never discussed poisoning Bruce with seeds she found on the property.

Hillier asked the defendant to describe the evening of Bruce's death. The witness painted a scene of blue-collar normalcy. A kiss, a glass of iced tea, and the tired working man sat in front of the TV before showering.

"When he finished his shower he came back out of the shower, walked through the kitchen, stopped at the end of the cook table, reached up into the cupboard above the counter, and he took some Excedrin."

Stella said her husband had been suffering "tension" headaches caused by the hectic nature of his job. He had also injured his foot.

The evening he died, he took four.

"I asked him, 'Why four?'" she recalled. "He said, 'That's what I need.'" Bruce walked into the den and sat down and finished watching TV.

Hillier's questioning would later be described as "gentle." The defendant choked back tears. She didn't seem to be the antifreeze-veined killer her daughter had portrayed.

"He went back into the living room and sat down to finish watching TV. He had on his bathrobe. I was finishing fixing dinner for him. Pretty soon he got up and he walked out onto the patio. I thought that he had spotted a hawk that we have out there on the property and that he was watching the hawk.

"He stood there for a few minutes with his hands on the railing. I was still working in the kitchen. Pretty soon he turned around like he was going to walk back into the house. He stooped at the doorway and he said, 'Babe.' I answered him. He didn't answer me for a minute, and I said, 'What do you want?'

"He was leaned over. He said, 'I feel like I'm going to pass out.' I went to him. I asked him what was wrong. By that time he had squatted down in the doorway and he just shook his head. He didn't answer me again. I told him to come in the house and lie down on the couch. We had a couch in the den right by the glass doors.

"When he stood up he started to walk off of the steps to the patio, and I got a hold of his arm and I pulled him back towards the door, and I said, 'Come in the house and lay down.' He followed, pulled on my hand, and got back into the house, and he started to reach for the couch. He put his hands on it to brace himself. As he put his hands on the couch to lay down, he collapsed."

"What did you do?" Hillier asked sympathetically.

"I tried to get him to get up, and he did not respond. I went immediately to the telephone and called 911."

The court proceedings ended there for the day.

Stan and Laurie Church drove their yellow '72 Chevy pickup home mostly in silence. Laurie cried part of the way to Pacific. She felt she had let her friend down, hadn't done her job. Her husband was angry over the whole trial fiasco.

"Why didn't he let me say something?" she asked about Tom Hillier.

It was so brief, so pointless.

Chapter Sixty

All eleven benches in Judge Dwyer's courtroom were wedged tight with spectators on the morning of April 28. Air-conditioning systems worked overtime to keep the heat of the courtroom in check.

Hillier had his client pick up her testimony at the point when she was en route to the hospital with her mother. She said she and her mother waited in an area outside of the emergency room because hospital personnel had preferred it. It was there they learned doctors didn't know what was wrong with her husband, and "they did not know if they were going to be able to save him or not."

Bruce was moved to another area for more tests—an EKG, she recalled. A social worker said she and her mother could go to the ICU and wait.

"We waited there to be notified that he had been brought up so we could be with him. The social worker came back in and said the doctors wished to see us downstairs, and he took us back down to the same room that we had been waiting in."

"What happened next?"

Again, Stella choked with emotion.

"The doctor came in and informed us that they had not been able to save him."

She said a doctor asked if she wanted to be with her husband, but the teary-eyed defendant declined because "I didn't think that I could at that time."

Every now and then Hillier paused to allow his client to get a grip on herself, underscoring her emotional delivery.

"The doctor said that they would like to perform an autopsy on him to find out the cause of death and asked me if I would sign the papers, and I told him yes, because I wished also to find out why my husband had died."

She told the court she went home, tried to sleep, and made the trip to Wenatchee to tell Bruce's folks the news.

"When did you meet with Cindy?"

"I don't know the exact time, but I met with Cindy that same day after I got home and relaxed from the long drive, trying to get myself together to go over to a friend's house where my daughter was staying and tell her that her dad was gone."

Stella said she had been concerned about telling her daughter. Cindy and her stepfather had become close.

"I was concerned on how she would take the news because shortly before that, right at Bruce's death, Cindy and Bruce were not getting along very well because she had, in his mind, shirked her responsibility and sent her daughter to California to stay with a friend of hers, and Bruce was upset because our granddaughter was in California."

"Do you remember what you told her?" Tom Hillier asked.

"I had sat down at the table and I asked her to sit down because I had something to tell her, and when she sat down and she saw the condition I was in, she asked me if something was wrong with Mom or Dad Nickell. I told her no, that it was not them. I said, 'It's your dad.' I said, 'He's gone.'"

Stella Nickell said she could not specifically recall making the "I know what you're thinking; the answer is no" statement.

"If I made the remark it was because, knowing Cindy, she was feeling bad about her and her dad not having made up before he died."

She told the court how, after seeing a TV report on Sue Snow and calling 911, King County police came out to pick up the bottles.

Later, the FBI and FDA called for an interview. She recalled the meeting with Ike Nakamoto and Kim Rice.

She provided all the information they requested, including where she shopped—Albertson's North Auburn, the Pay 'N Save South Auburn, and Johnny's on the East Hill of Kent. She had shopped in about "every store in Auburn."

When asked about the third bottle found in her bathroom, Stella said she didn't know anything about it. She could not recall if she had purchased it or not.

"Do you know who else had access to your house during that time period? Say from May to early June?"

The defendant rattled off the names: Jerry Kimble, Cindy Hamilton, Wilma Stewart, A.J. Rider, Cora Lee Rice.

Further, the defendant said she met with the FBI after she had met with her lawyer. She said she did not know Bruce had died of cyanide poisoning until after she and Bill Donais discussed problems with the insurance policies.

Hillier brandished the June 16, 1986, letter from the state concerning the physical exam Bruce was to take. "Did you receive that letter before or after meeting with the FDA and the FBI on June 19?"

"I received that letter afterwards."

"What action, if any, did you take in response to that letter?"

"I didn't take any action, because there was none to take because it had to do with a physical examination that Bruce was supposed to take, and by that time he was already dead."

Stella told the jury how she had met with Dick Johnson and others at the Department of Transportation to learn what was required to file a claim. She said she was told it would be easier for her to go to Olympia in person. She was also told to bring a certified copy of the death certificate, "and they said that if I had any, to bring with me some newspaper clippings."

She testified that she made follow-up calls to the state, but it was because the "lady in the office" told her the insurance board would make a decision on the policy and when she didn't hear from them, she called. She also made other follow-up calls, because she had been told to do so in the event she didn't hear from them.

It was time for Hillier to focus on SAs Cusack and Nichols's interview of November 1986.

While the defendant admitted the subject of her late husband's state insurance policy had been broached by the FBI, "it never went into any detail."

"I told them that as far as I knew, the only coverage that he had was approximately $25,000 in coverage." She said the FBI had never indicated it might be worth more.

"I told them that there was no other policies because there wasn't, other than what Ike and I had already talked about, which was the credit card policy and Bruce's state insurance."

When Hillier pointed out that she had written to All American prior to her FBI interview, the defendant said she still hadn't heard back from the company until after the interview with Cusack and Nichols.

It was time for the defense to go back to the daughter.

Regarding Cindy's move from California in December 1982, Stella said her daughter "was having problems down there with the gentleman that she was living with. She wanted out of the area, and I told her to come up. Bruce and I talked about it. She could stay with us because she was my daughter."

The defendant testified she did what any mother would do, despite finances that "were not the greatest." Tom Hillier asked why she allowed Cindy to live at the Nickells' for four months.

"Because Cynthia had had a rough life when she was younger. We were trying to make it better for her. I was quite young when I had Cynthia. I know that I wasn't the greatest mother, as most young girls are not, but we wanted to help Cindy as best we could to get her feet under her and get her situated up here where she was close to us and we could be together."

Stella said her daughter had a "natural talent for being a beautician" and so they enrolled her in a beauty college. They bought her a car.

"We knew that she was still young and she needed to do her running around, meet new friends, get herself situated, and go back and forth to beauty college."

Why did the living arrangements change in April 1983?

"Cindy and I had gotten on the outs a little bit because of what she was doing. I had volunteered to take care of [her little girl] and she was taking advantage of that situation, coming in at all hours. The only restriction that we really put on her, we requested that she call if she was going to be extremely late so that we would know that she was safe. She was ignoring that point, and Cindy and I had a few words about it.

"Then, Bruce had also stepped into it with me and told me that I was not going to be taken advantage of and be a built-in babysitter for her. We decided that it was time that she start looking for an apartment of her own."

Stella said after she "calmed down and after Cindy got over her mad spot, we became close again like we were, mother and daughter."

The federal public defender brought up the subject of drugs.

Stella claimed she and her daughter had first discussed drugs during Cindy's teen years in California. The discussions continued after she moved to Washington. Drug use, the defendant said, was one of the reasons Cindy moved back to the Seattle area. After a while, the defendant said, her daughter got back into cocaine through one of her boyfriends. Beyond that, the two did not discuss drugs.

Next, Hillier hauled out Cindy's testimony checklist. No, Stella said she never discussed hiring a hitman to kill her husband. No, she did not tell her she wanted to get someone to run him off the road.

"Run him into a semi-truck or some sort of head-on collision?"

"No."

"Shoot at him during rush-hour traffic?"

"No."

"Did you ever discuss anything remotely connected with that testimony Cindy offered here?"

"No. I have never discussed anything of that sort."

Stella shook her head with great certainty.

"The thought had never entered my mind and never would, because I loved Bruce too much. There is no way that I could even possibly think of getting rid of him." She denied telling her daughter she was going to Texas as an alibi.

Tom Hillier asked his client a series of questions about the phone call she and Wilma Stewart shared in May 1986. The defendant "vaguely" recalled it. She was angry and upset with Bruce at the time, and told Wilma she might end up on her doorstep one day. It was fleeting, not a real threat. And, she said, she had no intention of making it a permanent split.

"When two people are upset and as angry as I was, I figured if we had a week or two of separation to make us realize what we actually had, that things would straighten out and we'd calm down and become closer."

The defendant concluded that by the end of the call her "mad spot" was gone, and of course, she never went to Texas.

"Did you ask her not to tell Bruce about that talk?"

The defendant nodded. Her husband was "extremely jealous," she said.

"I told her not to mention it to her uncle Bruce because I didn't want him to probably get the wrong idea that I was talking about leaving him, which I wasn't. It would have been a little bit hard to explain to him why I was so angry."

Though she recalled Jeanne Rice's frequent conversations about the bodyguard venture, the defendant also denied discussing it with her daughter. She never considered the job as something she'd like to do.

Hillier asked about Jeanne Rice's testimony citing confessions of an unhappy marriage.

"It's possible that we could have mentioned having problems in our marriage, because when you get two women together and they have a few problems in their marriage to begin with, you end up starting to grumble and gripe about your men in common conversation."

Was it true, as her daughter had testified, that she wanted out of her marriage but didn't want to lose community property? The defendant again made a flat denial.

She never told her daughter she hoped to end the marriage by poisoning her husband.

"Did you ever tell Cindy that perhaps you would simulate the Tylenol-type murders that occurred back east because that would be easy?"

"No."

"Did you ever tamper with the capsules that were in fact tampered with, that have been introduced into evidence through the five bottles that are in court here today?"

"No, I haven't."

"Did you kill your husband, Bruce Nickell?"

"No, I did not."

"Are you responsible in any way for the death of Sue Snow?"

"No, I'm not."

"Did you place the bottles that were found at Johnny's and Albertson's and that are in evidence today on those shelves?"

"No, I have not."

"Have you ever touched or come in contact with cyanide?"

"No, I haven't. Not to my knowledge."

"Are you responsible in any way for the crimes charged?"

"No, I am not."

Chapter Sixty-One

As expected, in her cross-examination, Joanne Maida hammered question after question as the defendant's rigid posture stiffened to near breaking.

"Mrs. Nickell, you told Wilma Stewart two weeks before Bruce's death that you were sick and tired of fighting with him. Correct?"

"Yes, I was sick and tired of fighting with him. I did not like to fight."

"And that you were very angry at him. Correct?"

She was angry, she said, but she wasn't going to leave her man.

Next, the prosecutor hauled out the April 25, 1986, letter to North Pacific Bank.

"The earlier letter that you wrote to them that came out to them between March and April 1986, do you remember telling them in that letter not to push?"

"If you just have patience ... I will eventually catch up. Just don't push ..."

"By May 1986, you were almost $1,900 behind in payments to North Pacific Bank, weren't you?"

The defendant couldn't recall the amount. To refresh her memory, Maida had pulled the government's exhibit, the North Pacific Bank letter from June 1, 1986.

The defendant was asked to read the last sentence into the record.

"*Thank you for your patience in this matter. My payments will stay current.*"

"This letter was written four days before your husband's death, was it not?"

"Yes, it was."

"And at the point in time that that letter was written and on the day that Bruce Nickell died, your financial situation was steadily deteriorating, was it not?"

"No, it was not steadily deteriorating."

"Was it steadily improving?"

"Not very fast, but it was improving."

Again, to refresh the defendant's memory, Joanne Maida pulled three more government exhibits: the Visa and MasterCard accounts, the delinquency letter from Pacific Coast Investment on the land, and the North Pacific Bank debt on the mobile home. All delinquent, with a total topping $8,500 and escalating rapidly the day Bruce Nickell died.

"Mrs. Nickell, in April to May of 1986, your financial situation had not been improving. It was steadily getting worse, was it not?"

"No, it wasn't."

The defendant would be damned before she'd give an inch.

It was time for Joanne Maida to bring out the books. Stella was presented with a copy of *Deadly Harvest.*

Joanne Maida pressed: "Did pages 88 and 89 of the book particularly interest you, Mrs. Nickell?"

"The whole book interested me."

The prosecutor sought an explanation for the large number of prints found on the two pages.

"I do not know which pages have the most fingerprints and which ones don't because I looked at the whole book."

The defendant was asked to read a passage on the odor of bitter almonds.

"Did the thought occur to you how it is that the pathologist missed the scent of bitter almonds during your husband's autopsy?"

"No."

Joanne Maida asked if the defendant knew if cyanide had an odor. When Stella Nickell said she did not know, she was asked to read.

After morning recess, Joanne Maida focused a great deal of attention on the encyclopedias, and more critically, her contention that the defendant had read the volumes as a guide to killing her husband.

She zeroed in on a palm print.

"Were you holding the page down, Mrs. Nickell?"

"Yes, I was."

"So you could take notes?"

"No."

Again, Stella Nickell didn't deny she read about foxglove.

"Is foxglove poisonous?" Joanne Maida asked.

"I don't know how poisonous, but it is dangerous, especially to children."

"It's very poisonous, ma'am, isn't it?"

Stella Nickell repeated her answer.

"What kind of seeds does foxglove bear?"

"I don't know."

"Little black seeds, Mrs. Nickell?"

"I have no idea."

"Does foxglove grow on your property?"

"Yes, it does."

"And you were familiar with it prior to June 5, 1986, were you not?"

"Yes, we were."

The "we" was an interesting choice of pronouns. Did she mean Bruce? Cindy, perhaps?

The overdue book, *Human Poisoning from Native and Cultivated Plants*, was discussed next. Stella Nickell did not deny reading that book either.

"Do you recall what the symptoms are of ingestion of the foxglove plant?"

"No, I do not recall."

"Do you recall that the book talked about children being placed in danger from sucking the flowers or eating the leaves or seeds of the foxglove plant?"

"Yes, I do."

As cross continued, Joanne Maida returned to *Deadly Harvest* and its passages on Indian tobacco, page 119 and its seven fingerprints. The defendant acknowledged that the text indicated lobelia, or Indian tobacco, was chemically similar to the nicotine of tobacco. And, in fact, nicotine was a powerful alkaloid.

Maida read a passage: "*Overdoses brought serious illness and sometimes death. Thus, lobelia received a reputation as a poisonous plant.*"

It was clear where the line of questioning was headed.

Stella did not refute that Bruce was a chain-smoker and there had been the presence of emphysema in his lungs, but she did deny a nicotine-overdose murder plan.

Now to put all of the defendant's interest in plants into some kind of context that would lead the jury to conclude murder. Joanne Maida questioned the defendant on her financial difficulties around the time she checked out the book *Deadly Harvest*, due June 16, 1983.

Stella Nickell said she could not recall any.

To jog her memory, Joanne Maida presented the Chapter 13 bankruptcy petition filed two weeks after *Deadly Harvest* was due back at the Auburn library.

The second time Stella Nickell checked out the book, it carried a due date of May 22, 1984. Bruce Nickell had been laid off the month before.

"Mrs. Nickell, do you recall complaining to your daughter that your husband wasn't trying hard enough to find work and you were unhappy with him just being around the house?"

"No."

"You weren't happy with his unemployment status, were you?"

"Nobody is happy to be unemployed. He was trying his best."

"I'm not talking about Bruce's unhappiness. You weren't happy with your husband's unemployment, were you?"

"That's a hard question to answer."

"Well, were you or weren't you?"

"No. Neither one of us were happy over the fact that he had become unemployed."

Joanne Maida had the clerk show the defendant the Nickells' 1984 tax return, showing $13,502 in total income. Of that amount, Maida pointed out, some $1,100 was earned by the defendant at Eddie Bauer.

"Mrs. Nickell, you weren't happy to go to work at Eddie Bauer; you did so because you had to, didn't you?"

"No, I did not have to. I did it to help relieve the financial situation we were in."

Joanne Maida turned to the Firemen's Fund/American Life Insurance application. "And was it applied for on January 20, 1984, a couple of months before Bruce was laid off from McDonald Industries?"

"Yes, it was."

Maida presented the form letter from Firemen's showing the $50,000 death benefit. "And throughout the life of that policy, you actively tracked its progress, did you not?"

"What do you mean by 'actively tracked its progress'?"

"When the premium payments went up, you immediately made a note of that and tried to call the insurance company, did you not?"

"I noticed it coming in on our bill, yes, and I wanted to find out what it was for."

"And you sent a letter to the insurance company after you received this notification of an increase in premiums, didn't you?"

"I do not recall receiving a notification of an increase."

"Nevertheless, you sent a letter to them asking about why the policy payments had increased?"

"Yes, I did."

Yes, the defendant said, she canceled the policy, signing her husband's name. The cancellation acknowledgment was dated July 19, 1985.

"Mrs. Nickell, a month and a half after you received that acknowledgment letter of cancellation from the insurance company, you signed Bruce's name to another insurance policy, did you not?"

"I do not recall."

The clerk was asked to hand the defendant the All American exhibits.

Now Stella remembered. It had been filled out and signed September 1985.

"A month after you signed Bruce's name to that policy, you signed his name again to another one, didn't you?"

"Yes."

It, too, was for $20,000.

"So you knew by October 14, 1985, that you had submitted and were in the process of submitting two different applications for two different life insurance policies, did you not?"

"I did not remember applying for the first one. I had not received a policy yet in the mail."

Joanne Maida was skeptical. "You had forgotten that?"

"I did not recall it in my memory."

"You did not recall that a month prior you had signed your husband's name on another $20,000 group term life insurance policy?"

"There was a lot going on in our life at that time."

"Do you recollect telling your niece, Wilma Stewart, that part of the life insurance total that you were tallying up was comprised of two $20,000 life insurance policies with a total amount of $40,000?"

"No, I do not recall that, and I never tallied up what I expected to receive from my husband's death."

Stella said her niece could have been confused, "because when she was talking to me at one time and said the FBI agents had been over to question her, they told her that the life insurance that I could expect from Bruce's death was over $200,000."

When asked, Stella said she could not recall Bruce's staying home ill in January, February, and March of 1985. Joanne Maida again jogged her memory with an exhibit; the sick-leave records from work. On January 21, Bruce Nickell was "sick to his stomach." On February 11, 1985, Bruce Nickell had written "stomach flu." On March 18–20, 1985, he wrote "sick to my stomach."

The defendant found the last entries, October 30–November 1. Her husband had written "flu."

"Mrs. Nickell, we've talked about what that *Human Poisoning* book says are the symptoms of foxglove poisoning. They include nausea and fatigue."

"Yes."

"Have you ever observed anyone who's exhibited these symptoms?"

"Not to my knowledge, no."

Under more cross, the defendant said that she could not recall telling SA Nakamoto she had called the insurance company's toll-free number and had been told there had been a clerical error.

Though the defendant had remained steadfast, her friends were glad it was time for afternoon recess. Some didn't think her defiant stance was doing her case any good.

At 1:30 p.m., the trial resumed with Joanne Maida picking apart Stella Nickell's claim that when she was asked by Equifax's Lynn Force, she declined to tell him of other policies, when, in fact, she knew of them.

"And that was a lie, wasn't it?"

Hillier objected; this time he was overruled.

"A lot of people look at it in a different way. I did not consider it an out-and-out lie, because I did not see where it was any of his concern that I had other insurance policies because he gave me no reason as to why he needed to know."

"It was a little lie, Mrs. Nickell?"

Another objection was lodged by the defense, and Judge Dwyer sustained it.

"It was not an out-and-out lie, Mrs. Nickell? Is that what you just told this jury?"

"Yes, it is."

"So although you had been—you tried to be helpful when you first visited the state insurance people who had asked you to bring some news clippings with you, when you talked to this insurance investigator the following month, you just chose to tell him something that was not an out-and-out lie?"

"I chose to tell him the way that I felt." The defendant said Lynn Force did not give her "any reason to need to know about any other insurance."

Again, Stella denied hearing Lynn Force say that her husband had been covered for $136,000 under the state insurance. Maida moved to the "third time" anyone asked about insurance policies—November's meeting with SAs Cusack and Nichols. "The only policy you told them about was a policy that you describe to have a $25,000 base coverage. Correct?"

"No, that's not the only policy I told them about. On that particular day they asked me about that particular insurance and asked me what the coverage was on it. I told them. They asked me if there was any other insurance policy, and I told them no."

She said she did not tell them about the two $20,000 policies because she thought they were referring back to Mr. Nakamoto's notes, where she had already mentioned them.

"When they asked you what other interest you might have with regard to your husband's death, what did you tell them?"

The defendant bristled. "What do you mean by 'what other interests I might have'?"

"Did you make an affirmative statement about any interest you might have or might not have in your husband's death?"

"I do not recall a question being put to me in that manner."

"And yet, Mrs. Nickell, six days prior to that interview in November of 1986, you had filed a claimant's statement against both of the All American Life insurance policies, had you not?"

The defendant admitted she had, but she was very confused at that time.

Joanne Maida challenged her. "You completely forgot, it completely slipped your mind, that six days before you had mailed in a claimant's statement against both of the life insurance policies on Bruce Nickell's life?"

"I told you I did not remember exactly what time I sent them in. I had sent in references to those policies, yes."

The defendant was reminded that she had testified the day before that she believed she had only one All American policy. The assistant U.S. attorney wondered how that could be. She asked the defendant to study the documents.

Stella Nickell looked up and conceded there were two specification schedules and two different policy numbers.

"That's correct. And you sent in both of those personal specification schedules attached to the claimant's statement, did you not?"

Stella Nickell said she was confused so she had copied the contents of both envelopes and, yes, sent in two specification schedules. She stuck with her story.

When Joanne Maida asked the defendant about her call to SEIB two days after seeing the FBI, she said she could not recall telling Pam Stegenga the investigation was over. "I do not recall making that remark to the lady." The witness was asked to review the statement of insurance from the state.

"Now, you've indicated to us that there was some amount of confusion on your part about the $100,000, the Part E that's referred to on this statement, accidental death and dismemberment coverage. Is that correct?"

There was.

Joanne Maida had the defendant read from the document.

"*The following optional life insurance coverages are available and you have selected the coverages that are indicated.*"

"Is there anything in that statement that leaves it in question about what the coverage was?"

"No, not on this statement."

Joanne Maida referred to the $100,000 optional life insurance.

"The statement says that these coverages are available and that you have selected the coverages indicated below. Correct?"

"Yes."

When asked how much money the defendant thought she was going to inherit after her husband died, Stella Nickell said from what she learned in court she thought the total was $125,000.

Joanne Maida approached the defendant and totaled the figures one by one for a grand total of $176,000. The June 16 letter referred to $25,000 supplemental life coverage.

"To your understanding, the letter refers to the $25,000 coverage that was incompleted due to a failure to take a medical examination. Correct?"

"I did not have that understanding. According to the letter, yes." The $25,000 was not even figured into the grand total.

"That's pretty close to the statements you made to Wilma Stewart about getting close to two hundred grand, isn't it?"

Tom Hillier objected to the argumentative question, and Judge Dwyer sustained it.

"Mrs. Nickell, you were preoccupied with getting paid on these policies, weren't you?"

"No, I was not."

"Isn't that why you called on September 26, September 29, October 10, and November 20th of 1986?"

"No. I was following directions from the insurance board to call back."

The defendant fumed when the prosecutor made mention of "a briefcase full of clippings," as had been seen by SEIB's Sandy Sorby. "I had some clippings in my briefcase. It was not full of clippings."

Stella said there were approximately fifteen to twenty clippings in her briefcase—nowhere near the number Sandy Sorby had said she'd seen.

"You were keeping a pile of them for proof when you filed your insurance claim?"

"I took them with me, yes, because they needed them. I didn't know what kind of clippings they might possibly need, so I took all of them."

"In fact, you told Sandy Sorby once you got down there that you waited to come in until you had gotten the revised death certificate showing cause of death of your husband of acute cyanide poisoning, didn't you?"

"I do not remember the exact phrase that I used, but I did wait for the death certificate because I was informed by Ms. Fligner that it would be sent out to me immediately."

"Didn't you wait until the authorities would catch up with their error and finally put the true cause of death on that certificate?"

"No, I did not wait for that purpose."

"Mrs. Nickell, you waited, didn't you, because you always knew that acute cyanide poisoning was the only true cause of death behind your husband's sudden collapse at home?"

The defense again objected to the questioning as argumentative.

"Overruled."

"No, I did not."

Stella Nickell did not deny making calls to the pathologists on June 7, and again a week later. Yes, she asked her family doctor about the plausibility of emphysema as Bruce's cause of death.

"Mrs. Nickell, you were trying, were you not, to reopen a closed file on your husband's death because you knew that the insurance paid out more than four hundred percent for accidental over a natural cause of death?"

"No, I was not trying to open anything."

"Mrs. Nickell, when you weren't getting the autopsy results back from the authorities on June 7 when you called, and again on June 13, isn't that why you mixed up another batch of potassium cyanide and planted those bottles on the store shelves in the Auburn-Kent area?"

Tom Hillier objected that the question was argumentative and inappropriate for cross-examination, but Judge Dwyer allowed it.

The defendant answered with an emphatic "No. I have never mixed up anything of that sort."

Next, Maida fired off questions concerning the placement of bottles on store shelves. One claim after another was denied by the defendant.

"If it could appear that someone else had died from acute cyanide poisoning by random chance, that was the only way that you could directly inform the authorities of your husband's own death without casting suspicion on yourself, wasn't it?"

"No."

"Mrs. Nickell, you knew that if you had suggested acute cyanide poisoning as the cause of your husband's death, that that would cast too much suspicion on you, didn't you?"

"There was no way that I could suggest that, because I had no idea what had killed him."

"When Sue Snow's death was first broadcast on Monday, June 16, 1986, you knew it at that time, didn't you?"

"No, I did not."

"You waited twenty-four hours before calling the police to turn in your two bottles of Excedrin so that you would not appear too anxious to turn those bottles in as to your own husband's death, didn't you?"

"No. I called the 911 number on the seventeenth, the same day that I saw it in the news report on TV."

"By the way, Mrs. Nickell, you do shop at the Pay 'N Save North?"

"I do periodically, but it is not a common place for my shopping."

"Do you recall, when you talked to Ron Nichols and Jack Cusack on November 18 of '86, that you told them you did not shop at the Pay 'N Save North store because you didn't like the physical layout of the store? That's why you shop at Pay 'N Save South only. Do you recall that?"

"I did not say 'only.' I said that is why I shop at Pay 'N Save South. That is my regular place of shopping."

"Incidentally, for the record, Pay 'N Save North store was where the Anacin was found."

Tom Hillier stood. "Your Honor, I would object to something for the record. I think it's improper for the prosecutor—"

The objection was sustained.

Maida asked about the third Excedrin bottle, the one Stella Nickell claimed to know nothing about. The "Cyanide-Laced Medications" chart was moved to the easel. "We're talking about a third bottle of Excedrin that was recovered in your house, the bottle that you indicate you knew nothing about: Lot no. 5H102 expiration 8-88, the bottle recovered from Johnny's Market.

"Mrs. Nickell, on June 3, 1986, two days before Bruce's death, you shopped at Johnny's Market, did you not, and purchased over ninety dollars' worth of groceries?"

"To the best of my recollection, yes, ma'am."

"That particular bottle has the same number of capsules as the one found in your house. Referring your attention to another sixty-capsule bottle, Excedrin 5H102, expiration 8-88, taken out of the Snow residence, and referring also to her purchase of that bottle from either Albertson's North or Safeway, ma'am, you shopped at Albertson's North, didn't you, from time to time?"

The defendant said she did.

When Joanne Maida asked if she had shopped at Safeway, the defendant said she hadn't in "a long time."

"When we found the bottle that's marked by the arrow, Mrs. Nickell, it still had sixty capsules in it. Mrs. Nickell, didn't you purchase that bottle as one of several bottles that you bought for the purpose of tampering with it?"

Another flat no.

"And when you had enough bottles that you had laced with cyanide, that bottle turned up to be an extra bottle and you placed that under your bathroom sink."

"No."

The defendant denied she purchased the Anacin-3 with her ninety dollars of groceries from Johnny's. She had no idea how the Anacin-3 wound up on the shelves at Pay 'N Save North.

"And as I understood your testimony from yesterday, you have never purchased Algae Destroyer for use in killing algae in your aquariums. Is that correct?"

"To the best of my knowledge, I have never purchased it." Stella Nickell continued her denials concerning Tom Noonan's purported recommendation to crush tablets.

"I have never used a solid algae destroyer. Whether we ever discussed an algae destroyer or not, I do not recall, because we have had far too many conversations about our fish tanks."

"Mrs. Nickell, can you think of any reason why Tom Noonan would be mistaken about your purchases of Algae Destroyer?"

"I have no idea why Tom Noonan would be mistaken. We may have talked about Algae Destroyer in our extensive conversations that we have had."

"Can you think—"

Stella interrupted, "I do know that I have been mistaken for another lady that does go in there. The only way they have separated us is when I speak or when I write out my checks and they see my name on the check."

Joanne Maida looked incredulous. "This is the first time you have ever made a remark in that regard, isn't it?"

Stella Nickell said she had told her attorney, but she didn't know who the woman was.

"Can you think of any reason why your daughter would be mistaken about your using Algae Destroyer?"

"As far as I know, she has never said that I used it. I have never used a solid algae destroyer."

"Mrs. Nickell, at home you kept a container or containers with some residue amounts of Algae Destroyer still left over from before you switched to liquid algaecide, did you not?"

"No, because I have not used it."

The prosecutor asked if the defendant had used the same contaminated container when she packed the capsules with cyanide. Stella Nickell again denied it. The litany of denials went on.

"You knew that you could get potassium cyanide from a photographer, didn't you?" Joanne Maida asked.

"The only way that I knew you could get it in photography was in the solution you develop film in, because there was an article on the front of the paper up at the airport that she and I both read that said it was very easily accessible to the public because it was used in developing film."

Yet, as Joanne Maida pointed out, the *New Caxton Encyclopedia* said the same thing.

Stella Nickell did not, however, deny discussing the Tylenol poisonings with her daughter. She said it was "one of the common conversations up at the airport." But she denied talking about the ease of putting things back on store shelves.

"Mrs. Nickell, do you personally know of any reason why your daughter would go through the ordeal of trial to testify the way she has?"

Tom Hillier objected. "Your Honor, I'll object. It's argumentative."

"Sustained."

After some thought, the question was rephrased: "Can you think of any reason why your daughter would have said all these things that you have now denied on the record you discussed with her?"

Stella paused; this answer slower in coming than the others. And of course, there was good reason for that.

"I have no reason to believe what she said. I have no idea as to why she would say the things that she has said to put herself and me through this situation."

"And the Mexico idea fizzled out when Jeanne Rice left town. Correct?"

"As far as she was concerned, yes. I never had the idea."

"This was a couple of months prior to your husband's death that Jeanne left town. Is that right, as far as you know?"

"I do not know. I didn't even know that she had left town, because she had quit working at the airport."

"By April 1986, a couple of months before your husband's death, you had made a decision that you would stay with the house in Auburn because you were committing yourself to the bank to make the financial payments they wanted, didn't you?"

"I was always committed to staying with my husband and the house and the land."

"That's why you wrote that letter under date of April 25 to North Pacific Bank saying that you had had marital problems, they were just about resolved, Bruce was no longer involved, and you had taken over the payments."

"What reason are you referring to?" Stella asked.

"The reason that you had committed yourself to pay off the delinquency payments on the property in Auburn."

"The reason I was committed to that was because Bruce and I needed to catch our payments up to date."

The jury departed down the steps to the right of the jury box for afternoon recess, and Stella managed a smile for her sisters. She felt she was holding her own.

Stella Nickell and Joanne Maida resumed their little drama after recess, with the Asst. U.S. Attorney running through the status of the Nickell marriage according to the defendant. It was a marriage getting better, not worse, when Bruce Nickell died.

Stella Nickell agreed.

"You recall that I directed your attention to the chart earlier and showed all of your credit card balances and how much you owed?"

"Yes."

"And that it had not changed in April-May 1986 from what it had been anytime earlier?"

"Those particular bills had not changed that much, no, but our financial situation was up the uphill grade."

"And yet by April you were telling the bank that Bruce was no longer involved. Correct?"

"Yes."

Joanne Maida distilled the letter's content for a reminder. "… The second-to-the-last sentence indicates that 'My payments will be on time in the future.' Correct?"

"Yes."

"What does the last sentence say?"

"It says, 'Thank you for your cooperation until I can get my feet under me again.'"

"'My feet under me'?"

"Yes."

It was shortly after Stella Nickell sent the letter that she phoned Wilma Stewart.

"You were very angry with Bruce and you were thinking about just packing up and leaving and coming down to live with her in Houston?"

Stella denied the idea of a Houston move.

"I don't recall her saying that I had thought about packing up … She had been trying for quite a long time to get us to move down there, and she was hoping that I might possibly stay."

"The reason why you called Wilma Stewart in May of 1986 was to ask if that was possible, if you could come and live with her. Correct?"

"No. If I had had any plans whatsoever of going to live with my niece, I would not have had to ask her if it was possible, because I knew it was."

By June 1, the prosecutor charged, Stella changed her plans. The defendant denied any plans to live anywhere else. She had gotten over her anger by the time she was off the phone. The prosecutor directed the defendant's attention to her June 1 letter to North Pacific.

"And throughout this letter, you're talking in the first person. I, I, my, my, all the way down, and what do you say in the very last sentence of that letter?"

"It says: '*My payments will now stay current.*'"

"Mrs. Nickell, by June 1, 1986, you wrote that letter four days prior to your husband's death; you had already decided that this property was going to be all yours, hadn't you?"

"'No.'"

"Three days after you wrote that letter dated June 1 of 1986, you set out to execute a plan by which the property would become all yours, didn't you?"

"No, I didn't."

By June 5, 1986, Joanne Maida pointed out, Bruce Nickell was "no longer involved."

*

Tom Hillier's re-direct was damage control. It was clear that while his client hadn't budged from her story, things still looked bad for her.

He went over the bank letter.

"Because you used expressions such as 'I would like a chance for me myself to prove my word,' did you mean to imply that you were intending to kill Bruce?"

"No. I phrased that letter—I have a bad habit of saying 'I' and 'me' as an individual because I wrote the letter. I cannot speak for somebody else."

She said she never meant to suggest that it was her property alone, or that it was about to be so.

"Ms. Maida talks about your financial situation in April and May, and we have an illustrative chart here. As evidenced by the April 26 letter, you enclosed a check for $800 to North Pacific, and then on June 1 you wrote again, indicating another payment and that by the end of that month you would be all caught up. So this figure by the end of May was not $1,892 in debt, was it?"

"No," she said, the figure would be less. In fact, she and her husband, both employed at the time, were trying to catch up as fast as they could. That was what she had meant by an improving financial situation.

Concerning the April 26 letter to the bank, the defendant said she was not suggesting she'd leave her husband. "Did you ever think of leaving him?" Tom Hillier asked.

"No, because Bruce was like a part of me."

By the time she hung up the phone, she said her niece had talked her "out of being angry" and put her "back into a good mood."

"Did you—again—are you responsible in any way for the crimes charged in the indictment the government has brought against you?"

"No, I am not."

Tom Hillier was finished. He thanked his client, who sat glumly, drained of the little color she'd had.

Joanne Maida said she had three more questions.

The defendant again denied telling her daughter of any cyanide research before Bruce died.

"Did you not tell her that you had learned that potassium cyanide could be obtained from photography?"

"No, I didn't. We read that in the newspaper."

"When you told your daughter the day after your husband died, 'I know what you're thinking, but the answer is no,' the import of what you were saying to her was clear, wasn't it, in light of these prior conversations with her?"

"I don't understand what you're getting at. If I made the remark, which I have no recollection of most of the remarks I make to her, I was trying to comfort her over a death in our family."

"Based on your prior conversations with your daughter about your husband, nothing more needed to be said between you."

Tom Hillier objected on the grounds that this was argumentative.

Judge Dwyer agreed, and there were no more questions. Stella Nickell stepped down as the defense rested.

The jury was excused, while over Tom Hillier's continued objections Joanne Maida reargued the admissibility of Katy Hurt Parker's rebuttal testimony. Judge Dwyer agreed that the testimony of the defendant conflicted with Cindy's testimony. He cited the defendant's denials.

Katy Hurt Parker would be allowed to testify.

Tom Hillier had lost that battle, but he pulled a reward from his threadbare bag of tricks. It was agreed the reward stipulation would be read to the jury before the government's rebuttal case.

The prosecuting attorney Maida made another play for the polygraph phone call, but Judge Dwyer held firm—the jury would not hear it.

The jury returned, and the judge read:

"Stipulation: The parties agree and stipulate that the Proprietary Association and Over-the-Counter Drug Trade Association advertised a $300,000 reward for information leading to the arrest and conviction of the person or persons responsible for the deaths involved in this case, and that information about the reward was published in both the *Seattle Times* and the *Seattle Post-Intelligencer* on June 20, 1986."

Katy Hurt Parker took the stand for the second time. The government's sole rebuttal witness told the jury she had lived with Cindy in the mid-eighties. Prior to that time, she said, she knew Cindy for about a year.

"About a year?"

"About a year, year and a half."

"Did you meet her in 1985?"

The defense objected. The witness was being led. Judge Dwyer agreed. Katy looked flustered, without a clear path to follow. She told the court she met Cindy in 1985 when they worked at 7-Eleven. The two women became roommates.

The witness figured they had lived together off and on for "approximately six months" since March or April of '85.

"Did there come a time, Ms. Parker, when Cindy Hamilton came home and shared with you a conversation she said she had had with her mother?"

"Yes, there was."

Her time frames were less than precise. She thought it was "about November" of 1985, reasoning, "Because she spent holidays with us, Thanksgiving and Halloween."

The specific conversation occurred at her kitchen table. It was Cindy who broached the subject. "She says, 'Katy, do you know what my mom asked me today?'"

Her voice was so soft, the jury strained to hear.

"'She asked me how much cocaine it would take to kill a person, and I asked her why.' She said that her mother had been talking about getting rid of her father and this was one way."

Joanne Maida asked if a reason had been mentioned as to why Stella would want to kill Bruce. "That she was getting tired of him."

The witness stated further that Cindy had told her that Stella was worried that her own mother wouldn't have a place to go if she lost her property.

"Did you talk immediately at that time to Cindy about whether there was a possibility of that happening?"

The witness said she had.

The judge interrupted the testimony to remind Maida that questioning be confined to the conversation between mother and daughter.

Maida promised clarification.

"Was that the end of the conversation, or did it go on?"

"It went on."

"Did you pursue the subject with her?"

The witness said she did. She said she asked if Cindy thought that her mother would really do it. "What did she say?"

"She said—"

Again, Judge Dwyer interceded and Tom Hillier objected.

"Did you continue your contact with Cindy Hamilton the year later, after Bruce Nickell died?"

"Yes, we did."

Joanne Maida switched tracks and asked if Cindy and the witness discussed her going to the authorities back in November of 1985.

She said they had. A few questions followed, and the witness was turned over to Hillier for cross-examination.

Tom Hillier had a chance to discredit the witness. She had been extremely vague in her recollections. He asked if she had been contacted and asked to come forward by Cindy prior to her appearance before the grand jury.

She said she had.

He continued but was unable to further pinpoint when Cindy moved in and how long she had stayed. Katy didn't agree that her friend had "an unstable lifestyle."

"Do you know whether or not she was using cocaine during that time frame?"

Katy didn't care too much for Hillier, and it showed. She admitted Cindy drank, but that was the extent of her drug use. "In all the time that I have known Cindy, I have never known Cindy to use any drugs."

"When you say she was visiting with you during the holidays, was she living with you?"

"I know that she stayed with me during, like, Thanksgiving, and she was there on Halloween because we got our kids together and got them dressed, but she wasn't actually living full-time with us."

Further questions showed only that the conversation didn't take place on either of those nights. "Didn't Cindy Hamilton tell you that her mom and her stepfather enjoyed a good relationship?"

"She never really said anything. Just, whenever she talked, it was 'my mom and dad.'"

That marked the end of Katy Parker's testimony.

*

With no more witnesses from either side, testimony was over. The next day, the attorneys would meet to go over the exhibits to go to the jury. Final arguments would wait for Monday.

Some stories never made it to court. Maybe it was because they didn't fit, or they impugned a witness's credibility. Katy Hurt Parker held one in her memory. It was a phone call she had received from Cindy back in June 1986. The two women seldom saw each other during that time. Some would say the contact was infrequent because Cindy no longer needed Katy's babysitting services—Cindy was living with Dee Rogers, and her little girl was off in Northern California.

It might have been a nice surprise when Cindy phoned if her news hadn't been so terrible. "Katy, my dad died a couple days ago," she said, sounding shaky. Katy gave her condolences, then blurted something that even surprised herself.

"Did your mom do it?"

"No. He dropped something on his toe at work, and it caused a blood clot and it went to his heart."

"Well, I don't think your mom could have something to do with that," Katy offered.

"'Course not. No way."

If Katy didn't question her friend because she seemed so upset by her loss, there was also another reason. "I didn't want to know any more than I already knew," she later said.

Chapter Sixty-Two

Stella Nickell's fate now rested in the hands of seven women and five men who had studied her every move, every gesture.

Joanne Maida started her closing statement with expressions of empathy, an emotion she seldom displayed throughout the trial. She said Sue Snow had died because Stella Nickell's plan depended on it and depended on her husband's death appearing just as random.

"But the so-called random killer made three fatal mistakes in the execution of an otherwise flawless scheme. The scheme was flawless because of its simplicity. It was flawless also because of its anonymity," she said.

The first mistake was the Algae Destroyer–contaminated bowl. The defendant, she said, had switched from the tablets to a liquid, leaving the bowl aside to dissolve the hard tablets. The bowl was then used to mix the cyanide for the capsules.

Stella's second mistake was not leaving the autopsy well enough alone. She had committed the perfect crime, and her husband's file had been closed. He had died of emphysema.

But he hadn't, and Stella was forced to bring the bottles to the authorities' attention.

Maida went through the evidence. The Anacin-3, found at the Pay 'N Save store, where the defendant claimed she did not shop—yet checks were written there. Pay 'N Save North did not stock that particular count-size of Anacin-3 found on their store shelves. A price sticker on the box showed it had originally been stocked by a member of Associate Grocers.

Johnny's in Kent, where Stella Nickell purchased almost a hundred dollars of groceries on June 3, 1986, stocked Anacin-3. Johnny's was an Associate Grocer.

Only five of the 15,000 bottles examined by the FDA were laced with potassium cyanide. Of the five, Stella Nickell produced two. That, Maida said, was her third mistake.

"The staggering odds were multiplied further because the defendant purchased them at different stores, at different times." Her husband dead, the defendant applied for the benefits ... money, money, money ...

First the state policy, then two All American insurance policies. There were two letters, two claims made by the defendant.

"It's crystal clear, ladies and gentlemen, that Stella Nickell is filing a claim against each of the two policies. She sends in two different specification schedules, two death certificates, and the two applications which she made separately in September and October 1985."

The defense's professed misunderstandings were dismissed as flat-out lies: to Ike Nakamoto, to Lynn Force, to Cusack and Nichols.

The defendant was not confused; she knew the state insurance was $136,000.

Happy or unhappy marriage? Joanne Maida told the jurors to use their common sense. Bonnie Anderson had said the defendant liked her work hours because she didn't have to deal with her husband. Jeanne Rice told the court of Stella Nickell's interest in packing up and leaving for Mexico—with her daughter, not her husband.

Maida went on, dredging up Cindy's charges against her mother: the hitman, Katy Parker and the cocaine, the Firemen's Fund insurance, Bruce's layoff, *Deadly Harvest*, the little black seeds, the bodyguard business, the Tylenol murders ... the comment "I know what you're thinking, but the answer is no."

"Nothing more needs to be said between mother and daughter for the significance of that comment to be grasped. It is not lost on Cindy Hamilton."

She reminded the jurors that Cindy came forward six months later and told her story to the FBI, providing information that suggested her mother researched the cyanide plan at a library.

The jurors were asked to examine the library books carefully—the positions of the prints; the number of prints on pages dealing with cyanide.

After four hours of closing, Joanne Maida put her case to bed.

"Two people died because Stella Maudine Nickell, with cool, chilling deliberation, set out to eliminate them because it behooved her interests to do so. Her acts reflect a human being without social or moral conscience—a hard, icy human being who was willing to adopt a horrendous course of action as was convenient to accomplishing her purposes. She has attempted to explain away all of her words and conduct just as she has attempted to explain away every shred of physical evidence in this case presented against her. But she attempts to deny and she attempts to explain away too much. Stella Nickell attempts to escape accountability for decisions which she made which had irrevocable consequences to Sue Snow and to Bruce Nickell."

The courtroom clock read 1:10 p.m. when Tom Hillier stepped up to begin his closing and immediately attacked the government's "close-minded" view of the case. Joanne Maida's opening remarks suggested Bruce died alone, without his wife at his side. The prosecution assumed Stella was lying and not confused. The prosecution assumed there was a bowl that was used to crush cyanide and algaecide together, and that that bowl had been lying around the house for up to six months or a year depending on whether Tom Noonan's or Cindy Hamilton's version was believed.

Further, Hillier said, the prosecution assumed the defendant called the pathology department in mid-June 1986 to press for autopsy results, when the pathologists suggested it was a reasonable concern.

"The prosecution, without acknowledging the lies and inconsistencies of Cindy Hamilton, doesn't talk about her character at all," he said.

The prosecution had argued that Stella's daughter in no way could have known about the cyanide research without Stella's having told her about that sometime prior to Bruce's death.

Yet, as Hillier pointed out, Cindy stayed with her mother after Bruce Nickell died. It was then, he said, that his client researched both cyanide and emphysema.

The government's case rested on Cindy's shoulders.

As the defense lawyer saw it, Cindy's time frame concerning the insurance was at odds with the government's theories.

"She testified first that late in 1985 or early 1986, 'My mom talked about overdosing Bruce with cocaine, but I told her that she couldn't do that because it might show up in his blood stream, and he might flunk his physical. Then I won't get any insurance.'

"So the best we have is a vague time frame of late December, early January, which doesn't tend to mesh very well with the government's proof, because it was January 2, 1986, that Bruce took his physical."

There was no way for the defense to challenge a vague time frame, he said.

It was also at odds with Katy Hurt Parker's vague testimony. Katy was unable to say exactly when Cindy moved in, or when she told the cocaine story.

"We also learned from Katherine Parker that Cindy Hamilton brought her forward to the FBI in August of 1987. A suspicious mutual vagueness is shared between the two."

The third reason to question the insurance motive, Hillier claimed, was that ample testimony suggested Stella Nickell did not know what her husband's policies were worth.

He pointed out that no one had told Stella Nickell the amount of the insurance, with the exception of Lynn Force. Yet Stella didn't hear him. When the FBI interviewed the defendant in November, they knew of the correct figure, but they didn't clue the defendant in.

"Because the government would choose to hold these cards close to their vest and then argue a conflict that they create because they don't have the courtesy or forthrightness to confront Stella Nickell with information that they think they have to try to get some clarity to this situation.

"The fact is, ladies and gentlemen, that there was confusion on that policy, and it was documented from day one and you heard it from witness after witness after witness, and from that fact reasonably follows the fact that Stella Nickell believed that the policy was worth $25,000."

He cited the All American policies. Stella was confused about their value, but she didn't conceal that she had them. She told SA Ike Nakamoto of the policy, even gave him its number.

Hillier disputed the prosecution's claim that Stella continued to conceal the existence of the policies when she met with SAs Cusack and Nichols. When asked if there were any other polices, she said no.

"She said, 'I said that because I assumed he meant beyond the information I had already provided.'

"Heck, ladies and gentlemen. Several days before, Stella Nickell had just sent in her claimant's form to the insurance company. Obviously she's not going to try to conceal that kind of information, having already provided the insurance numbers to the FBI." The jury was asked to put themselves in Stella Nickell's chair as the FBI interrogated her.

"Are you going to try, when a week [earlier] you sent in an application for insurance proceeds, to lie and conceal, knowing these gentlemen have been investigating the heck out of the case for the last five months?"

Concerning the letters to North Pacific evoking the Nickells' financial problems, Hillier sarcastically dismissed the prosecutor's insistence that they were confessions of murder.

"We're having problems in the marriage. Don't worry about it. I'm getting rid of Bruce. Boy, I'm going to get the life-insurance policies to you in a hurry, so hang in there, please."

Such talk, as evident in her letters, suggested Stella Nickell was a direct person, a take-charge woman. She was upset with her husband and she was pretty vocal about it, but she had taken the bull by the horns and would get caught up on their bills.

Hillier suggested that Maida's cross-examination on the Nickells' financial problems, beginning in 1983 and followed by books on poisonous plants, were an attempt to "bootstrap" and "shore up" Cindy's time frame on her story "that Stella Nickell was going to poison Bruce anytime she's got a problem with the money."

Hillier shook his head. The facts were, he said, that Stella Nickell was spending time babysitting in 1983, and when the Nickells moved to the property a year later, she was concerned about her granddaughter getting into poisonous plants.

"The time frame concerning the checking out of the book is absolutely consistent with what Stella Nickell said as to why she checked them out."

He pointed out that the government's testimony concerning the foxglove was placed in the context of sick-leave records from early 1985. But Cindy said the seeds conversation occurred at the airport, within six months of Bruce Nickell's death.

"So according to Cindy's own testimony and the government's strained theory as to the significance of these physical papers, Bruce was sick in January and February of 1985, and if Cindy Hamilton is believable at all—and she's not—this occurred in January and February of 1986, a full year later, according to the only basis for even making that argument, and it's a strained argument to begin with. Flat contradiction by the government's star witness. Flat contradiction because Cindy Hamilton is not telling the truth."

The prosecutor had cross-examined the defendant at length about the problems in 1983 and '84 with finances and about Indian tobacco and emphysema. "What are we supposed to guess here? That Stella was going to roll up some Indian tobacco and give it to Bruce and to use the emphysema as a cover for that? Or that she would cause his death and argue that he had emphysema?"

What of the notes Stella had allegedly taken as she plotted to kill her husband?

"Who among you didn't expect some notes to appear in evidence in front of Stella Nickell in a dramatic proof that she is lying?" But there were no notes in evidence.

"The prosecutor planted seeds in your minds without proof in the hope that you will abandon your common sense, your experience, and your reason and join the prosecutor in her murder mystery."

Tom Hillier had never given a lengthier argument, and he told the jury so. Yet he had more. The details of the case alone would free his client.

He brought up the algaecide and Tom Noonan. He said he sold the defendant Algae Destroyer beginning in October 1985, before moving to a new store by January 1986.

"Cindy Hamilton says that twelve months before Bruce died, during the summer of '85—and again, your recall is critical, twelve months before Bruce died—she told her mom to use a liquid algae killer produced by Aquatronics Products, and that her mom had used tablets before. Cindy Hamilton never mentioned a brand name. Never mentioned a brand name. To the extent that Ms. Maida suggests otherwise, she's wrong. She wasn't questioned about it, and I mentioned this in sort of my rebuttal remarks earlier this afternoon. She wasn't shown 12-1, the picture of Algae Destroyer, and asked, is this it? That's telling proof that even Cindy Hamilton wouldn't have confirmed the prosecutor's theory."

Public defender Hillier also emphasized that the FBI's Roger Martz couldn't offer a reason for the algaecide's presence in the cyanide. His witness, Dr. David Honigs, insisted the green particles were not placed in there by accident. Tom Hillier invoked Tom Noonan's testimony about Stella Nickell's first purchase of Algae Destroyer.

"Remember what he said? He paused. He looked up. Paused. October 1985. October. Right out of the blue, out of nowhere, he came to October. Is that the quality of information that a woman's liberty depends upon? Right out of the blue!"

The testimony was at odds with Cindy's testimony. She said she talked with her mother about algae problems caused by sunlight, a problem of the summertime. Not October.

Stella said she never discussed crushing any tablets with Tom Noonan.

"Who do you believe? Out-of-the-blue-October Tom Noonan? Or Stella Nickell?" After chiseling away at Tom Noonan, Hillier went after Cindy's testimony.

He questioned if his client's actions were consistent with her daughter's characterizations. Greedy? When she had little or no money, she helped Hamilton buy a car, offered free daycare for her granddaughter, school tuition.

Bored with her husband? When Bruce hit rock bottom, it was the defendant who helped him dry out.

"Does it make sense that a strong woman, a direct woman, would cater to every whim of her husband to the point of obnoxiousness, by some standards of liberation, if she hated him?

"Does it make sense, ladies and gentlemen, that Stella Nickell would ask Cindy Hamilton where she could acquire heroin, cocaine, speed, and other drugs for, as Cindy Hamilton figured, the purpose of resale because, as Cindy Hamilton testified, it could supplement her mom's income? Is that reasonable? Or is it more reasonable that Stella, knowing of her daughter's problems with drugs, would talk to her about her drug use?"

He called her reasoning on why she didn't do anything to save Bruce "absolute insulting nonsense, and suggests how truly detached from reality that troubled young woman is."

"Why does the prosecutor change its theory three and four times during this case from Stella going to poison her husband Bruce back in '83, to going to leave him, going to divorce him, going to go to Mexico, going to kill him, going to Texas, going to kill him? The reason is they've got to keep up with Cindy Hamilton and her oscillating details.

"We're talking, from the prosecutor's theory, of a woman driven to kill. Where is there anybody other than Cindy Hamilton? We've got a lot of people saying, 'Yeah, Stella had her gripes.' She voiced those gripes to Wilma and Jeanne Rice. That's consistent with the normal marriage, ladies and gentlemen, with the usual ups and downs, with some frightful financial stress?

"Don't buy into this theory that there's just too much there. Analyze each piece of evidence one by one. What are you left with? Cindy Hamilton."

After fifty more minutes, Tom Hillier was finished.

A ten-minute break allowed Joanne Maida to prepare a rebuttal. She defended Katy's and Cindy's time-frame testimony.

"Both of them have approximately the same time frame. No one two years ago was taking notes at the time that certain conversations occurred."

The assistant U.S. attorney addressed the reward.

"It is too late now to hurl that charge or any insinuation against any witness who has testified, who has not been given the opportunity to respond to that accusation. Without that, the record is absolutely bald that any witness called by the United States has testified for any other reason than to report the facts as facts must be reported."

In defense of Cindy: "If you bring to your deliberations your commonsense perceptions of human behavior, based on your collective life experiences, you will find that Cindy Hamilton would not have put herself through the anguish of the last two years and the ordeal of this trial unless she speaks the truth. She has no motive to incriminate her mother, and the fact that the discussions with her mother were too important to disregard were reason enough for her to come forward, and come forward she did."

The prosecutor told the jury that Cindy did not stand alone. Physical evidence and the testimony of others backed up her story.

"Not a single witness, not a single witness has disparaged her ability to tell the truth or any reputation for doing so except the defendant, who has a direct interest in the outcome of this case," she said.

"When the whole picture is put together, piece by piece, detail by detail, there is undeniably only one person who had the motive, the inclination, and the opportunity to commit these crimes. The real killer, who Mr. Hillier suggests is still out there on the loose somewhere, is sitting within the four corners of this courtroom, and she knows it."

It was four o'clock, and rather than have the jury deliberate for an hour, Judge Dwyer adjourned.

Whether he was sending a heroine or an accomplice home, when SA Jack Cusack put Cindy Hamilton on a flight headed for California, he did so with relief. He had kept his promise to watch out for her and see her through the ordeal of the trial, but he was tired. He had had to handle the tiresome personality of a young woman out of control.

He waited for her plane to leave, then returned to Seattle to phone Joanne Maida with the word that Cindy was on her way back to Garden Grove.

"You know, Joanne," he said, laughing. "I've never been divorced before, but I have a hunch the way I feel right now is pretty close to the feeling."

Chapter Sixty-Three

The Nickell trial jurors filed into court single file. It had all come to this moment on May 3, 1988. Some were eager to get going, others somewhat excited by the culmination of their responsibilities. Most were concerned that whatever came from the deliberations, it be the right decision. After instructions from Judge Dwyer, they were excused to the jury room. It was time to get busy.

Being on a jury is not a life of courtroom drama. It can be quite dull. Twelve jurors and two alternates had been thrown together to weigh the evidence. Fourteen people with little in common.

The waiting game between rulings had been boring, and the fact that the case could not be discussed had been excruciating. Small talk passed the time for some, reading for others.

Jurors talked about their jobs at Boeing, a law office, the state, real estate, even unemployment. Those who had them discussed their kids and grandchildren.

It was all so quiet, so anonymous.

And yet within that group, one would emerge during deliberations. Once in the jury room it was apparent, nearly immediately, that one person had broken from the feeling that Stella Nickell was guilty.

It was the real estate saleswoman, Laurel Holliday.

Yes, the defendant came off as glacially cold. But that didn't mean anything, most of the jurors agreed as they sat at the table to begin deliberations. Most knew a courtroom was hardly the most comfortable venue for the accused.

"She was under max control, everyone was watching her ..."

"She did cry."

"Right. So what?"

"She's innocent, I tell you."

The last comment was made by Laurel Holliday.

And as they went over the evidence, a juror asked: If the defendant had been so innocent, why had she lied about shopping at that particular Pay 'N Save when checks proved otherwise?

Laurie Adams took it further: "It was the closest to her house ... she didn't have to deny going to the store. It would have been very reasonable to say she went there."

Others agreed.

"They had those canceled checks. Did she forget about them?"

The argument resumed the next day.

Laurel Holliday maintained such a response pointed to innocence. Her reasoning confused other jurors.

Juror Adams later recalled Laurel Holliday's conclusion: "'The woman is innocent, the end justifies the means.' It is okay for her to lie on the stand to get herself off, to get a not-guilty verdict. She even said, 'I'd do the same thing.'"

Hands went up in the air and jurors stood away from the table as a show of protest. Sighs were as loud as screams.

The foxglove was another case in point. The defendant's prints were on the books, on passages about foxglove. She told the court she had read about dangerous plants to protect her granddaughter.

One juror said that it would have been totally reasonable for Stella to say she recalled information about the plant.

"Why deny it now?"

And so it went, the clock counting the hours, the jurors waiting on the holdout to declare Stella guilty, or at least offer a valid counterpoint to any argument being discussed.

Five and a half hours in the jury room had passed as the group considered evidence and listened to recollections and views on the evidence. At 4:30 p.m., the jurors gathered their things to leave. Clear in their minds were Judge Dwyer's precise admonishments to avoid the news and any discussion of the case.

Laurie Adams took the bus to her home in Redmond. Those single drove home alone. They were lucky. No one would ask them any questions.

Jurors spent some of their time trying to prove to Laurel Holliday that Stella Nickell had a reason to kill her husband. But she just didn't seem to get it.

"It was almost like she was playing dumb. It was very clear to all of us that this woman took out insurance policies on her husband that he knew nothing about," Marcheta Cruse said later. Yet Laurel Holliday questioned them.

"What do you mean?" Or, "I don't understand."

She gave the same response when the jury reviewed the flurry of checks presented by SA Marshall Stone. Murray Andrews kept things going as smoothly as he could, as some of the older men in the group grew agitated when the real estate agent went over the same thing again and again.

One of the women suggested a flip chart be procured to help organize questions about cyanide-laced bottles, the stores where they had been purchased, and the proximity to places frequented by the defendant.

A couple of the men rolled their eyes upward. Why bother? They knew Stella Nickell was guilty. But, at 11:00 a.m., Murray Andrews wrote out a note on a slip of paper for the bailiff.

We would like to request a large note pad (or easel) and marker pen, if available. Signed, Murray M. Andrews, Foreman. After clearing it with counsel, neither of whom had any objections, Judge Dwyer had the materials sent to the jury.

The jurors decided the only way they were going to convince Laurel Holliday was by working through every bit of evidence. And so they did.

"Are you satisfied that it all points to the fact that she's lying?"

"Or do you have any more questions about the checks?"

"What else would you like to look at?"

It was obvious that something was off with juror seven. Nobody knew what it was.

Laurie Adams thought nothing of the file folder Holliday kept in front of her during deliberations. And as people tend to do, jurors Holliday and Adams both sat in the same seats both days.

Yet Laurie noticed that the title on the folder had something to do with real estate taxes, which seemed like such an odd subject to read during deliberations. As Holliday sat reading one of the single-spaced typed pages, a curious Laurie Adams looked over her shoulder and read. Later, she recalled the gist of what she saw. It made her recoil as if she had seen a rattlesnake. Laurel had written:

And these jurors, one of them reads the National Enquirer! *[...] And the only one that's close to my intellectual equal reads a Robert Ludlum novel! [...] And that Vietnamese guy...*

Appalled, Laurie quit reading.

Later she summed up what the notes had meant to her: "It just spoke volumes of her negative attitudes of everyone who was on the jury. It said a lot in terms of why she was so difficult... She was there with a major responsibility, it wasn't something to be taken lightly. You leave your preconceptions, emotions behind. You need to do the job."

Laurie took a couple of deep breaths and moved to a seat away from Holliday and her little folder. The young woman told herself she wasn't going to say anything to anybody. She didn't want to harm the deliberations.

But it was only the beginning.

At 5:00 p.m. it was time to call it a day. Again, the twelve left after being dismissed by Judge Dwyer in his courtroom—eleven frustrated jurors and one isolated juror.

The next day the jury focused on Cindy Hamilton.

Murray Andrews considered the daughter's testimony to be the most damning. The case was circumstantial, but Cindy had put all the pieces together. He spoke for the majority of jurors on this.

Some of the female jurors were skeptical of Cindy's testimony due to their firsthand understanding of the sometimes volatile dynamics of a mother-daughter relationship.

Others wanted further clarification; whether Cindy had come forward of her own accord, or whether the FBI had contacted her and got a confession out of her. Just after three o'clock, Foreman Andrews sent a note to Judge Dwyer:

5-5-88.

Please provide the testimony that will help clarify (1) Did Cindy come forward voluntarily to the FBI or did they contact her at which time she offered information about Stella's conversations with her. (2) What date did Cindy provide this information to the FBI?

Signed, Murray M. Andrews, Foreman.

Judge Dwyer knew such questions are routinely answered, but a better approach would be to refer the jury to their collective memories. His note, under Maida and Hillier's approval, responded:

To the jury:

It is not feasible to try to locate, select and read back the parts of the trial record that bear on these subjects. The jurors must rely on their collective recollection of the evidence presented during the trial.

Back to deliberations, and no one, it seemed to the foreman, was more disappointed than Laurel Holliday.

The reward was discussed, but most didn't feel it had been the motivation. While it was true the daughter was in line for some of the reward, she also had much to forfeit.

One juror considered how difficult it would be to turn a parent in when, no doubt, it would lead to an irrevocable estrangement. "She had a lot to lose if she was making all this up."

By five o'clock, Judge Dwyer dismissed the jury again, reminding them not to discuss the case outside the jury room. "As time goes on, it might seem difficult to abide by this instruction, but I must keep giving it. It is very important that you comply with it one hundred percent."

That night, the *Seattle Post-Intelligencer* readied its edition for the next day.

JURY REBUFFED IN BID TO REVIEW TESTIMONY OF NICKELL'S DAUGHTER

Speculation immediately arose that the jury is deadlocked over the issue of the credibility of the 28-year-old daughter Cindy Hamilton, whose testimony was challenged on the witness stand by her mother...

The next day, still, Laurel Holliday held tight to her beliefs.

Just as deliberations were getting underway on May 6, the real estate agent nervously said she had something to read for the group. Laurel pulled out a letter she said she had written at her word processor the night before.

Later, jurors would remember the tone of its content, if not the exact words.

"I think she felt we were all against her, making life difficult for her," foreman Andrews recalled. "I don't think she was a strong person. She couldn't come up with that extemporaneously. She needed to write it down."

Marcheta Cruse was put off.

"It was a letter voicing her opinion more or less of all of us as being against her. She didn't like the tone we used with her during deliberation. I think she resented the men's attitude against her more than the women's. I think in her mind they were badgering her."

Juror Holliday wanted another definition of reasonable doubt.

Marcheta asked Laurel Holliday to tell the others what her personal definition was. The woman said she had some doubts; she was only at fifty percent sure that Stella Nickell was the guilty party.

"I have to be ninety percent sure."

Some wondered how in the world someone could measure their doubts in percentages.

"That's awfully strange when eleven of us are ninety percent sure," Marcheta answered back. "How can eleven of us be ninety percent sure and only one of us fifty percent sure?"

It went on and on. Finally, peacemaker and foreman Murray Andrews said he'd write another note to the judge.

May we have more detailed explanation on what constitutes "reasonable doubt"? Signed, Murray M. Andrews, Foreman.

He knew a mob scene in the jury room was not the way to get a conviction.

That afternoon, the judge and counsel met over Andrews's note. Stella Nickell interpreted the words as an indication that things were going her way.

The federal judge was reluctant to offer clarification, preferring that the jury review the instructions he had already provided. "Experience has shown it doesn't add anything really to pile on more definitions; that these words mean what they say and they should decide the case accordingly . . ."

A supplemental instruction was a possibility, but Tom Hillier objected to its wording. Judge Dwyer said he would send a note back to the jury telling them to consider the instructions they had already received.

Further, he told counsel that should circumstances suggest the jury was deadlocked, he might make available Cindy Hamilton's testimony regarding the FBI and the timing on her coming forward. It would be a lot of work, but, of course, it would be worth it. Nobody wanted a retrial.

The jury got their answer in the form of a typed response on a page with their original note affixed. As Murray Andrews read it, he thought he noticed Laurel Holliday slump a bit.

And around they went. Another vote was taken, and again there was the lone dissenter. "I'm not convinced," Laurel said.

"If you want to see a smoking gun," the foreman said, "it is here. It is the total evidence and testimony that shows us Stella Nickell is guilty." One of the men cursed and walked away from the table. Laurel Holliday said nothing further. She held firm.

"She didn't do it," she said.

At 3:15 p.m., Judge Dwyer read the note without a trace of resignation:

5-6-88, 2:50 p.m.

After three votes taken over the last three days, we have been unable to reach a unanimous decision. No juror has changed his/her vote during this time. We await your instructions.

Signed, Murray M. Andrews, Foreman.

Again there was hope. For Stella Nickell, there was a chance that the jury had not believed Cindy's tales of cyanide and murder. Perhaps they believed her.

The judge was adamant deliberations continue. It was premature to give up and accept a mistrial, and the expense of the inevitable retrial. He proposed that the jury retire early for the weekend, rest up, and resume deliberations on Monday.

Further, the judge proposed to read the supplemental instruction on reasonable doubt, and offer an explanation concerning the "technical difficulties" of searching Cynthia Hamilton's testimony when a transcript didn't exist. Counsel agreed to meet early Monday to discuss the court reporter's transcript, in advance of the jury's continuing deliberations.

The jury returned and Judge Dwyer offered a supplemental definition of reasonable doubt. He was clear, however, that it was not meant to replace the existing instruction.

"A reasonable doubt is one for which a reason exists and may arise from the evidence or lack of evidence. It is such a doubt as would exist in the mind of a reasonable person after fully, fairly and carefully considering all of the evidence or lack of evidence. If after such consideration you have an abiding belief in the truth of the charge, you are satisfied beyond a reasonable doubt."

Regarding their request for clarification of Cindy's testimony, the court reporter would look for the proper passages over the weekend.

Though the jurors had gone around and around with Laurel Holliday as they tried to get her to see what they saw, it was clear by Friday afternoon she was not going to make a decision to convict. Murray Andrews thought the holdout was simply unable to make the decision. It was something personal.

She was trying to wriggle out of it.

Chapter Sixty-Four

Stella Nickell looked better after her weekend of hope than she had in the three weeks of trial. Her black hair was shiny, the gray streaks appearing more like highlights than an indication that she had run out of L'Oreal soft black long ago. She wore a maroon skirt, floral blouse, and a knit acrylic sweater vest.

It was May 9, 1988.

U.S. marshals escorted the defendant to her chair as Tom Hillier, Joanne Maida, and Judge Bill Dwyer remained embroiled in hammering out the scope of her daughter's testimony, based on the notes taken by the court reporter.

Hillier's preference was that a stipulation be made to simply give the answers to the jury's questions. He considered the court's ruling when the questions were first asked to be the best tack—reliance on collective memories. He was uncertain that all the appropriate references could be found, given the lack of a complete transcript.

And though Maida had no problem with a stipulation, Judge Dwyer had told the jury they were going to get the testimony, and that was what was going to happen.

By 9:00 a.m. the testimony was ready for the jury.

Of course, none of those in the courtroom could have foreseen what was about to happen that Monday morning. Eleven jurors, however, wouldn't have been surprised. They knew something was up with Juror Holliday when she abruptly left the jury room with a bailiff.

She did not say a word. ·

In the courtroom, moments later, Judge Dwyer read a note the troubled juror had written on Sunday and submitted to him through the court clerk.

Dear Judge Dwyer:

I am a juror in Stella Nickell's trial. Something happened on Friday which I must tell you about. A woman called me at home about 7 p.m. and said, "Don't you [all] know that she failed the lie detector test." (I can't remember whether she said "all" or not.) She hung up before I even had a chance to realize what she was saying. I have tried to think who it could have been but I did not recognize the voice.

It frightened me that someone sought out my home number and called me like this. I told my roommate about it shortly after this woman called but I haven't told anyone else. I left a message for you on the phone machine for jurors Friday night, but then I remembered that we are only supposed to write to you.

Sincerely, Laurel Holliday.

While the defendant sat confused and quiet, unsure of what to make of the letter, the judge proposed to question the juror to discern whether she should continue deliberating or be excused.

Hillier didn't see how the issue of the polygraph could be covered at all. As far as he was concerned, his client never failed the polygraph—he saw only a summary, never a full report.

The judge planned to tell the juror that polygraphs were inadmissible, and nothing on the record indicated she took one anyway. Maida, who clearly could see a verdict in jeopardy, was concerned that other jurors might have heard about the phone call.

It was agreed that each would be questioned after Laurel Holliday.

As Laurel Holliday was seated in the witness box, Judge Dwyer reminded her that her oath from her original impaneling still applied. He started off asking her if she had told any other jurors about the phone call.

She said she hadn't.

"It's very important that you not do that. Don't mention anything about it at all. Okay?"

She agreed. The juror told the court she had no idea who made the call. It happened too quickly.

Judge Dwyer told the juror that nothing in the testimony, the court record, or the exhibits indicated that the defendant had taken a lie-detector test. She was to decide the case solely on the record. Further, he offered a comment that would have put Jack Cusack in another line of work:

"Also, you should know that in any case the law provides, and has provided for many years, that the results of these polygraph tests, if a person has taken one, are not admissible in evidence, and one reason they're not admissible is that their scientific reliability has never been established."

Laurel Holliday was emphatic when she told the court she could go forward and decide the case.

After talking with his client, Hillier made the surprise announcement that the juror could remain on the jury. Maida pressed hard for an alternate.

"Simply because the information received is a matter that is absolutely inadmissible. It may not be humanly possible for the juror to disregard the information she's heard."

Judge Dwyer suggested another option: using a jury of eleven. He recessed to think it over.

The troubled juror returned to the jury room in silence. She looked straight ahead, presenting a stoic front.

When they convened later, Maida asked that the juror be excused and deliberations continue with eleven. It was too risky, considering what might happen "in the heat of deliberations."

In addition, she said, there was the concern of future calls.

If both sides wanted her off the jury, the judge said, it would be done without hesitation. Tom Hillier, however, wanted her to stay on.

"What we have here is a situation in which a juror has been exposed to an outside influence about the case but has also given very firm and clear commitments in answer to questions that she can and will decide the case strictly on the evidence amid the instructions. Under those circumstances, I think it is required that I keep her on in light of the defendant's request that she be kept on. The information—alleged information—to which she was exposed in the telephone call ordinarily would be information that would cut against the defendant. But under the circumstances, I am satisfied that her assurances should be accepted and she should continue deliberating with the other eleven."

Hillier was reminded that counsel were not permitted to interview jurors after a verdict. He found the rule "offensive" to the First Amendment. He said he wasn't willing to abandon any rights.

"Well, let me put it this way," Judge Dwyer said, "do you still want the juror on the panel, knowing that this incident that we've been talking about this morning will not cause the Court to make an exception to the usual rule about post-verdict interviews?"

Tom Hillier said yes.

When the jury returned, the judge announced that one among them had received an inappropriate anonymous phone call concerning the case. Yet the juror stated she could put the call out of her mind and decide the case based solely on the evidence.

"Neither side in the case was responsible for this incident, and it has nothing whatever to do with your deliberations," he said.

When asked for a show of hands from other jurors who might have received a communication outside of the courtroom, no one raised a hand.

That said, the Court moved on to Cindy's testimony. The court reporter was sworn as a witness and instructed to read from his shorthand notes:

"Q: (by Ms. Maida) You have told us that when you were first questioned by the FBI shortly after your dad's death, that you denied any involvement your mother had in your father's death. Did we understand you correctly?

"A: Yes.

"Q: Did there come a point in time after that that you came forward with information to the FBI, basically what you've testified to in court today, that information?

"A: Yes.

"Q: The second time that you talked with the FBI, was that in January of 1987?

"A: Yes, it was.

"Q: That's about a six-month lapse between interviews, is that correct?

"A: Yes.

"Q: Did you do a lot of serious thinking in those six months?

"A: Yes, I did.

"Q: And by January 1987, had you decided to tell the FBI what you knew?

"A: Yes, I did.

"Q: After you told the FBI what you knew, did you tell the grand jury?

"A: Yes, I did."

Next, the court reporter read from Tom Hillier's cross-examination:

"Q: (by Mr. Hillier) In addition to that conversation with the grand jury—well, let me back up. You were sworn and took an oath to tell the truth during that testimony?

"A: Yes, I was.

"Q: Before that you had, I thought I heard you say, two major conversations with FBI agents?

"A: Yes.

"Q: And those would have occurred in January of 1987?

"A: Yes.

"Q: So about two months before you testified before the grand jury?

"A: Yes."

At 10:30 a.m., the court reporter stepped down and deliberations resumed.

Of course, the attorneys and the judge didn't know it, but some of the jurors who had been deliberating with Holliday seriously doubted there had been a phone call to a juror at all. Outside the people in the jury room, who really could have known that the greatest trial in the Federal Courthouse occurred after the government and defendant rested the Nickell case?

Marcheta Cruse didn't say anything to the others, but inside she was hopping mad.

"When this deal about a phone call came through, then things started clicking in my mind ... this lady has just been bamboozling us all the way through here," she said later.

Marcheta worried that the jury would end up hung because it was probably the oddball real estate saleswoman who had received the supposed phone call.

What is going on in this woman's mind? Marcheta thought. *No one knew who the holdout had been.*

It seemed suspicious that no one else on the panel had been called.

Had there even been a phone call?

SAs Cusack and Stone thought the phone call story was ridiculous.

"There is no way she could have gotten a call. No way anyone would have known she was on the jury. No goddamn way!" Cusack told the younger agent.

At 3:35 p.m., the verdict was in.

The courtroom was full, with media cameras outside ready to pounce on jurors as they left.

Stella Nickell was expressionless. She closed her green eyes for the verdict. Tom Hillier put his arm around her.

Murray Andrews gave the verdict to the clerk, who stood and read:

"CR87-276WD, United States versus Stella Maudine Nickell. We the jury find Stella Maudine Nickell guilty of the crime as charged in Count I; guilty of the crime as charged in

Count II; guilty of the crime as charged in Count III; guilty of the crime as charged in Count IV; guilty of the crime as charged in Count V of the indictment."

Stella clenched her hands slightly, lowered her head, and bit down on her lower lip. It was over. It had been mother against daughter, and daughter had won. She kept her eyes down as the jurors were polled.

What had promised to be a day of hope ended with guilty on all counts.

Courtroom observers noticed something peculiar about Laurel Holiday.

She was crying.

Tom Hillier immediately asked for a sidebar. In light of the unusual events of the morning, the defense wanted to question the jurors to find out if Laurel Holliday had been the holdout.

"I think that raises the probability beyond any possible odds that we have a juror-misconduct issue that ought to be ferreted out in the interest of justice," Tom Hillier said.

He wanted to know if it had been another juror who had made the call. Joanne Maida balked. "Their verdict should remain inviolate; and I would oppose any attempt of counsel to go behind the verdict at this point." The judge sided with the assistant U.S. attorney. He refused to "violate the sanctity of the jury's deliberations." The judge moved on to thank and excuse the battle-weary jurors. Sentencing would take place on June 17.

Bright sunshine and microphones assaulting his face, Murray Andrews was the only juror to speak to reporters on the courthouse steps. Others were still reeling from the experience of deliberations, not to mention the theatrics of sobbing juror number seven.

"When did you find out she failed a lie-detector test?" a reporter asked.

"Right now," he said. "You are the first one to tell me that…" The foreman was quoted in an article in the following day's Auburn edition of the *Valley Daily News* headlined:

NICKELL GUILTY IN CYANIDE KILLINGS

"Cindy's testimony obviously was the key that brought things together," Andrews said. "We felt we had to link together a whole chain of circumstances to get beyond a feeling of reasonable doubt. Without her [Hamilton's] testimony, there was not the thread that carried through all the evidence."

When Fred Phelps saw Stella after the verdict, she seemed all right. Upbeat, even. "She was planning her appeal," he said later.

While Paul Webking stood on his doorstep and spoke to the media on his emotional reaction to an expected verdict, Sarah Webb, reached by telephone, could find few words for a reporter: "Oh, my God. Oh, my God. Oh, my God. Oh, my God."

Hayley Snow cried when she learned of the verdict. It was supposed to be over, but deep down she knew now it would never be over. A guilty verdict didn't make her feel any better.

In Garden Grove, Cindy Hamilton surely must have been a mire of relief and worry. It was true the verdict was guilty, but what of the mess with the juror?

Her stepfather also had mixed feelings.

"After watching TV, listening to the FBI and Cindy, reading the papers, I've come to my conclusion: I don't know who did it," Bob Strong said later.

Chapter Sixty-Five

If it hadn't been one of the jurors, could someone from inside the courthouse have passed on the information that juror Laurel Holliday was the Nickell holdout? News reports suggesting someone who knew of the jury's split during deliberations had added to the legal maelstrom. In advance of court with the convicted and her attorney, Judge Dwyer made a check of his own staff—from law clerks to courtroom personnel.

No one knew anything.

Other court staff also denied any knowledge.

The U.S. Marshal's office queried all eight of the court security officers under its jurisdiction. Again, nothing.

At 2:30 p.m. on May 11, 1988, Stella Nickell sat quietly in her seat while Tom Hillier argued his motion for an order granting permission to interview jurors. His original concern had been over whether Laurel Holliday, who had received the phone call, had been the holdout. Since news reports now stated that with absolute clarity, he no longer needed to query the jury on that point.

Instead, he requested the court to hold an evidentiary hearing to determine if there had been juror misconduct.

Joanne Maida disagreed. The jury had followed their oaths, and it was pure speculation they had not. Juror Holliday reported the call in good faith, and the court accepted it.

"In spite of information learned by this juror that was prejudicial to the defense, Mr. Hillier insisted on her remaining on the panel. He took an awful risk, but not only did he not object to her remaining as a juror, he adamantly objected to her excusal. He did this after consulting with his client. At that time I believe I advised the Court that we had a real mess on our hands: in the event of a guilty verdict, having sent this woman back to continue deliberations with the rest of the jurors, that Mr. Hillier would ask to interview the jurors, which would be unlawful."

Maida suggested that Hillier set aside his second-guessing and learn to live with his decision to keep her on the jury. The U.S. Attorney's office would not sanction any jury inquiry into the verdict "based on pure speculation and conjecture."

Though he doubted any juror had made the call or that any had told someone outside the court where they stood, Judge Dwyer had no choice but to question each juror under oath. The possibility of juror misconduct had to be investigated.

*

No one outside of the Nickell jury knew of Laurel Holliday's strange behavior during deliberations: the letter she read, the journal entries she made, the professed feelings that all were against her, the tears during the verdict. No one talked about it. It had been bad enough.

And it was about to get even worse.

A *Seattle Times* reporter who had heard about the mysterious phone call drove over to the courthouse a half hour before closing, just to see if there was anything on the Holliday woman.

It was the kind of thing a good reporter does as a matter of course. It seldom pays off as big as it did.

A quick records search indicated a single case, a civil suit, with her name.

He learned that juror Holliday had filed a lawsuit against Pepperidge Farms. It stemmed from an incident occurring on the last day of July 1986.

A thirty-eight-page deposition she gave in *Laurel Holliday v. Pepperidge Farms* on August 19, 1987, detailed how Holliday claimed to have bitten into a Goldfish cracker during a broker's open house. The crackers were hard, the taste bitter, followed by a burning sensation. She spat them out.

"I saw a pill inside the cracker."

Panic ensued, and she called poison control.

"I pretty much figured I was dead. This was right after the cyanide poisonings in Auburn."

Right after the poisonings in Auburn!

It was unbelievable that she could ignore a lawsuit in which she cited the very case she was impaneled for! Most prospective jurors go out of their way to tell the court of incidents that are even remotely suspect. Laurel Holliday, for some reason, hadn't.

Later, FDA labs identified the pill as ibuprofen.

On May 12, 1988, the *Seattle Times* ran a copyright story:

NICKELL JUROR HAD ACCEPTED SETTLEMENT IN PRODUCT CASE

In the article, she told the reporter she never told the judge about the case because "I was never asked ... There was no reason to . . ." The case was assigned to arbitration and settled out of court, with Holliday getting only $500.

She told the reporter she had discussed the incident just before impanelment but felt it didn't apply to the Nickell case. It was a manufacturer's error, not product tampering.

Talk around Seattle was that Pepperidge Farms's attorney had questioned whether the incident ever took place at all. A pill could not survive the steel rollers cracker dough is pressed through during manufacturing.

Jurors were aghast after they saw the news report.

Marcheta Cruse felt betrayed. Holliday could have had the whole thing end in a hung jury. And for what purpose?

"How did she even get on that jury?" she asked.

Murray Andrews had some thoughts on why Holliday did what she did.

"I think she wanted to be there to write the story, but not to have to make the decision. She suddenly realized, 'My God. I've got to be part of the decision process.' She was basically stalling for time because she didn't want to do it," he said later.

Chapter Sixty-Six

It was not a happy reunion for the Nickell jurors. Before filing back into the courtroom on the afternoon of May 13, they waited in familiar, and frankly, depressing quarters—the jury room. Everyone was on edge. Laurel Holliday, dressed in a dark V-necked vest over a white long-sleeved blouse, looked physically ill. She said her answering machine had been jammed with phone calls from the media the past couple of nights.

Talk about creating your own problems, Laurie Adams thought.

Joanne Maida, Tom Hillier, and Stella Nickell listened as Judge Dwyer went over the afternoon's plans. The jurors would be brought in as a group, re-sworn, then individually questioned from the bench.

Laurel Holliday was first. Judge Dwyer opened the hearing by asking a pale and nervous juror if she had indeed received the call. In a voice just barely audible, she said she had, and she still had no idea who had been on the other end of the line. She did not tell the other jurors about the call. She also insisted she had not told anyone where she stood, innocent or guilty.

"I suspect my feelings were obvious to everyone who knew me, but I said nothing about my intended verdict," she said.

Concerning notes she might have made indicating how the deliberations stood, the juror said she took them home most days, though there might have been one day she did not.

"Was there anything in your notebook that would have shown anybody, if anybody read it, how the jury stood?"

"It's possible. It's possible."

Judge Dwyer turned to the subject of the impanelment process, reminding the juror that she was placed under oath at the time she was first questioned. He pulled Court's Exhibit I, a copy of Holliday's impanelment.

Q: Have you yourself, by chance, or anyone you know been the victim of a product-tampering incident?

A: No.

She maintained her answer was true, despite news reports about the Pepperidge Farms incident. The judge pulled Exhibit 2, her August 19, 1987, lawsuit deposition. He read the passages where the juror had cited the Auburn poisonings.

"Now, at that point—that is, when you bit into the cracker and had that thought—did you believe you were a victim of product tampering?" the judge asked.

She did think she was a tampering victim, but she wasn't sure.

"And when was it then, if you recall, that you decided this was not product tampering but something else?" the judge asked.

"I knew within seconds. Poison Control said I wouldn't be calling them if it were cyanide, and the FDA report came sometime later—I don't remember exactly when—but then we knew that it was just actually a pill that I take for headaches myself."

Judge Dwyer moved on. Why hadn't she considered mentioning her lawsuit?

"It occurred to me... but I was trying to be very exact and to the point, and listening to your question, and I knew this had nothing to do with the federal tampering law, which is the law that you had just read us, I believe."

She said she had mentioned the Pepperidge Farms case to reporter Kristin Jackson of the *Times*, the day before impanelment.

"I said, you know, I wondered if it would matter, but I just listened to the questions and if it didn't come up, it wasn't important to me and it would have no impact at all on my feelings about this case."

"Can you recall what, if anything, she told you when you asked her?"

"She said that she thought the important thing was to answer directly to the questions, and that only I would know whether anything in my life had biased my ability to be on the jury."

"Then, when you were asked the question I just read, did you believe that the 1986 incident and your lawsuit did or did not come within the scope of the question?"

"I thought that it was completely outside the scope of the question."

The judge read from Exhibit I, questions from impanelment:

"Q: Can you think of anything in your life experience that you feel would affect your ability to be anything other than an impartial juror?

"A: I can't. My job involves having two sides see each other's point of view when I negotiate an offer, so I think I would be fair."

Laurel Holliday stuck by her answer.

Judge Dwyer returned to the lawsuit deposition, reading juror Holliday's professed "paranoia" concerning packaged products and her anxiety, entailing less trust in the world.

Why hadn't she considered those feelings when the defense asked his question concerning life experience?

"I don't see the relationship. To me, the anxiety I felt at that time was over, for one thing. This took place, I believe, the last day of July in '86. This deposition was taken in August, I guess, of '87. I eat Pepperidge Farms Goldfish now. The feeling had changed, and I still don't understand . . . no one has explained to me how that relates to Stella Nickell and any feeling I might have about whether she would be guilty or innocent."

She also admitted she had talked with others about writing about the case, including a San Francisco–based literary agent.

Had any discussions concerning writing about Stella Nickell's case occurred between impanelment and her discharge as a juror? "Well, yes. As I said, I think I did mention that I did consider writing an article if anything came, I probably mentioned it to three or four people."

"During the trial?"

"Just—yeah, probably I did say that. You know, I was thinking about it." She did not, she insisted, reveal anything about jury deliberations.

"Any other conversations you've had with anybody on the subject of books or articles?"

"Well, I can probably name some more names of people who—because I know that I keep a journal every day and that I do write that I might have mentioned it to close friends."

"During the trial or after?"

"Probably both."

*

After Laurel Holliday returned to the jury room, the others, one by one, were called in. None knew anything about the phone call.

And certainly none had told anyone where individual jurors stood for conviction or acquittal.

All were excused.

Drained by more than an hour of questioning, Holliday left the courthouse by the back door, declining to talk to the media.

And that, for once, seemed like a good idea.

SAs Cusack and Stone shared a sense of disbelief back at the FBI offices down the hill from the courthouse. They had come so far in the two years since Seamurs began, and now this juror might screw it all up.

A week later, Tom Hillier filed a sixteen-page brief seeking a new trial for Stella Nickell, citing that juror Holliday "willfully concealed material information during jury selection…" The brief was convincing. Talk circulated around the courthouse and the jail that in the event of a mistrial, murder charges might be filed, in King County, with Joanne Maida named special prosecutor.

"Ice" Maida would go after the death penalty.

There was one hitch: Would Cindy co-operate if called on again? She had told Dee Rogers she couldn't do it if her mother might be executed.

Maybe now such sentiment didn't matter. Push had come to shove.

Friends who visited Stella in jail during this time reported that the woman was doing great considering all she had been through. It was true she didn't have her hot rollers, but now she had a chance for freedom. She was even upbeat, as she had been when Harry Swanson kissed her goodbye the day she took the polygraph a year and a half before.

Stella shared her hope with Wilma Mae that the Laurel Holliday fiasco might be the answer. Stella's niece prayed alongside her.

Her aunt might go free after all.

Just before lunch on June 3, the council met in Judge Dwyer's courtroom for brief oral arguments on the defense motion for a new trial. The focus was Hillier's argument that Laurel Holliday had withheld information during impanelment questioning and therefore should not have been seated on the jury.

Joanne Maida disagreed.

The hearing ended with the distribution of copies of a letter written to Judge Dwyer. It was from Laurel Holliday. Holliday claimed *Times* reporter Kristin Jackson called her when she saw her name on a list of potential jurors—provided to the *Times* by the court.

The reporter later denied any such list.

Laurel Holliday blasted the media for their "witch hunt" tactics. She wrote about voting guilty and whether she had made the right choice.

"I'll never know for sure . . . I am constantly agonizing over whether I was correct in my assessment of 'reasonable doubt.'"

Chapter Sixty-Seven

Wilma Stewart cried a Northwest downpour when her aunt was sentenced on June 17. Joanne Maida had done all she could to ruin an innocent woman, and Tom Hillier had failed miserably in getting a mistrial out of the juror debacle. And there was nothing Wilma could do about any of it. She felt disgusted by the sea of betrayal that had swallowed her aunt. Cindy was going to get reward money and the FBI agents were able to stand proudly and give Americans everywhere the all-clear signal—a madwoman was going away for a long time.

After brief oral presentations from both sides, Judge Dwyer pronounced a sentence of ninety years, with parole a possibility at thirty years.

Stella would be at least seventy-four before she had a chance for freedom. Tom Hillier announced he had filed an appeal, as his client looked on stoically.

Judge Dwyer agreed to recommend that during the time of the appeal, Stella would be incarcerated at the Washington Correction Center for Women in Gig Harbor.

Stephenson girls never give up. And Stella Nickell did not disappoint her tribe. Just as mother Cora Lee had bucked up time and time again when trouble befell her, so did her youngest daughter. From the bank of pay phones in the prison, Stella placed numerous collect calls to Wilma. A new trial was the usual topic of discussion. Both women held great hope that the Laurel Holliday affair would eventually win a new trial. Other times she even suggested that maybe Cindy would "come to her senses and say she lied."

Stella asked her niece to call famed San Francisco attorney Melvin Belli to see if he'd take the case. Wilma made the call, only to learn he wouldn't even take a look at the case unless she could come up with a $5,000 retainer. There was no money for that.

One time, she asked her aunt if she had heard from Cindy. "No, but I'd like to."

"How can you want to still see her after what she's done to you?"

"She's still my daughter."

On her own, Wilma pursued other avenues. She tried to find out if maybe Sue Snow and Uncle Bruce were having an affair, but that led her nowhere. Her aunt wasn't dead but as the weeks passed, people sometimes made it seem that way.

With the Nickell mobile home about to be hauled off the Auburn property, Wilma had been power of attorney with the responsibility of collecting her aunt's belongings. She wanted to save the mobile home from repossession, but she simply didn't have the money.

Fred Phelps, the dutiful boyfriend who had been to every day of the trial, hadn't helped matters. Stella claimed Fred hadn't paid a bill since she was arrested in December.

Wilma had to move fast, or there wouldn't be anything left.

Stella said Fred could have a few items—the wall unit, the davenport, and some other furniture. Wilma wanted the

Commodore 64 computer and asked for the refrigerator and some of her aunt's CorningWare, and her aunt said she was glad to let her use it.

"I'll need some of those things back when I get out," she said.

When Wilma got to the mobile home she noticed the Commodore 64 was already gone. Fred told her Stella had given it to Jim McCarthy.

Surrounded by boxes in the middle of the living-room floor, Wilma distributed her aunt's considerable collection of bric-a-brac into containers. Among the boxes was a safe. Inside, there was a shoe box. Inside the shoe box Wilma found a denim-blue five-year diary, the kind young girls often keep. It was fastened with a tiny gold-colored lock. Also inside the box were several small bottles.

She scooped all of it up and put it in her car bound for Eastern Washington.

It took a week and three trips over the Cascades to bring all of the Nickells' belongings home for storage. Stella's loyal niece stacked it all in the garage and a bedroom closet. She planned to go through it later.

The next time her aunt called from prison, Wilma asked about the computer. Stella told her that she had, in fact, let Mac have it.

"He'll give it back to you," she said. "He'll call and get it to you."

Wilma wondered why she had given it to him in the first place. She was family; Jim McCarthy was just a friend. As she came to and from the property, it crossed Wilma's mind that it might have been her grandmother and aunt who had done the crime. Cora Lee had said little, if anything, about the case—at least not to Wilma. It seemed as if she was holding back, not because she was ignorant, but because she knew something.

"Grandma stood to lose more than Aunt Stella did—her whole investment."

When Stella finally came to accept Fred had taken her for a ride, there was very little she could do about it. He was on the outside, and she was in prison. She wanted Bruce's guns back, but Fred said he had sent them out to be cleaned. She even asked Wilma to hot-wire the truck and steal it back, but her niece refused.

Wilma had learned a lot of things at the Maple Lane reformatory; hot-wiring, however, was not among them.

Chapter Sixty-Eight

Cora Lee was never the same after her fall at the courthouse. The old woman, as formidable as she was, couldn't put all the pieces together again. After the trial, after she lost everything she had, Cora Lee split time between her daughters, living in spare bedrooms or basements. It was a useless, defeating end for a woman who had worked so hard everywhere, from sawmills to pea fields. Her knotty hands were idle. Her mind was growing frail.

By July the year after her youngest daughter was sent to prison as the nation's first convicted federal product tamperer, Cora Lee could last no longer.

Though doctors said it was cancer, Stella had other ideas about the cause of her mother's death.

"For me to end up in a prison and my daughter's the one that put me there—and her favorite grandchild on top of that, it's part of what killed Mother," Stella said later from prison.

"I can't prove it," she went on, "medical science might not be able to prove it. Nobody has said anything about it. But in my own mind, I'm sure that when Mother fell and hit her head and bruised the brain, somehow that upset the body to the point where it started the cancer in the top part of her lung. Because Mother had no traces of cancer before that. None. Mother fell in April, hit her head, she contracted cancer in October, and by the following July, she was dead. And when they found the cancer in October, it was only the size of a quarter.

"But see, if she hadn't have been at the courthouse to begin with, she wouldn't have fell on those steps. So when you come right down to the knotty nitty-gritty, all circumstances involved, Cynthia is basically the reason for our mother's death."

Stella phoned Stan and Laurie Church and told them she wasn't going to go to the funeral. There had been a big media frenzy over whether or not she'd make an appearance and she wasn't going to let anyone take pictures of her.

"I'm not going to glorify it for those newspaper people. I'm not going to my mother's funeral in shackles and chains," she said. Her sisters wanted her there, though they understood her presence would alter the mood and meaning of the service.

"We all agreed," her sister Berta said, "that if she wanted to be there, we would surround her and be there. We'd be there for her."

Cindy Hamilton talked with Dee Rogers around the time of her grandmother's death.

"Dee," Cindy said, "the thing that hurts me most is my grandmother died hating me."

Dee insisted that couldn't be true. Cora Lee would have backed up her favorite granddaughter if she had known the truth.

Years later, Berta recalled her mother's feelings about Cindy. Cora Lee, in fact, had talked about her favorite grandchild the week before she died.

"'When Cindy gets off these drugs, if she's on drugs ... she's going to have to live the rest of her life with these memories,'" Berta recalled her mother saying.

Hate her? Never. Cora Lee adored her granddaughter.

"I don't want to give her any relief," Berta said years later. "I wouldn't want to tell Cindy, but Mother did not die hating her. She kept her picture in her wallet. I love the kid too. But she's done wrong."

Years later, Stella summed up her feelings for her daughter: "Even though there were times that I used to get so angry at Cynthia that I could snap her little head off just like a grasshopper's, I don't have any hate in me for Cynthia."

*

In July 1989, Cora Lee was laid to rest in a south Tacoma cemetery. She was dressed in the pretty, full-length dress she had planned to wear for her last wedding. With her burial went family secrets. And, Stella later lamented, all of her hope.

"Mother knew for a fact that I didn't do this," she said. "She knew it."

It was late summer-early fall 1990 when officials from somewhere—Bob Strong never caught exactly who they were—called the house on Ranchero Way in Garden Grove, looking for Cindy. Despite Laurel Holliday's shenanigans, 6th Circuit Appellate Court had upheld the conviction in the *United States of America v. Stella Maudine Nickell.*

Now there was money to be handed out.

Bob didn't know where Cindy was. He wished he did. He and his stepdaughter had had a falling-out over drug paraphernalia he claimed she brought into their house. Cindy said it was a set of scales used to weigh the gold chains she was selling. Bob wasn't anybody's fool and told her he didn't think so. Cindy left in a bitter huff, and never came back to the house. When the folks from up north called about the reward, he didn't have a clue where to find her.

"It took them a long time to locate her just to give her the money. That itself seemed kind of strange to me," he said.

The Nonprescription Drug Manufacturers Association's dispersal of the money following Stella Nickell's failed appeals in 1989 and 1990 brought joy and disappointment to its recipients. Cindy Hamilton got the lion's share, $250,000; Tom Noonan, $15,000; Bonnie Anderson, $10,000; Dee Rogers, $7,500; Sandy Scott, $7,500; Katy Parker, $5,000; Gerry McIntyre, $2,500; Lynn Force, $2,500.

It brought outrage to those like A.J. Rider who had been left out in the cold.

"I never got shit! They never even gave me an application," A.J. Rider said, unable to disguise her bitterness.

She smelled a rat named Cindy.

"They had to have done something drastic to get her to testify, as much as she was trying to hide and evading them. Somebody made some deep promises somewhere."

Jack Cusack was uncomfortable with the split. He felt it should have been divided more evenly.

The greatest surprise to some was the fact that Dee Rogers had been awarded so little. No matter what anyone thought of her personality, her somewhat pumped-up stories, the fact remained undisputable—without her, there would have been no Cindy. And without Cindy, there would not have been a winnable case.

Dee Rogers paid some bills and blew the rest of her share on luxuries. The trust funds for the kids and the country farm without men was a dream that was not to come true.

Although Sandy Scott was glad to get her share of the reward and had come to accept her neighbor as "Cyanide Stella," some of the convicted's actions still confounded her.

Why hadn't Stella disposed of two of the bottles of Excedrin capsules recovered from her home? It was easy to reconcile why she kept one—to prove her story that Bruce had been the victim of a tampering—but why the others?

Stella clearly hadn't known the third bottle was under the sink.

"I knew it was in there," Sandy said later. "Why wouldn't she have known it was in there? She wouldn't have left it sitting there. Why have evidence against yourself? It had to be a plant."

Sandy also wondered about Cindy's behavior the day the FBI and FDA came out to the Nickell place. "Why are they accusing my mother?"

"The thing that got me about Cindy from the very start was that attitude she had when she came that day, automatically assuming that they were accusing Stella. That would lead me to believe she knew something ahead."

At one point Sandy Scott believed Cindy might be an accomplice.

"It's not right. Cindy not only got away with something, she got paid a quarter of a million dollars! Who says crime doesn't pay?"

Once Stella Nickell's daughter got her bundle of money, she was gone.

The California woman who had cared for Cindy's daughter off and on was heartbroken when, after two years, Cindy came one December day and took the pretty little dark-haired girl away. Before Cindy showed up, the friend had asked for permanent custody papers.

Instead, the little girl left with her birth mother. She has not seen her since.

"I still have her pictures on my wall," the foster mother said. "I wasn't a blood relative, I simply took that baby because somebody needed to. I loved her ... Cindy used me as a dump."

Leah Strong had not heard from her sister either.

"I've been thinking about Cindy. It makes me mad because she's not wanting no one to know where she's at. It's like she's doing it on purpose. Like, to hell with you all. I ain't done nothing to her. She don't even know I'm pregnant.

"That's why when I went out there Christmas [1990] before last, I tried working things out with her. I thought things were worked out. As soon as I come back out here, I haven't heard nothing from her. It hurts me. I wonder why? We were talking. Getting along. It made me feel good. It was like I did it all for nothing. She don't call me anymore to let me know where she is. It wouldn't hurt her to call or write me something."

It has been years since Katy, Bonnie, or even Dee has heard from Cindy.

"Last time I saw her was right around the time of the trial," Dee said. "It wasn't goodbye, but it was different. This chapter is closed, now it's done. But that's okay. I know I'm always in her heart. I know if Cindy needs me, she'll call."

She clings to the hope the cycle of abuse and neglect has been broken and Cindy and her daughter are living on a ranch somewhere in Oregon, raising animals and never thinking about Stella.

Wilma stood by her aunt, bitter beyond words over Cindy.

"I can understand her being angry at her mother for raising her the way she did. I'm trying to understand that she could be so angry that she could turn against her and put her in prison."

The money was insignificant when the Snow/Webking out-of-court settlement with drug giant Bristol-Myers was paid. No amount could replace Sue. Hayley and Exa both used some of the funds to pay for schooling. Paul went on with his life too. He had the greatest bitterness to set aside. Few could imagine the stress of being accused of killing a loved one, by the very people to whom he was closest.

*

Stella Maudine Nickell: Lone killer, or did she have an accomplice in her daughter? SA Jack Cusack had been troubled by that idea from the very beginning.

His children watching television, his wife clearing the dinner dishes, SA Cusack took his place in his trophy-filled office. His old ham radio sat idle.

Only mother and daughter knew what the hell they had said out on the concourse, or when they rode to work. When conversations ranged from screwing with Bruce Nickell's brakes, to hiring a hitman, to re-enacting the Tylenol murders, it wasn't likely that it was a one-way conversation. There had to be a dialogue of some sort going on.

What had Cindy omitted from her story to the FBI?

It seemed doubtful that someone would discuss the utopian outcome of a murder plot—the insurance money, the fish or ceramic store—without having been involved in it more than Cindy maintained she had been.

The question SA Cusack later posed was "just how deep was Cindy into it?"

No one knew. Nothing tied her to the actual plots; no evidence, no testimony.

A few things stuck in his mind. Here's a woman that was privy to a lot of inside information about a murder she says she wasn't involved with. She testifies against her mother and rides out into the sunset with a quarter of a million dollars.

Why had Stella's daughter turned her mother in? Some close to the case suggested it was far from her story of doing "the right thing." Cindy also might have come forward to save herself. The FBI investigation was not going to go away. No stone was going unturned, and after a few months of watching the feds get closer, closer... dangerously closer... she decided to tell her story.

Stella might have done the same thing and saved herself. All of her arguments could have been believed—she always signed Bruce's name, she was confused about the insurance amounts, she researched the cyanide *after* Bruce died. Who had the contacts with drug dealers? It was Cindy, not Stella. There are plenty of reasons why Stella would never point the finger at Cindy. A mother's love was possible, though far-fetched. One scenario could be that if Stella and Cindy had in fact done it together, Stella might entangle herself by implicating her daughter. And Stella was too smart for that. She took her chances that Cindy would change her mind; she gambled on her daughter's love and loyalty.

And she lost.

*

Wilma Stewart began the lonely task of going through her aunt's belongings, mementos of a life: refrigerator magnets, two Tri-Chem liquid embroidery kits, tropical fish paraphernalia. Her bowling ball, her leather tooling kit, even her aunt's saddlebag purse with its jingling cat bell were sorted into piles for Goodwill, for posterity, and for the garbage man.

Late one night, while smoking a cigarette and sucking on her usual eucalyptus cough drop, Wilma Stewart sat in her upstairs bedroom and pored over the legal papers that had filled the box whose contents had come from the minisafe out at the property in Auburn. Divorce papers, insurance papers about Stella's claims on Bruce's policy, even military records suggesting Uncle Bruce's discharge had been without honor.

Among the papers she found items that would break her heart.

Several small amber prescription bottles, stripped of any pharmacist's labeling, were in a clutch in a shoe box. A couple of the bottles were full of small, blackish seeds. A single bottle was marked: "Foxglove." Wilma couldn't discern whose hand had written the label. Stella's? Cindy's? Cora Lee's?

But there was more. She picked up the five-year diary, the one she had seen back at the property when she moved her aunt's belongings but hadn't had time to read. Seven or eight pages had been filled out. What Wilma read then would haunt her forever.

"*I'm getting strange phone calls . . .*

"*There's a strange man watching me from across the street . . .*

"*. . . work the other day and there was a car parked across the street . . . it followed me . . . I ditched him . . .*"

Then the writings simply ended.

At first, she thought the entries had reflected something that was happening to her aunt when she was with Fred Phelps.

There had been several media creeps hanging around for a story. She looked at the date again.

1986.

It had been written before Bruce had been murdered.

When she first read it, however, nothing clicked. It was as though she had two pieces of a puzzle without the interconnecting piece. She couldn't put it together. Wilma kept thinking about it.

"There's a strange man watching me from across the street…" Where had she heard the story before?

The answer that came later was Cindy. It was Stella's daughter, the apple of Cora Lee's eye, the woman who betrayed the family, who had said Stella had been planning a kidnapping and had poisoned Bruce with seeds she gathered on the property.

Wilma's discovery added credibility to someone she chose not to believe.

"I had heard during the trial Aunt Stella had originally schemed at this idea of a kidnapping," Wilma said some years later. "She was going to journal that someone … was kidnapping. It was confirmation of what Cindy was saying about Aunt Stella being kidnapped and going to Mexico."

The discovery ate at her. Aunt Stella was not stupid, and she surely had time to get rid of anything so incriminating. How could she have forgotten the diary and the seeds? She had more than a year and half, why hadn't she destroyed them?

In the pile of mementos was also Aunt Stella's white leather-covered Bible.

Fred Phelps had claimed Stella found more time for Bible study after she took her leave from Burns. She was private about it, not saying what she was really looking for. Yet a slip of paper she kept inside the Bible betrayed her search. On it she wrote:

Death in family Ps 29
1 Cor 25
Lying detected Ps ci
Acts 5, Rev 21 Repentance:
Ps Ii, xxxii, lxxxiv, cxxx, cxxxix Babtism [sic]: Mark X,
39, Etc;
Acts ii 37 Etc. Marriage:
John ii, Eph V Thanks: 2 Sam vii

Stella also pressed Bruce's obituary between the pages: *Bruce Edward Nickell, 52, a former Winthrop, Peshastin and longtime Seattle area resident, died at Harborview Medical Center…*

Wilma threw away the diary and the little black seeds. If there was another trial, she was not going to give anyone the chance to force her into testifying. One time had been more than enough. The Bible, of course, could not be burned. She stored it in a box in her adopted father's basement.

Guilty or innocent, her aunt was a woman she loved. She never told Stella about her discovery, even though they wrote and had frequent phone contact. What Wilma had discovered helped to make some things seem more plausible, but in the end, who but God knew if Stella really had killed Bruce and Sue?

Or if she had done it alone.

Afterword

Stella Nickell and the people surrounding her landmark federal case have been a part of my life for more than three decades. Over that time, two things remained constant.

Stella maintained her innocence and her daughter had vanished for good.

All of that changed recently.

A couple of years ago, I got the surprise of my life when I received a message from Cindy Hamilton. I had searched for her relentlessly when I started writing the book.

She was looking for an oil painting of herself as a baby, one that Dee Rogers had long insisted was the key in getting to talk to Cindy. Unfortunately, I didn't have it. I did, however, have photographs from Cindy's tumultuous childhood, her wedding, and of her daughter. We exchanged a few instant messages and emails and finally, talked on the phone.

It's funny how wrong you can be about someone. I'd often thought that it was possible that Cindy and her mother were in cahoots on the murders. I wasn't the only one with the theory, either. The FBI hinted as much too. I could see how that might work—their relationship had been love/hate since the day Stella beat her black and blue with a hairbrush. And when the FBI cajoled her into taking the reward money, she took it and ran.

And never surfaced again.

Cindy was funny. Stand-up comedian funny. And smart. And despite all that she'd been handed in life, she didn't make any excuses or blame anyone. It is what it is. She'd just turned sixty and like everyone who has not had it easy, was doing the best she could. The *best* meant cutting all ties with her family and the friends she'd had when her mom killed Bruce and then Sue.

She never saw her mother again after facing her in that Seattle courtroom. Never corresponded. And has never wanted to. That's not cold. It was smart. It was the only way to protect herself and move on.

We talked awhile and I sent the photos as soon as I could.

She messaged me when she got them: *OMG!!!! Thank you sooooo much! I'm crying right now. (Happy)*

Her past had been stolen by her mother.

Later, when I learned that her little sister, Leah, had died unexpectedly at fifty-three, I sent flowers to Cindy. We talked about how it was living with a mother who put partying ahead of her children's well-being. How she used to Dumpster dive for toys for Leah. How the women who worked at the Dennison's cookie plant saw a big sister looking out for a little one and often gave them cookies. How she tried to make a life for a five-year-old in the trailer parks of Kent.

Cindy had never forgiven her mother for killing Sue Snow; for dragging an outsider into her scheme for a tropical fish store or ceramics shop.

"Honestly," Cindy told me, "if she had only killed Bruce, I'd probably never told anyone. Never gone to the FBI. Just keep it in the family, you know. That's how I was raised. Keep everything locked up."

She sent me another message: *Been watching you all day. They are having a 'Deadly Women' marathon on the ID channel.*😄

She also told me that she'd found out that her mother had lied about who her father had been. She took a DNA test and found a familial match—and it wasn't Lester Slawson. Instead of finding her father, she was able to connect with several siblings, including a brother to whom she's become close.

"That's the only good thing," she told me. "Finding family when I no longer thought I had any."

Then there is Stella.

I met her several times at the federal prison near Pleasanton, California. It is one of those prisons invariably described as resembling a college campus or a country club. It is neither.

Here are some notes on the first of our visits:

She surprised me in both her appearance and demeanor. I had seen only her driver's license photograph; this Stella Nickell looked better than ever. Blue jeans flattered her forty-nine-year-old figure and her trademark long wavy black hair, now streaked with gray, was pulled back in a barrette. Earrings she had made herself dangled.

"It is not in me to kill anyone," she told me.

Stella said she was the victim of some kind of a plot or a frame-up. Though she had several years to conjure one up, she had no pat answer to explain why she was arrested and convicted of five counts of product tampering.

But part of the puzzle, she said, rested with her daughter. Though she never came out and said it, the implication was always that Cindy had set her up. The betrayal hurt her deeply, but Stella always knew it would end that way.

"Everybody was sure she'd back off, change her mind and change her story. I said no. Once Cynthia starts something she will not back off. Because Cynthia is not one to admit that she's wrong. Even though she might know that she's wrong, she will never admit it. She's been that way all her life."

Looking back, I realized it was Stella talking about Stella. She wasn't going to back down. And for more than thirty years she didn't.

Hayley Snow Klein, now a mother of a college-bound son, and I have stayed in touch all these years. She knows, like I do, that we are bound forever by this book. We also know that the story has never felt completely over. Loose ends on loose ends.

She let me know in 2018 that Stella was going up for parole, a day that when I was writing the book, I honestly never thought would come. Having long accepted that Stella, and not Paul Webking, was her mother's killer, Hayley and Aunt Sarah drove up from Artesia to Albuquerque for a closed-circuit TV hearing from the prison in Dublin, California. Stella appeared on the monitor telling the examiner and parole board that she was a good person, an excellent inmate, and, of course, completely innocent. Her hair was white, and she looked like the elderly woman she was. Gone was the last image most had seen of her—long dark hair and red lipstick.

"She never even said my mom's name."

On May 9, 2019, Stella was up for parole, once more on closed circuit TV from the prison to federal offices in Albuquerque. We had talked before the hearing, and again, expected more of the same—complete denial.

Hayley texted me from the hearing:

"She's admitting it!!!!"

My response: "Wow!"

Hayley and I talked while she and her aunt drove back home to Artesia. They were as shocked as puzzled as I was. Stella confessed, but not completely. Once more, she was uncertain about how things happened or why she did it. To make matters worse, the video feed failed and the hearing ended without the requisite follow-up that might have provided more detail.

"Half-assed confession," I said.

Sarah agreed.

"Still a liar," she said.

"She's old and she wants to get out," I said.

"Right," Hayley answered. "We didn't even get to give our impact statement."

We all agreed that she'd never get out.

Hayley, ever vigilant about her mother's murder, wrote to the parole board after the hearing:

> … *Ms. Nickell admitted that she tampered with Excedrin bottles with the intent to kill her husband. She misinformed the examiner as to the number of bottles she contaminated with cyanide and falsely stated that she did not believe her husband was covered by life insurance. She says she does not know why she did it. Furthermore, she claims she is not a violent person, yet she criminally beat her own child years before she committed two murders. While trying to make a confession, I believe only to please the Parole Commission,*

she continues to lie about the details to disguise the malicious premeditated nature of her crimes. She also still fails to simply and outwardly face the fact that she murdered someone else, a perfect stranger, to gain more for herself personally. Her casual attitude toward her actions that rocked the nation and resulted in two murders is shocking and more insulting than when she just simply denied her responsibility all together.

Hayley went further, reminding the court about the nature of the crimes.

They were not crimes of passion. She had to scheme, plan, research, find her poison, and take many steps over time to pull off the crimes she committed. Then, she stood by and watched her husband die after he ingested the cyanide-laced Excedrin. For me, watching my mother die was a nightmare. It created images I cannot erase from my memory. What was Stella thinking as she watched her own husband die in the same way?

Listening to her, watching her, and knowing she cannot face her victims makes it clear to me she has no remorse. She has not accepted and come to terms with the damage she caused to my family, her family, and really to the psyche of the nation.

Stella Nickell is an uninvited, unwanted part of my life, and yet I cannot let her go. She has caused a permanent scar and absolutely does not appreciate the impact of her calculating, sociopathic behavior. Although she refuses to acknowledge us, she cannot be forgotten by us. She is the person we must face every opportunity we are given to bring any amount of justice possible to the dear person we lost, Sue Snow.

And then in May 2022, Stella made a plea to the feds for compassionate release. She had health problems and said she didn't have much time left. She wrote how she made arrangements to live with old pal A.J. Rider in Las Vegas. She can get a job. Model prisoner. Blah, blah, blah. In her plea for mercy she talks only of herself—of what she's missed out on being incarcerated for more than thirty years—her grandchildren, family members who she's not seen since going to prison.

She's all about Stella.

Like she's always been.

Hayley made a statement to the press and in this afterword, I think her words should be the final word on the subject of freedom for her mother's murderer.

"I used to wonder if she had served enough time. And I would ask myself what difference it made to me whether she was in or out. But, that was before her parole hearings. I've participated in all three of her parole hearings to date. Each time her story changed, and she clearly lied. And each time, I could feel a deep cold-heartedness in her that no amount of grandmotherly behavior or manufactured sobbing could disguise. It is something anyone with any intuition at all can sense. It is hard to feel compassion or sadness for someone like that. So, I believe that, after a lot of consideration over the years, she is where she needs to be. She is not remorseful, and that is evident in her parole hearings."

Note: In June 2022, Stella Nickell was denied compassionate release. She will have another parole hearing in 2024.

A Letter from Gregg

Dear reader,

I want to say a huge thank you for choosing to read *American Mother*. If you did enjoy it and want to keep up to date with all my latest releases, take a moment to sign up at the following link. Here is a promise: Your email address will never be shared, and you can unsubscribe at any time.

greggolsen.com

I loved writing *American Mother* because it is the ultimate challenge when it comes to true crime writing. It is complicated. It is full of memorable characters. But mostly because it is a puzzle—no one can say with complete certainty what exactly is true. That's not because of the case, but because of the mother and daughter involved. Which is a liar? Both? Or only one?

I hope you loved *American Mother* and if you did, I would be very grateful if you could write a review. I'd love to hear what you think, and it makes such a difference helping new readers to discover one of my books for the first time.

I love hearing from my readers, and you can get in touch on my Facebook page, through Twitter, Goodreads or my website.

Thanks,
Gregg

Keep in Touch with Gregg

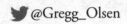 GreggOlsenAuthor

@Gregg_Olsen

www.notorioususa.com

ACKNOWLEDGMENTS

This is a work of nonfiction and as such it is only as good as the author's sources. I have been very fortunate in that regard. Nearly all of the people cited in these pages were interviewed specifically for this book. Two names have been changed. Where possible, verbatim testimony was used to reconstruct conversations. In other cases, I relied on the recollections of sources directly involved in such conversations.

I regret I was unable to reach Cindy Hamilton. None involved in the case, her life, her family knew—or would say—where Stella's daughter was living. I tried every legal means to locate her.

Over the years of researching and writing this book, I have had the pleasure of meeting and getting to know dozens involved in this tragic, very American drama. I appreciate the time and effort given so freely by so many seeking the answers to questions of their own.

I have also been inspired by some, in particular, of Sue Snow's survivors—Hayley Snow, Cindy "Exa" Snow, Sarah Webb, and Paul Webking. Hayley's anguish and confusion over family loyalties, as written in her diaries, shaped this book tremendously. Sarah Webb's devotion to her twin sister's memory and her pain over her loss touched me profoundly. Guilty of nothing but the kind of personality that might rub some the wrong way, Paul was always honest, thoughtful, and direct.

The many contributions Wilma Stewart made to this book are immeasurable. Stella's niece, now happy and successful in her career, put me in touch with relatives and friends who filled in the gaps. Whenever I had a question, Wilma was always ready to search for an answer. Wilma, in many ways, is my hero, the hero of this work. I'd also like to acknowledge Sandy Scott and Dee Rogers for their help, as well as Seamurs Case Agent Jack Cusack, and the many others at the FBI who assisted me throughout the project, including Ron Nichols, Dave Hill, Dick Thurston, and Bobbi Cotter.

Update, 2022:
For this edition, I give my biggest thanks to Claire Bord, publisher of Thread, who provided heroic support and amazing insight to get *American Mother* into the hands of readers all over the world. I'd also be remiss not to mention Susan Raihofer of David Black Literary Agency, my literary agent for nearly three decades. Finally, a shout-out to my UTA film agent, Addison Duffy, who supports each project with enthusiasm and smarts.